THE ART OF THE TEXT

STUDIES IN VISUAL CULTURE

STUDIES IN VISUAL CULTURE

THE ART OF THE TEXT:
Visuality in Nineteenth- and Twentieth-Century Literary and Other Media

edited by

Susan Harrow

Cardiff
University of Wales Press
2013

www.uwp.co.uk

British Library CIP Data
A catalogue record for this book is available from the British Library

ISBN   978-0-7083-2659-6
e-ISBN   978-0-7083-2660-2

The rights of the Contributors to be identified as authors of this work have been asserted in accordance with sections 77 and 79 of the Copyright, Designs and Patents Act 1988.

Typeset in Wales by Eira Fenn Gaunt, Cardiff
Printed by CPI Antony Rowe, Chippenham, Wiltshire

Contents

Contents

Series editors' preface

Studies in Visual Culture provides a forum for ground-breaking enquiry into visual-cultural production in its social, historical and cultural contexts. The series places particular emphasis on the exchanges, transactions and displacements that link Europe to wider global contexts across the visual-cultural field. The series seeks to promote critical engagement with visual media as ideological and cultural as well as aesthetic constructs, and foregrounds the relationship of visual cultures to other fields and discourses, including cultural history, literary production and criticism, philosophy, gender and sexuality research, journalism and media studies, migration and mobility studies, social sciences, and politics. The Studies in Visual Culture series thus focuses on exploring synergies and key debates between disciplines, concepts and theoretical approaches, and offers an exciting new arena for testing and extending disciplinary, theoretical and conceptual boundaries.

Acknowledgements

Many people, not least the twelve contributing authors, have worked with insight, energy, and commitment on the project that has become *The Art of the Text*. I am deeply grateful to Jean Duffy for her precious support and encouragement. I thank all the team at the University of Wales Press, especially Sarah Lewis.

Illustrations

Contributors

Jørgen Bruhn is Assistant Professor at Linnaeus University, Sweden. He has written monographs on Marcel Proust (with Bo Degn Rasmussen) and on M. M. Bakhtin. In addition, he has published articles on the theory of the novel and intermediality as well as on medieval literature and culture, Cervantes and Cassirer. His study entitled 'Heteromediality' appeared in Lars Elleström (ed.), *Media Borders, Intermediality and Multimodality* (Palgrave MacMillan, 2010) and he has also recently produced a book-length study entitled *Lovely Violence: The Critical Romances of Chrétien de Troyes* (Cambridge Scholars Publishing, 2010). With Anne Gjelsvik and Henriette Thune he has published 'Parallel Worlds to Possible Meanings in "Let the Right One In"' in *Word & Image* (2011). Jørgen Bruhn is currently writing on intermedial theory and adaptation.

Jenny Devine completed her doctoral studies at Royal Holloway, University of London. She is a former pupil of the Ecole Normale Supérieure, Paris, where she received the *Certificat d'étudiante étrangère*. Her academic specialisms are modern and contemporary French literature and visual arts, as well as Nietzschean philosophy. She has been involved in a variety of contemporary art projects in London, and has worked at the South London Gallery and at Elastic Residence, where she was Writer in Residence.

Anne Freadman is A. R. Chisholm Professor of French at the University of Melbourne, Australia. She has published widely in semiotics, including a book on Charles Peirce, *The Machinery of Talk* (Stanford University Press, 2004). She has also written on genre theory and on French women's writing. Anne Freadman is the author of several articles on Colette's journalism. Her study on Colette's memory books appeared in 2012 with Legenda.

Kate Griffiths is a Lecturer in French at Cardiff University. She is the author of an AHRC supported monograph, *Emile Zola and the Artistry of Adaptation* (Legenda, 2009), and of articles on nineteenth-century French literature, adaptation across different media and French film. With David Evans, she is co-editor of two volumes: *Pleasure and Pain in Nineteenth-Century France* (Rodopi, 2008) and *Haunting Presences: Ghosts in French Literature and Culture* (University of Wales Press, 2009). She is a member of the executive committees of the Society for French Studies and the Society of Dix-Neuviémistes. Her current projects include monographs on cross-media representations of nineteenth-century France and on Zola and television.

Susan Harrow is Ashley Watkins Professor of French at the University of Bristol. Her research interests lie in modern poetry and narrative with a particular focus on the interrelation of literary modernism and visual culture. She is the author of *The Material, the Real and the Fractured Self* (Toronto University Press, 2004), of *Zola, The Body Modern: Pressures and Prospects of Representation* (Legenda, 2010) and of a short study of Zola's *L'Assommoir* (1998). She co-edited with Tim Unwin, *Joie de vivre in French Literature and Culture* (Rodopi, 2009), and with Andrew Watts, *Mapping Memory in Nineteenth-Century French Literature and Culture* (Rodopi, 2012). She served as joint editor of *Romance Studies* (1999–2008). She has served as president of the Society of Dix-Neuviémistes (2008–10) and as president of the Society for French Studies (2010–12).

Peter Hawkins is, since 2008, Senior Research Fellow in French in the School of Modern Languages at the University of Bristol. During his long academic career he taught degree-level courses on surrealist poetry and introduced the poetry and aesthetics of Paul Éluard to first-year undergraduates. His other research interests concern popular French *chanson* and postcolonial literatures in French, with particular reference to the Francophone Indian Ocean area. He was awarded the French academic distinction of *Chevalier dans l'ordre des palmes académiques* in 1998 and was promoted to the grade of *Officier* in 2009.

Contributors

Michelle Henning is Associate Professor in Visual Culture at the University of the West of England, Bristol. She is the author of *Museums, Media and Cultural Theory* (Open University Press, 2006) and of numerous articles and chapters on photography, media, museums and modernity. Her essay in this volume is part of a project funded by the Arts and Humanities Research Council (UK) on symbolism and modernism, which focused on Otto Neurath's 'picture language' of Isotype and its connections to Romanticism and to older symbolic systems, such as Egyptian hieroglyphs. She is currently working on a book on Otto Neurath and Isotype.

Áine Larkin is Lecturer in French at the University of Aberdeen, having begun her academic career at Trinity College Dublin where she studied for her doctorate on Proust. In 2008 she was awarded a postdoctoral research fellowship by the Irish Research Council for the Humanities and Social Sciences. Together with text/image relations, her research interests include literature and medicine, the literary representation of music and dance and contemporary women's writing in French. Her book *Proust Writing Photography: Fixing the Fugitive in Proust's 'À la recherche du temps perdu'* appeared with Legenda in 2011.

Nina Parish is a Lecturer at the University of Bath, where she teaches French Cultural Studies and translation. Her research interests include twentieth-century French literature and the visual arts, especially modernism, the avant-gardes, modern and contemporary poetry (especially experimentation with electronic forms) and artists' books. She is the author of a monograph and several articles on Henri Michaux (*Henri Michaux: Experimentation with Signs*, Rodopi, 2007). More recently she has published on digital practice: 'From book to page to screen: poetry and new media', in *Yale French Studies*. She is a founding member of the 'Poetic Practice and the Practice of Poetics in French since 1945' network (*http://frenchpoeticpractice.wordpress.com*).

Karen Quandt undertook her doctoral studies at Princeton University researching 'Landscape and the imagination: expressive aesthetics in French Romantic poetry'. She teaches in the Department of Foreign Languages and Literatures of the University of Delaware. Her research interests concern the relations between the arts, Romantic aesthetic theory and theories of vision. She has given a series of papers on the uneasy relationship between painting and poetry in the nineteenth century.

Katherine Shingler is a Lecturer in French at the University of Nottingham. Her current research project, funded by the Leverhulme Trust, moves from poetry to prose texts and focuses on the development of the 'art novel' in the period 1900–30. The art novel undergoes a series of modifications in the early twentieth century, as the new popular art form of the cinema competes with painting as the primary reference point for writers. This project examines the interaction of still and moving images in fiction by Guillaume Apollinaire, Blaise Cendrars, Louis Aragon and André Breton. Katherine Shingler's broad interests are in word-and-image studies, visual poetry, Maurice Denis's work as an illustrator and psychology as a critical tool for literary scholars.

Timothy Unwin is Emeritus Professor at the University of Bristol, where he was latterly Ashley Watkins Professor of French. Prior to his arrival at Bristol he was James Barrow Professor of French at the University of Liverpool. His books include *Art et infini: l'œuvre de jeunesse de Gustave Flaubert* (1991), *Textes réfléchissants: réalisme et réflexivité au dix-neuvième siècle* (2000), and *Jules Verne: Journeys in Writing* (2005). He was also volume editor for *The Cambridge Companion to the French Novel: 1800 to the Present* (1997) and *The Cambridge Companion to Flaubert* (2004). He is currently completing a critical edition of Jules Verne's *Une ville flottante*. He is a member of the editorial board of the *Australian Journal of French Studies*, and co-moderator of the Francofil electronic bulletin board for French studies. He is general editor of *French Studies* journal.

Michael Williams is a Senior Lecturer in Film Studies at the University of Southampton. His monograph *Ivor Novello: Screen Idol* was published by the British Film Institute in 2003. He has edited (with Mike Hammond) a forthcoming volume on British Cinema and the First World War for Palgrave Macmillan and is currently completing a monograph on classicism and the development of stardom in the silent film era. Other work includes writing on landscape and sexuality in British cinema; Belgian film maker Bavo Defurne;

adaptations of Patricia Highsmith's *The Talented Mr. Ripley*; Anton Walbrook; and stardom and antiquity in *Ben-Hur* (1925) and *300* (2006). He is an editorial advisor for *The Velvet Light Trap*.

Introduction

Susan Harrow

The Art of the Text contributes to the fast-developing dialogue of textual studies with visual culture studies. Its focus, via a series of detailed readings, is the processes through which writers think visually and the practices via which readers respond visually to the verbal medium. 'Readers' may be film makers, essayists, painters, printers, cultural commentators, academics, or may belong to that most elusive of all categories 'general readers': all participate in the work of discerning and determining the visual quality of texts and other media. *The Art of the Text* aims to capture the creative impulse and the critical reception that privilege the visual, and to relay something of the disciplinary and interdisciplinary investment in visuality studies that engages the full range of practitioners and respondents today. Where an intensity of concern with the visual is formative of the culture of the twenty-first century, it is – as this collective project reveals – equally foundational in the nineteenth- and twentieth-century texts and the other media explored here.

The primary aim of this volume is to probe the visual capacity of literary texts and related writing (journalism, film-fan magazine, art criticism, literary manifesto, philosophy, letter, memoir) and to explore the visual capacity of textual works through analysis of the processes of creative transformation and adaptation. This reverses the practice of reading visual images, of 'cultivating picturacy' to reprise the term and the concept developed by James A. W. Heffernan.[1] In his brilliant 2006 study, Heffernan is working in an interartistic space, teasing out the subtle, often subversive relations between images and words, but the priority that he gives to visual images negotiated, as Heffernan puts it, 'with the aid of words', articulates the primacy of the properly visual over the written or textual in the continuing resistance to ekphrasis that has defined visual culture studies since the late 1970s.[2] The primary focus of *The Art of the Text* on the visual capacity of *textual* images does not imply a nostalgic return to traditional ekphrasis with its emphasis on the conflict between media or on inter-art rivalry. Rather, across the chapters of this book, an international group of researchers re-engage with the ekphrastic impasse in order to consider how the literary or literary-related text develops its own visuality, how it seeks to make visual analogues in the medium of words.[3] As the turn to visual culture becomes more pronounced across our disciplines, so the visuality of text has become an urgent area of textual focus. This group of researchers from UK, USA, Australia, Ireland and Sweden developed the collaborative project that is *The Art of the Text* following a conference organised by the Centre for Visual and Textual Studies in France at the University of Bristol in 2008. The contributors research across a variety of media and disciplines, although their primary ground of enquiry is textual. Whilst the essays reach out to non-literary disciplines, they focus on the visuality of the text, on 'the art of the text', and its capacity for translation, adaptation and transformation through other media. Active in areas as supple and porous as intermediality studies, adaptation studies, thematic criticism, philosophical readings and word-and-image studies, the contributors to this volume lift the debate out of the conflict zone of traditional ekphrasis: their concern is with how texts and other media cohabit and interact with visual images, and with how those texts and media embrace or resist pictorial images in the conscious development of the visual capacity of their own medium.

The Art of the Text explores a series of interrelated questions, questions that traverse differences of media, mode, century, culture, language and genre. The researchers ask how words relate to – or retreat from – pictures. How do *actual* visual images – those of art or cinema – respond to the texts that seek to accommodate them or appropriate them? How pertinent are concepts of adaptation, alteration and migration for understanding the visual project of a text and the reception of that text? And how salient are those concepts for understanding the textual project of images? What is lost and what is (re) gained in the process of cultural or interartistic translation and transformation when visual images inspire or inform images shaped through words?

The twelve researchers whose work is presented here reflect on the *lure* of the visual for writers and intermedial practitioners. What compels writers and seduces practitioners in visual terms? What is the value of the visual and what are its formative values? The chapters of this book explore this question from a variety of perspectives that are epistemological (Modiano), physical and lexical (Verne), memorial and erotic (Proust), ludic (Michaux), graphological (Neurath), photographic (Proust, again), historical and poetological (Hugo, Éluard), ekphrastic (Colette), sculptural (film-fan magazine), cinematographic, televisual and adaptive (Akermann, Cardinal). Beyond their differences and coincidences, the perspectives are always existential, experiential, imaginative, creative and humanistic.

Key questions are posed for each of us as readers. How do we read visually? What is visual about a written medium? Having traced a definition of the visual in texts, how do we explore that visuality? What desires and motivations – social, cultural, erotic, commercial, ideological – guide our reception? How does the visuality of a text relate to its subsequent transformation, translation or adaptation through a series of primarily visual media? The contributors to this book develop approaches that track the visual in terms of the represen-tation of processes (cropping in Zola's *L'Œuvre*, for example), genres (portrait and landscape in Michaux's 'Grande Garabagne', for example), colour and structure. A plastic and sculptural approach is taken to the iconography of the film-fan magazine by Michael Williams; a comparative reading of Modiano and Nietzsche is offered by Jenny Devine; the colour-saturated rhetoric of Colette's appraisal of fabric is tracked by Anne Freadman; a reading of Chantal Akermann's filmic interpretation of Proust is developed by Jørgen Bruhn, extending theoretical boundaries in intermedial studies.

In pliant ways the essays map to the five domains identified by W. J. T. Mitchell in *Language of Images*: the graphic domain (which makes explicit reference to painting and photography); the optical domain (which mobilizes the lexicon of visual instrumentality such as mirrors, screens, projections, viewing instruments, lenses and glasses, photographic film); sense data (which relates to the sensorium and acts of perception); mental images (which materialize in the form of dreams, memories, fictions and fantasies and their representations); and finally the verbal domain (metaphors, rhetorical figures and descriptions). Yet to categorize and typologize is to elide plurality and misrepresent complexity. The readings developed here reveal the *traffic* between those domains, the criss-crossing of influences, the ricocheting of media and modes, the meshing of processes and perceptions, and the inter-action of forms of making and forms of becoming. Thus, in the opening reading of visuality in Verne, Timothy Unwin ranges from optical to philosophical, epistemological to poetological, demonstrating from the inception of this volume that no single analytical method prevails or is privileged.

Visuality is appraised here, not as a state, but as a set of *processes*, processes of adaptation, resistance, negotiation and transformation. The contributors' alertness to the visual project of texts and other media foregrounds both actual visuality and visual capacity. The contributors show how the aesthetic projects resist and subvert traditional assumptions about the linear influence and the mimetic translation of visual material. They explore the ways in which texts and other media themselves unsettle, challenge and 'complexify' trad-itional assumptions about word–image relations, about ekphrasis, and about the enduring *ut pictura poesis* principle. In this the contributors respond to – and, in turn, extend – the discipline-defining work in intermedial studies of Mieke Bal, James W. Heffernan, and W. J. T. Mitchell and of the Scandinavian group led by Lars Elleström. But their methodology is also wider and more flexible, ranging from Roland Barthes and Stephen Bann to Peter Brooks and Susan Sontag, and taking forward the pluralist and painstaking practice of close reading. In the process of reading visually, the twelve researchers have fresh things to say about visual–textual relations in canonical texts drawn from Romanticism, naturalism, surrealism and high modernism, and across a range of media from film, textiles and television, to film-fan literature, picture language and painting. The time frame is broadly nineteenth- and twentieth-century, with a particular focus at the centre of the volume on cultural interactions of the 1920s: this tightly defined historical focus allows for a correspondingly broader geographic remit that reaches out to Viennese and British and American culture in this period and begins to challenge – from the inside – visions of French cultural hegemony.

As they probe key issues at the visual–verbal interface, the contributors to *The Art of the Text* identify and explore sites around which visuality is concentrated or which it shapes and informs. Their work converges on three defined but mutually permeable sites: Thinking the Visual Image; Intermedial Migrations in the 1920s; Visual Negotiations and Adaptations.

Thinking the visual image

This section considers the import of visuality in its physical and its metaphysical resonances in four canonical French authors representative of the development of literary modernity (Verne, Proust, Michaux, Modiano). The contributors to this section are concerned with perception and its textual inscription in the frustrated writerly desire to seize and articulate visual sensation. Epistemological concerns about how we see the world and how we know it visually, and how we bring that experience to language, inform each of the readings offered here. This sequence of essays is united by a concern for how visuality is captured in language and how, also, it 'gets away', and the implications for literature's incompleteness. Timothy Unwin's close textual study of Jules Verne's scopic voracity, in its optical and epistemological manifestations, reveals the paradoxical silence and the ultimate incompleteness of Verne's visual rhetoric. Unwin begins chapter 2 by arguing that sight, seeing and visuality are central connecting strands in Jules Verne's writing. First, they are crucial to the unfolding of Verne's stories, while also decisive in the way that his characters interact with others; secondly, they account for the descriptive prolixity of Verne's style; and thirdly, they drive the metaphysical vision that ultimately emerges from the *Voyages extraordinaires*. Seeing or being seen (and sometimes not seeing and not being seen) are recurrent elements; for the characters themselves, seeing and observing are obsessive, even neurotic practices, and the sights of the natural world are absorbed with almost bulimic intensity. One central lesson of the *Voyages extraordinaires*, for both characters and writer, is that the world is to be beheld as though it will never be seen again. Its sumptuous variety must be recorded with urgency, and Verne's writing emphasizes the boundless proliferation of nature while also placing on display the cornucopian lexicon. Yet this chapter also stresses that, for all its visual vitality, the Vernian text conveys a sense of its own incompleteness: the infinite spectacle of nature can never be fully apprehended. While, for Verne, nature and the lexicon may each abhor a vacuum, the eyes and the pen are unequal to the task of capturing all the sights and all the words that are available. The extraordinary energy and optimism of his writing are, in the end, counterbalanced by a sense of powerlessness.

Áine Larkin in chapter 3 approaches photographic practice in *À la recherche du temps perdu* as a model for the protagonist Marcel's process of apprehending and recollecting his experience. The heterogeneity of photography and its registering of spatio-temporal fragments map analogically to the narrator's quest to capture and to rework, in the dark room of his memory, images of the beloved. The significance of the visual in the Proustian narrative and the diversity of systems of visual representation which were exploited by Marcel Proust have been affirmed by many critics. Larkin explores the appropriation of one type of visual image – the photograph – in *À la recherche du temps perdu* as a model for the protagonist's way of apprehending and recollecting his experience. The photograph is described by Susan Sontag in *On Photography* as 'a thin slice of space as well as time'. The intricate temporal relations inherent in photographic practice and the photographic image are made manifest in the stylistic representation of Marcel's process of perceiving and remembering. His visual perception of the objects of desire that are Gilberte, Albertine and the *petite bande* at Balbec is characterized by alertness to effects of light and framing that is suggestive of photography; while his explicit awareness of temporal continuity is frequently mirrored in the syntax of the long, sinuous Proustian sentence. Informed by the work of Mieke Bal, Philippe Ortel and Malcolm Bowie, Larkin's reading explores several key episodes where photography is evoked in relation to Marcel's obscure objects of desire, in order to point up the significance of this system of visual representation in a work devoted to the search for lost time.

Nina Parish's reading in chapter 4 of Henri Michaux throws the spotlight on the poet–painter–travel writer's complex, often paradoxical relation to visuality where the very absence of visual images exposes the text's visual capacity and spurs the reader to adventurous participation in developing that capacity through the act of imaginative reception. From 1936 onwards, Henri Michaux published books containing both verbal and visual content, and continued to do so until his death in 1984. In 1936, he also published the first of his imaginary journeys: 'Voyage en Grande Garabagne'. This text does not contain any concrete visual images, although an *Atlas de Grande Garabagne (cartes, portraits, croquis)* is alluded to in the introduction. Parish argues that this failed attempt at incorporating both text and image within the book is highly relevant to the representation of Michaux's fictional stay in Garabagne. Using Mieke Bal's visual analysis of Proust's *À la recherche du temps perdu* as a starting point, Parish demonstrates how physical elements, such as portraits and the evocation of faces, provide a visual structure for Michaux's text and deepen its otherness. Michaux's neologisms participate in this text's alterity and can be considered as precursors to the eruption of images in his work. Parish's interdisciplinary approach to 'Voyage en Grande Garabagne' makes a return to Roland Barthes's *L'Empire des signes*, which opens with a reference to Michaux and to the founding of 'une nouvelle Garabagne'.

Jenny Devine's comparative reading of the 'black hole' of nihilism explored by Nietzsche and Patrick Modiano in chapter 5 focuses on the writers' harnessing of light and dark, of planal flattening and of perspective(s), as the nineteenth-century German philosopher and the contemporary French novelist visualize the *idea* of self-dissolution. Readers of Modiano are familiar with the recurrent evocation in his writings of a 'trou noir'. Following the dissolution of their world, Modiano's protagonists find themselves plunged into a dark void; their values shattered, they struggle to overcome an ensuing disorientation. In communicating these distressing existential states, Modiano relies heavily on visual devices: he evokes scenes of shifting perspectives and disquieting modulations of light, which challenge and undermine narrators' perceptions of reality. Informed by Nietzschean philosophy, Jenny Devine's essay explores Modiano's adept treatment of light and perspective and suggests that, while words and concepts necessarily distance us from our 'vivid first impressions', the visual can, on the contrary, take us closer to what Nietzsche terms 'the nerve stimulus'. Devine argues that visual language acts as a bridge between ideas and sensual reality, between the theoretical and the experiential. Modiano's visual language brings us closer to the experience of dissolution and disorientation and, thus, it forms a complement to Nietzsche. Modiano's visual depictions of the descent into a 'trou noir' effectively communicate those fundamental existential states on which philosophical discourse focuses but for which it struggles to find adequate linguistic and conceptual expression.

Intermedial migrations in the 1920s

This section examines the dialogue between specific media, the migration from one medium to another, and the productive if conflicted relationship between visual and textual forms in the international context of 1920s Paris, Vienna, London, and Hollywood. The contributors to this section have a particular concern with the interface between textual and material culture, specifically graphic communication, textiles, and fan literature, as well as film and painting. A concern here with social impact, technology, and audience reception brings into focus the role of commodity culture, markets, publics, and mainstream reception.

Katherine Shingler's work on Louis Aragon in chapter 6 probes the rivalry between painting and cinema in the surrealist writer's first novel *Anicet ou le panorama, roman* (1921), focusing on the displacement of outmoded pictorial ekphrasis by the fresh pursuit of cinematic technique. *Anicet* is structured around a competition between different artists and their respective art forms, each seeking 'la beauté moderne', represented here by a young woman, Mirabelle. The young Anicet identifies the painter Bleu (a fictionalized representation of Picasso) as his strongest rival for Mirabelle's affections. Ultimately, however, Anicet discovers Bleu's painting to be stuck in an aesthetic dead end, unable to respond to the demands of modern beauty. Correspondingly, Aragon's own writing turns away from the visual model of painting and towards the new art of the cinema. The visuality of Aragon's text hence consists not in the creation of static images but, rather, in techniques aiming to capture the experience of the filmgoer. Aragon frequently identifies narrative perspective with the camera's gaze, and parts of the narrative are constructed as cinematic sequences projected onto a screen for the reader to 'see'. Aragon's focus on cinematic tricks and special effects, which combine the privileged relation of film to reality with the creation of fantastic worlds, is linked to the surrealists' concept of the surreal as rooted in the real. Shingler thus demonstrates the importance of film in the development of the surrealist writerly aesthetic.

In chapter 7 Michelle Henning examines picture language and, specifically, the standardizing Isotype method of Otto Neurath, which she compares to Neurath's quirky creative signatures, revealing their Barthesian *scriptible* quality in contradistinction to the utilitarian monologism of Isotype. Henning begins by describing the Isotype method of pictorial statistics, invented in 1920s Vienna by the Vienna Circle philosopher and sociologist Otto Neurath, and compares it to Neurath's own signature drawings of a cartoon elephant. Isotype was among the first standardized systems for representing social facts in pictures. Neurath presented it as a picture language, an artificial language like Esperanto. Although he did not draw the symbols, he exerted a strong influence on their visual appearance and established the basic principles and conventions of Isotype. In his correspondence he did draw, signing his letters with a distinctive cartoon of an elephant. Henning uses these two different practices to consider what a picture language might entail. In particular, she addresses the differences between the standardized geometric appearance and systematic method of Isotype and the playful, improvised and amateurish signatures. She shows how the signature drawings came closer to natural language by becoming dialogic or 'scriptible', as Neurath's correspondents began to draw in response. This quality is absent in the methodical, impersonal Isotype, but Isotype has had an enduring influence on contemporary visual icon systems, while the elephant died with its author.

Anne Freadman explores Colette's work as a literary critic and her specific engagement with textiles both as producers of meaning and as products involving the visual actions of makers, sellers and consumers. In chapter 8 Freadman reminds us that Colette was, amongst other things, a professional critic. Her journalism, which is occluded in many critical appraisals, is placed centre stage here. Frequently Colette wrote about fashion, commenting on parades, on private showings, and on trade displays of fabric. Her work is satirical, in the sense in which literary criticism was a subject for satire in ancient Rome, and it is as satire that we can understand its generic operations.

Reading her work on textiles, we learn not only about their aesthetics, but also about the social conditions of high fashion – its modes of production, the temporality of fashion and the mediation of the relation between the high visual arts and consumer taste in the luxury fashion market. Freadman probes the multidimensionality of Colette's appraisal of fabric and fashion, revealing its complex rhetoric, its probing of the sociological, economic, cultural and perceptual values of cloth and clothes. At the same time, Colette's mastery of the descriptive arts – her verbal discernment, her colourist brio, her talent for articulating texture – is matter for sheer readerly pleasure.

Turning to the Hollywood star system, in chapter 9 Michael Williams examines the mediation, through sculpture and concepts of classical plasticity, of the outward beauty of film stars in interviews published in British and American fan magazines of the 1920s. André Morin wrote in 1957 that the beauty of film stars was 'as eloquent as the beauty of statues'. Morin's phrase not only alludes to the ideals of 'classical beauty' by which stars are valued, but suggests that stars themselves are works of art. Could the film-fan magazine interview, in elucidating the persona of the star as a work of art through heightened and often mythologized visuality, offer an equivalent to ekphrasis? Michael Williams draws from archival research into British and American film-fan magazines of the late 1910s and 1920s, a period that saw the consolidation of the star system and the refinement of a discourse through which stars could be constructed. In order to establish an appropriate visual and written discourse for the nascent art of stardom, studios and journalists looked to the aesthetics of fine art, and particularly classicism, for inspiration. For the printed page, they appropriated a language of description that could elevate, and animate, the screen idol for its audience, as a counter to stardom's fragments. Drawing from interdisciplinary work on ekphrasis and the iconotext, Williams argues that star studies can learn much from placing the discourse of stardom within a wider art-historical tradition.

Visual negotiations and adaptations

This section widens once more the temporal and aesthetic scope as it explores the negotiation of visual media in material drawn from romanticism, naturalism, surrealism, and the high modernism of Proust. The intermedial frame expands here from canonical literature to include television as well as film. First, in chapter 10, Karen Quandt observes that Victor Hugo said little about painting, but his *Orientales* (1829), in their attention to the visual and the image, afford us ample reason to wonder about this omission. Quandt assesses Hugo's resistance to the explicitly pictorial in *Orientales* through a comparative reading of poem ('Mazeppa') and painting (Delacroix's *La Mort de Sardanapale*, 1827): Hugo's resistance to translation and his flight from constraining plasticity are his means of negotiating, negating even, *ut pictura poesis*. Quandt argues that, in the *Orientales*, Hugo's neglect to acknowledge painting's obvious influence on his lyric reflects a persistent neoclassical tradition of hierarchy in the arts, where poetry sits at a categorical pinnacle. As experimental as they may be, the *Orientales* reveal a poet who remains unconvinced by the effects of the image; its seductive imprint pales in comparison to the sublimity of the drama that unfolds throughout the book. A meta-poetic commentary on the advantages of verse, the *Orientales* shelter the lyric from the threat of a mimetic enterprise and from oppressive plasticity. A comparison of Hugo's 'Mazeppa' and Delacroix's *La Mort de Sardanapale* (Salon of 1827) demonstrates how the similarities between poem and painting lead to their essential differences. Hugo's insistence on movement in 'Mazeppa' is a gesture of provocation, one that responds to Delacroix's tableau by highlighting its spatial and temporal limitations. Hugo's claim for liberty in the preface to the *Orientales* can thus be read as a response to 'ut pictura poesis': 'L'espace et le temps sont au poète'. Using the pictorial to his advantage, Hugo shows – through the device of narrative – that the poet is impervious to limits.

Kate Griffiths takes a multi-level approach in chapter 11 to the televisual adaptation of a French classic novel, Zola's *L'Œuvre* (1886). She evaluates the process of small-screen adaptation as it elides the epic and panoramic and re-focuses the personal and, like Zola's novel itself, develops a reflection on the intermediality of artistic creation. Adaptations, whatever their intentions, inevitably revise the original vision of the text they seek to adapt in a new medium. Pierre Cardinal's 1967 television production of Emile Zola's 1886 novel *L'Œuvre* is no exception, argues Griffiths. Cardinal's production, a piece reliant on short, boxy shots and interior scenes, crops the panoramic aspirations of Zola's text surveying art and life in nineteenth-century France.

However, Cardinal's piece brings the viewer closer to the novelist's textual vision in three key respects. First, the intimacy and claustrophobia of the adaptation echo Zola's intention to provide, in invasive close-up, a dissection of his characters under the looking glass of his fiction. Secondly, whilst Zola's novel explores the power of characters' vision and of its own pages to capture reality, Cardinal's production self-reflexively assesses the power of its own adaptive vision, its ability to render Zola in a different medium. Finally, Cardinal's piece, whilst it does revise Zola's novel, echoes and furthers the author's notion of authorship, not as a moment of originary purity, but as an intrinsically revisionary process. Zola adapts the techniques of art to his fiction, evaluating and inhabiting the interstices between pen and paint. Cardinal's work probes the boundary between painting and television, dramatizing the interaction of canvas and camera in an adaptation, which, like its source text, assesses the adaptive nature of artistic creation.

Paul Éluard worked closely with many of the visual artists associated with the surrealist movement, such as Max Ernst, Salvador Dali and Pablo Picasso. In chapter 12 Peter Hawkins reads Paul Éluard's *Donner à voir* (1939) as a heterodox collection of writings – poetry, prose, lecture and fragmentary reflections – that conceives of poetic writing as an analogue of surrealist painting and modern art, and as a form of aesthetic and visual resistance to revolutionary political orthodoxy. Éluard's earlier writings on the relation between poetry and painting are brought together in the 1939 volume *Donner à voir*, yet they are dispersed across a range of texts drafted at different times. Hawkins sets out to align them and to interpret them, showing the ways in which they differ from the surrealist orthodoxy imposed by André Breton in his manifestoes and theoretical writings. *Donner à voir* was published after Éluard had broken with Breton and the surrealist group, but before his subsequent membership of the Communist Party. *Donner à voir* shows how Éluard's ideas grew out of his close collaboration with visual artists: this is illustrated by Hawkins with reference to 'L'Attente', a text written to complement a drawing by Man Ray. Hawkins demonstrates how aesthetic principles are maintained even after Éluard's subsequent communist commitment, in spite of the party pressures to conform to Stalinist notions of socialist realism.

In chapter 13 Jørgen Bruhn contributes to the intermedial work of this volume by evaluating the 'mixed media' quality of Chantal Akerman's film adaptation of Proust's *La Prisonnière*, focusing on the productive tensions between narrative and screen projects, and between canonical modernist literature and its *sceptical* cross-media reception. Bruhn enters the lively field of adaptation studies. Eschewing the more conventional methods developed in adaptation theory and intermediality studies that deal with the relations between novel and film, Bruhn focuses on the media relations *inside* the text. By applying what Bruhn terms a 'heteromedial' approach, new aspects of the adaptation process come to the fore. The chosen example is Chantal Akerman's adaptation of Marcel Proust's *La Prisonnière*, a perplexing novel that Akerman has turned into a suggestive and intellectually challenging filmic work in its own right. Bruhn suggests that Akerman's film, renamed as *La Captive*, shows the inherent conflicts of almost all adaptations for it is a metafictive commentary both on the novel in question and on the medium of literature and film. Bruhn argues that adaptations tend to form an inter-medial constellation, *La Captive* underlining the struggle for dominance between literature and cinema. For the case study the author draws on Martine Beugnet and Marion Schmid's *Proust at the Movies*, but the results and final conclusions depart clearly from the work of Beugnet and Schmid.

Notes

[1] James A. W. Heffernan, *Cultivating Picturacy: Visual Art and Verbal Interventions* (Waco, Texas: Baylor University Press, 2006). Mieke Bal's influential study, *Reading 'Rembrandt': Beyond the Word–Image Opposition* (New York and Cambridge: Cambridge University Press, [1991] 1994), has done much to challenge traditional resistance to literary and visual intermediality.

[2] Heffernan, *Cultivating Picturacy*, p. 7.

[3] Developments in the wider field of visuality studies are reflected in the projects of these authors and the institutional research centres in which they are active: the prominence of intermedial studies in Sweden is noted, particularly the work of the group around Lars Elleström represented here by Jørgen Bruhn; Katherine Shingler's work has been developed in the context of an Early Career Fellowship awarded by the Leverhulme Trust for her project on the art novel of the early twentieth century and the interaction of still and moving images in fiction. University institutional structures such as research centres have given an important impetus

to these fields of enquiry: the Bristol Centre for Research in the Visual and Literary Culture in France, founded by Richard Hobbs, is an established forum for text–visual studies in the United Kingdom; Cardiff University launched its Institute for the Study of Visual Cultures in 2006 with lectures by Mieke Bal and developed a key book series, Studies in Visual Culture, published by University of Wales Press; Manchester University's Centre for Research in the Visual Cultures of the French-Speaking World (CRIVCOF) takes research in directions that include and extend beyond the *hexagone*.

I

Thinking the visual image

Jules Verne: The Unbearable Brightness of Seeing

Timothy Unwin

The sumptuously bound and lavishly illustrated volumes in Hetzel's 'Biblio-thèque d'Education et de Récréation' offer an unambiguous signal that visual enjoyment is crucial to our experience of reading Jules Verne's *Voyages extraordinaires*.[1] But Verne's texts also depend intrinsically on visuality, first because they so fulsomely detail the sights of nature throughout the known world, and secondly because sight and seeing – and on occasions their opposite, blindness – are key to the unfolding of many of the plots. Vantage points are essential: ships' prows, mountaintops, privileged views through a submarine porthole or the hatchet of a lunar missile, or from the basket of a hot-air balloon. So too are hideouts where the observer can enjoy invisibility while assessing danger, preparing escape or meditating strategy. The appear-ance of death itself turns out, on occasions, to be the ultimate vantage point. In *Mathias Sandorf* (1885) the motto of the eponymous hero, whose future son-in-law rises Lazarus-like from the dead to right all wrongs, is: 'la mort ne détruit pas, elle ne rend qu'invisible'.[2] To see but not be seen confers ex-ceptional and sometimes magical powers.[3] Conversely, to be seen and watched without knowing it can be a fatal disadvantage. In one of Verne's last novels, *Les Frères Kip* (1902), the identity of two murderers is revealed when their image, fixed on the retina of the victim's eyes in his dying moments, is rediscovered in photographs of the dead body.[4] Thus the criminals are seen and denounced from beyond the grave.

Not all of Verne's novels offer such a dramatic encounter with human sight and its ability to defy death or provide crucial knowledge; but visual curiosities, optical or ocular eccentricities and unusual visual faculties are a constant in his work. In *Cinq semaines en ballon* (1863), the manservant Joe who accompanies Samuel Fergusson on his balloon trip across Africa possesses 'une puissance et une étendue de vision étonnantes', enabling him to see Jupiter's moons without a telescope (*Cinq semaines en ballon*, p. 38). The eccentric geographer Paganel in *Les Enfants du capitaine Grant* (1866–8) is blessed with night vision, even though his eyes – like those of a number of other Vernian heroes – 'se dissimulaient derrière d'énormes lunettes rondes' (*Les Enfants du capitaine Grant*, p. 53).[5] Paganel, though, delivers the central Vernian lesson when he stresses the importance of seeing correctly: 'Tout est curieux à l'œil du géographe. Voir est une science. Il y a des gens qui ne savent pas voir, et qui voyagent avec autant d'intelligence qu'un crustacé' (*Les Enfants du capitaine Grant*, p. 71). Accurate vision, in the sense both of perception and of understanding, is the essential attribute of the scientist-explorer, and often depends in the first place on those instruments that facilitate sight and insight or give objective measurements or detail of the reality that is seen: sextants, telescopes, microscopes, periscopes, theodolytes, mirrors and lenses of all kinds. Sometimes these are allied to exceptional or implausible powers of vision. In *Le Pays des fourrures* (1873), the astronomer Thomas Black is obsessed with viewing the lunar halo during a solar eclipse, and seems almost conjoined with his telescope: 'C'était un homme à vivre dans une lunette. Mais quand il observait, quel observateur sans rival au monde!' (*Le Pays des fourrures*, p. 28). Such, indeed, is his ocular power that he is able to look directly at the sun through his own telescope, without any apparent damage to his eyes. In the case of Phileas Fogg's manservant Passepartout, on the other hand, the eyes signal in a different way that he is seeing 'properly', when in the early stages of *Le Tour du monde en quatre-vingts jours* he senses that Fogg is the right master for him: 'Passepartout eut comme une sensation d'humidité autour de la prunelle. Son maître avait fait un pas dans son cœur' (*Le Tour du monde en quatre-vingts jours*, p. 27). Often, though, the need to see in Verne is bound up with the need to classify, to create maps and to document the observed world in objective terms. The world has not only to be seen, but the memory of what has been seen must be officially recorded.[6]

Throughout the *Voyages extraordinaires*, the processes of observation are obsessive and driven. The sights of the natural world are taken in and positively consumed by the eyes, which sometimes appear to wear themselves out in over-enthusiastic contemplation or to risk damage through imprudent scrutiny. In the case of Hatteras, the obsessive desire to see the North Pole results in what appears to his colleagues to be both blindness and madness when he stares into the crater of a volcano (*Les Aventures du capitaine Hatteras*, p. 606). Hatteras discovers here not the unbearable lightness of being, but the unbearable brightness of seeing, and this extraordinary vision costs him his sight and his sanity. It is an indication that visuality in Verne is voracious, exuberant and almost always excessive. The spectator often devours shapes, colours or sights, just as the traveller consumes distance. The expression 'dévorer des yeux', frequently used in the *Voyages extraordinaires*, might seem a banal and lifeless metaphor, but it is frequently reinvested by Verne with its original connotations of physical appetite and hearty consumption. In *Vingt mille lieues sous les mers*, the harpoonist Ned Land, ever eager to cook and to consume the creatures of the sea that he beholds, watches a whale with a visual intensity that anticipates his Gargantuan appetite: 'Ned Land n'entendait pas. Il n'écoutait pas. La baleine s'approchait toujours. Il la dévorait des yeux' (*Vingt mille lieues sous les mers*, p. 465). It is as though the eyes reach out to touch and to draw in the prey. Verne underlines the active, near-bulimic involvement of sight. On other occasions, the consuming appetite of vision may lead to a sense of fatigue or wear, as the eyes weaken from the effort of sustained concentration. When Professor Aronnax scours the waves in search of the strange creature (in the event, the *Nautilus*) that has been sighted at the beginning of the story, voracious scrutiny (the culinary metaphor is again used by Verne) is accompanied by an anxiety that his visual powers will diminish through excessive use: 'Tantôt penché sur les bastingages du gaillard d'avant, tantôt appuyé à la lisse de l'arrière, je *dévorais* d'un œil *avide* le cotonneux sillage qui blanchissait la mer jusqu'à perte de vue [...] Je regardais, je regardais à en user ma rétine, à en devenir aveugle' (*Vingt mille lieues sous les mers*, p. 38, my emphasis). In the Vernian world, seeing is as essential to survival and good health as eating, and the visual variety of the world is one of the prime sources of textual proliferation in those copious lists and descriptions that characterize Verne's writing style.[7] The abundance of the visualized world is rivalled by the wealth of the lexicon itself, and Verne's writing thus generates a sense of cornucopian generosity. The eye, or the gaze, is in this sense central to his very approach as a writer. As Christian Chelebourg points out, the eye is 'l'organe par excellence de la reconnaissance, et c'est l'organe primordial de la science vernienne. Les *Voyages extraordinaires* forment une œuvre du regard.'[8] Not for nothing is Passepartout's reaction to the news that he is about to depart around the world conveyed with the comment that he has 'l'œil démesurément ouvert, la paupière et le sourcil surélevés' (*Le Tour du monde en quatre-vingts jours*, p. 25). The eyes have it: they not only receive but also tell a story.

Voracious visuality in Verne is apparent not merely because the eyes are ever eager to take in whatever enters their field of vision, but also because, in Verne's cosmology, the world is so abundant that passive spectatorship is simply impossible. The eyes must work overtime if they are to perceive all that is present before them. The human gaze is endlessly solicited, and there is urgency in this. As Michel Strogoff, denounced as a Russian spy, is about to be blinded by his enemies, the leader of the Tartar uprising, Féofar-Khan, famously commands him to use his last moments of sight with the words: 'Regarde de tous tes yeux, regarde!'[9] Sadistically, Féofar-Khan then lays on a pageant of colourful dances and other performances, in order that Strogoff may feast his eyes – for feast is indeed the word – one last time before he loses his sight forever. The sights and colours that are described are, for Strogoff, almost excruciating in their variety and intensity. The brightness is, for all its bewitching fascination, unbearable. The description of the dancers is sumptuous and pulsating. Glittering jewellery, shimmering light and profuse, vibrant colours mingle confusingly in the movement of heads, hair and limbs:

Elles portaient le costume national, et des bijoux les ornaient à profusion. De petits triangles d'or et de longues pendeloques se balançaient à leurs oreilles, des cercles d'argent niellés s'enroulaient à leur cou, des bracelets formés d'un double rang de gemmes enserraient leurs bras et leurs jambes, des pendants, richement entremêlés de perles, de turquoises et de cornalines, frémissaient à l'extrémité de leurs longues nattes. (*Michel Strogoff*, p. 333)

For Michel Strogoff, this is indeed exquisite torture, punctuated as it is by the repeated injunction by Féofar-Khan to enjoy this, his last spectacle, with 'all' his eyes. The imperative 'regarde!', featuring at the beginning and the end of a mere six-word sentence, underlines the extreme urgency of vision in these last moments, the need to take in everything and preserve the sense of it, and thus hold on to the visual imprint. But the plural, too, 'de tous tes yeux', is striking: two eyes may be better than one, but even two eyes, it seems, cannot possibly be enough to take in all the sights that the world has to offer. Each eye must multiply and match the spectacular variety of the display, and there is perhaps a memory here of the all-seeing hundred-eyed giant of Greek mythology, Argus Panoptes, whose miraculous powers of vision extended even to watchful alertness in his sleep, since the eyes themselves rested at different times. So the much quoted command in this chapter of Verne's novel (the phrase will be used by Georges Perec as an epigraph to *La Vie mode d'emploi* in 1978) sums up the appeal throughout his work to strive for a panoptic vision which is equal to the variety of the world.[10] Yet it also conveys the underlying sense that, however many eyes we might have, and however acute our vision might be, the world is always too profuse to be definitively taken in. The world is blindingly bountiful, over-generous in the sights it offers, overwhelmingly and unbearably intense.

The knowledge that vision may not ultimately be equal to the task of beholding all that is before it is, in Michel Strogoff's case, the most horrible of tortures. If, as he is about to discover, there is total blindness, there is also no such thing as total vision. The eyes cannot consume the fare that is placed before them. Nonetheless, certain images sear themselves upon the eyes, leaving a kind of 'imprint' similar to the one in the victim's retina in *Les Frères Kip*. As Strogoff is about to be blinded, a woman leaps out of the crowd and he recognizes his own mother. The alimentary image returns in the description of this, his last vision: 'Plus rien n'existait à ses yeux que sa mère, qu'il dévorait alors du regard! Toute sa vie était dans cette dernière vision!' (*Michel Strogoff*, p. 342). Whereupon he is blinded by the traditional Tartar method, a white-hot sabre being passed so close to his eyes that it destroys them with its heat. However, as is so often the case with Verne, things are not as they seem. In a neat variation of the Oedipal legend, the tears that Strogoff sheds for his mother as he is being blinded are just enough to reduce the effect of the heat from the blade and, although he is left temporarily unsighted, his vision later returns. So, while Strogoff regains the sight that he had thought lost, he is also able to learn the crucial Vernian lesson, which is to behold the world at every moment as if it were never to be seen again. To be overwhelmed by the visual variety of the world, to feel that the eyes are not enough, is also to be aware of its richness.

The sublime visuality of the world, and the need to apprehend it by every means possible, is thus a central message of *Michel Strogoff*. It is also one of the key messages of Verne's writing more generally. The universe of the *Voyages extraordinaires* is brimful of beauty, and the narrator or his characters are almost perpetually amazed by the spectacle that is offered to their gaze. The feeling of the sublimeness of creation is, for example, repeatedly evoked in *Autour de la lune* (1870), as Michel Ardan and his fellow travellers marvel at the celestial scenes before them. In highly charged passages like the following, Verne mixes astrological and scientific erudition with a quasi-mystical response to what is beheld:

> En effet, rien ne pouvait égaler la splendeur de ce monde sidéral baigné dans le limpide éther. Ces diamants incrustés dans la voûte céleste jetaient des feux superbes. Le regard embrassait le firmament depuis la Croix du Sud jusqu'à l'Étoile du Nord, ces deux constellations qui, dans douze mille ans, par suite de la précession des équinoxes, céderont leur rôle d'étoiles polaires, l'une à Canopus, de l'hémisphère austral, l'autre à Véga, de l'hémisphère boréal. L'imagination se perdait dans cet infini sublime, au milieu duquel gravitait le projectile, comme un nouvel astre créé de la main des hommes. Par un effet naturel, ces constellations brillaient d'un éclat doux ; elles ne scintillaient pas, car l'atmosphère manquait, qui, par l'interposition de ses couches inégalement denses et diversement humides, produit la scintillation. Ces étoiles, c'étaient de doux yeux qui regardaient dans cette nuit profonde, au milieu du silence absolu de l'espace. (*Autour de la lune*, pp. 420–1)

The Pascalian confrontation of the smallness of man with the vastness of space (though without the anxiety, since the stars are seen as gentle eyes staring back at the observer) is underpinned in Verne by a pedagogical mode of presentation and by the erudition on which this depends. Seamlessly woven into his description of the vastness of the heavens, there is detail of key stars and constellations, and an explanation of what causes the stars to twinkle when observed from below the earth's atmosphere. But the scientific and the poetic are interconnected, each relying on the other for its impact. For Verne, demonstrable scientific reality is itself proof of the miraculousness of the universe we live in, and there is no need to seek any philosophical or religious explanation beyond nature's observable manifestations. The apparent absence of God in Verne's world does not render creation any less godlike, for the cosmos itself is a divine spectacle.[11]

The sense of the boundless beauty of nature, a defining feature of Verne's writing, is probably nowhere more clearly conveyed than in the stunning lists in *Vingt mille lieues sous les mers* which describe the flora and fauna of the ocean beds. Perec, one of Verne's great admirers, once wrote: 'Quand, dans *Vingt mille lieues sous les mers*, Jules Verne énumère sur quatre pages tous les noms de poissons, j'ai le sentiment de lire un poème.'[12] The world that Verne describes in this novel is certainly one of magical abundance, in which the writing itself, with its repetitive and rhythmic lexical combinations, provides a clear textual correlative to the density of physical reality. Whatever the eye can behold, there is always more to be seen. The experience of reading Verne's lists gives a very real sense of the endless variety of nature, and that is indeed partly because it is textually quite impossible for the reader to process every lexical detail that is placed on view in the text. Just as the Vernian traveller's gaze is besieged by an over-abundance of sights, so too the reader's capacity to visualize is unsettled by rampant verbal proliferation. These lists may appear in one sense to be dispensable, for they have no direct impact on the unfolding of the plot, and like classic descriptive passages they may seem to have a rhetorically ornamental function. In another sense, though, they convey something absolutely essential and yet deeply paradoxical, namely, that the world is so profuse that it is impossible ever to 'write' it, or even to capture it momentarily in words. What is seen and reported is only a minute proportion of what exists. For all its astonishing vitality, Verne's writing thus intimates its own powerlessness, and indeed rests on the premise that it cannot bring the visual variety of the world within its compass. Even if the writer had the hundred eyes of Argus Panoptes, he would need a hundred pens to convey what each eye saw. There are not enough eyes to see the world, and perhaps not enough words to write it – or at least, there is not enough time to draw all of the words out of the lexicon. Verne's strikingly powerful representations of marine life thus carefully position themselves as partial reflections of reality, and implicitly recognize how much more lies beyond the range of the text, even though the text itself may seem to overwhelm us in its profusion.

In these lists, then, light, colour and movement are allied with exotic terminology, and with arresting sounds and rhythms, reinforcing the mood of fascination that is sometimes openly articulated, too, by an observer in the narrative. In the following passage, precise visual details are accompanied by a sense of variety and vitality. If the technical vocabulary and exotic or unusual names of sea creatures create an aura of strangeness, the overall sense of this visual spectacle is unmistakably joyous and intensely colourful, and is summed up in the simple yet enthusiastic response of Aronnax, who is mesmerized by the sheer multiplicity and diversity of the scenes that he beholds:

> Pendant deux heures toute une armée aquatique fit escorte au *Nautilus*. Au milieu de leurs jeux, de leurs bonds, tandis qu'ils rivalisaient de beauté, d'éclat et de vitesse, je distinguai le labre vert, le mulle barberin, marqué d'une double raie noire. Le gobie éléotre, à caudale arrondie, blanc de couleur et tacheté de violet sur le dos, le scombre japonais, admirable maquereau de ces mers, au corps bleu et à la tête argentée, de brillants azurors dont le nom seul emporte toute description des spares rayés, aux nageoires variées de bleu et de jaune, des spares fascés, relevés d'une bande noire sur leur caudale, des spares zonéphores élégamment corsetés dans leurs six ceintures, des aulostones, véritables bouches en flûte ou bécasses de mer, dont quelques échantillons atteignaient une longueur d'un mètre, des salamandres du Japon, des murènes échidnées, longs serpents de six pieds, aux yeux vifs et petits, et à la vaste bouche hérissée de dents, etc.
>
> Notre admiration se maintenait toujours au plus haut point. Nos interjections ne tarissaient pas. Ned nommait les poissons, Conseil les classait, moi, je m'extasiais devant la vivacité de leurs allures et la beauté de leurs formes. (*Vingt mille lieues sous les mers*, p. 153)

Verne's 'poetry', to echo Perec's term, certainly imparts a mood of astonishment. Enumeration and accumulation are central to its effect, and the use of the apparently banal 'etc.' at the end of the list has the crucial function of suggesting that it could continue indefinitely, that closing it has to be an arbitrary matter, and that there can never be enough words on the page to bring the description of this underwater world to completion. All that the writer can do is to suggest its infinite scope, and convey the desire for a panoptic, all-consuming vision, while in a sense also delegating all further description to the reader through this 'etc.', which might be considered a curiously postmodern and performative flourish. Totality is, though, beyond the range of the eyes and beyond the reach of the pen. There are always more details to behold and to gather into the gaze, always more words that are needed to fasten the image or suggest its vibrancy.

However, one of the constants in these lists in *Vingt mille lieues* is the emphasis on colour and on light. This regularly reinforces the sense of the magical beauty of nature. Even in the darkest ocean depths, light occasionally arrives (sometimes because of the bright electrical glow of the *Nautilus* itself) and brings what seems like a whole new universe to life. The vocabulary of abundance and colour is also linked on such occasions with scientific terminology that offers an explanation of the effects of light in the water. When, for example, Aronnax is taken by Nemo on a walk on the ocean bed, we read:

> Les rayons du soleil frappaient la surface des flots sous un angle assez oblique, et au contact de leur lumière décomposée par la réfraction comme à travers un prisme, fleurs, rochers, plantules, coquillages, polypes, se nuançaient sur leurs bords des sept couleurs du spectre solaire. (*Vingt mille lieues sous les mers*, p. 173)

This reference to the phenomenon of refraction through a prism, and to the solar spectrum of colours, is included to give a sense of objective authority to the vision that Aronnax enjoys, by way of explaining in rational terms the play of light and colour. But, as in the descriptions of the stars in *Autour de la lune*, scientific erudition also increases the awareness of nature's beauty. And this is further reinforced by a sense of movement and interplay, in which a dazzlingly mobile spectacle is offered to the eyes, as in this sentence where Verne evokes a heady riot of colours:

> C'était une merveille, une fête des yeux, que cet enchevêtrement de tons colorés, une véritable kaléidoscopie de vert, de jaune, d'orange, de violet, d'indigo, de bleu, en un mot, toute la palette d'un coloriste enragé! (Ibid.)

While painting is called upon as an appropriate point of comparison, the emphasis is in particular on the interaction of effects ('enchevêtrement', 'kaléidoscopie') and on the variations of colour and light that this produces. Aronnax appears, if anything, to be watching a motion picture.

Scientific erudition is again enlisted as an aid in describing the quality of light in chapter fourteen, 'Le Fleuve-Noir', where Aronnax comments on the diaphanous, phosphorescent qualities of the ocean depths. Here he refers to the discoveries of the naturalist Christian Gottfried Ehrenberg (wrongly – or perhaps mischievously – called Erhemberg in the text), whose interest in microscopic organisms had led him to demonstrate that these were the cause of phosphorescence in the sea. Verne's text appears to move swiftly beyond the scientific reference in order to concentrate on the dazzling qualities of the spectacle and on the movement of light:

> Si l'on admet l'hypothèse d'Erhemberg, qui croit à une illumination phosphorescente des fonds sous-marins, la nature a certainement réservé pour les habitants de la mer l'un de ses plus prodigieux spectacles, et j'en pouvais juger ici par les mille jeux de cette lumière. (*Vingt mille lieues sous les mers*, p. 146)

However, the reference to Ehrenberg is in reality a studiously casual one – a trick often used by Verne to conceal his dependence on a source. Ehrenberg's discovery was more than a hypothesis, for it had been scientifically demonstrated. The proof is summed up by Verne himself, without acknowledgment, in the previous paragraph where he points out: 'On sait que sa limpidité [that of the sea] l'emporte sur celle de l'eau de roche. Les substances minérales et organiques, qu'elle tient en suspension, accroissent même sa transparence.' But the scientific explanation of the sea's luminosity, dispersed throughout this long passage, is essentially there to support the sense of the miraculous quality of nature and of the magical spectacle that it offers the eyes. Despite appearances, Verne is suggesting, this is not a hallucination or a dream: it is the reality of our world, and is there to be observed by anyone who may have the privilege of an underwater journey. Few, of course, have the vantage point that Aronnax is able to enjoy, even though he is Nemo's prisoner:

De chaque côté, j'avais une fenêtre ouverte sur ces abîmes inexplorés. L'obscurité du salon faisait valoir la clarté extérieure, et nous regardions comme si ce pur crystal eût été la vitre d'un immense aquarium. (*Vingt mille lieues sous les mers*, p. 146)

But, with vantage points and hideouts, we return to our starting point: the position of the observer in Verne is vital, and once a privileged observation post has been established, the wonders of the world can be truly (if only ever incompletely) perceived.

In Verne's work, the eyes devour the beautiful spectacle of nature with all its movement, light and colour, and are often overwhelmed by the interplay of different sights. For Verne, the world is bright, colourful, vibrant and, above all, sublimely visual. It is a true feast for the eyes and offers to this most optimistic of writers an endlessly positive show. But, while the gaze senses the prodigious variety of the world, the observer knows, like Michel Strogoff, that it can never be completely taken in. There is no end to seeing, for the human observer does not have enough eyes to feast fully on the huge variety of spectacles that nature offers. By the same token, there is no end to writing, for the process of turning sights into words is by its very nature infinite. Yet, as I have suggested, Verne's writing depends fundamentally on this tension and this sense of incompleteness. The world is endless, self-generating, self-perpetuating. Just as the author of the *Voyages extraordinaires* can never complete his gigantic task of describing the whole world in his novels, despite his professed ambition to do so, so too, it is implied, the world that is visualized (either within his fiction or beyond it) is inexhaustible.[13] For Verne, as for Spinoza, nature abhors a vacuum, and his writing offers the precise stylistic equivalent of a metaphysical vision.[14] The extraordinary energy of Verne's writing is itself the clearest expression of his vision of nature and the world. Jules Verne's pedagogical mission, prescribed for him at an early stage by his editor Hetzel, was to instruct the youth of nineteenth-century France about the world at large. But one of the more lasting lessons of his work is that, beyond all the factual knowledge that may be assimilated, there is always more to be seen. Those who do not see and who fail to contemplate the miraculous world around them are implicitly mocked in the *Voyages extraordinaires*. Phileas Fogg is, for all his qualities, the most passive of travellers, always immersed in his games of whist, even delegating the business of sightseeing to Passepartout because he belongs to 'cette race d'Anglais qui font visiter par leur domestique les pays qu'ils traversent' (*Le Tour du monde en quatre-vingts jours*, p. 47). To see what is not truly there, on the other hand, could be a good deal more tragic, as is demonstrated in *Le Château des Carpathes* (1892) where the hero makes do with an artificial vision of his dead fiancée (a diva who is artificially 'revived' through a combination of phonograph and mirrors creating a hologram effect). Yet sometimes too – just sometimes – in Jules Verne's work we are given the message that there may be good reason not to see, or at least to look elsewhere. In *Le Rayon vert* (1882), the heroine Helena Campbell travels to the Scottish Highlands in search of the famous but elusive green ray that is, she is told, visible for a brief moment at the setting of the sun. The green ray does indeed appear, but Helena Campbell misses it because she has fallen in love and is staring into the eyes of her paramour at the critical moment. But there she sees another miracle, and that, suggests Verne, may well be just as enriching a sight as the beautiful spectacle of nature.

Notes

[1] References to the novels of the *Voyages extraordinaires* are taken from *Les Œuvres de Jules Verne*, 50 vols (Lausanne: Rencontre, 1966–71), and are given in brackets with the title of the novel following quotations.

[2] Verne, *Mathias Sandorf*, I, p. 324.

[3] The theme of invisibility will take a curious turn in one of Verne's last novels, *Le Secret de Wilhelm Storitz*, published posthumously in 1910. In this story, sometimes seen as a response to Wells's *The Invisible Man* (1897), the young hero appears to lose his fiancée who is made permanently invisible on consuming a potion concocted by an unhappy rival for her affections. But, despite her invisibility, she remains alive and the relationship between the couple continues.

[4] Verne thus uses a concept that was widely believed to be a scientific truth in the latter part of the nineteenth century, namely that at the moment of death the retina retained an imprint of the last object sighted. For an analysis of this theme and its uses by various writers, see Arthur B. Evans, 'Optograms and fiction: photo in a dead man's eye', *Science-Fiction Studies*, 20/3 (1993), 341–61.

5 Christian Chelebourg expresses this widespread Vernian phenomenon in a concise formula: 'Point de savant sans particularité optique. Le monde, pour être compris, doit être l'objet d'une vue singulière', in *Jules Verne. L'Œil et le ventre, une poétique du sujet* (Paris: Minard, 1999), p. 38.

6 For further examples and comment on the eccentricities of vision in the *Voyages extraordinaires*, see Chelebourg, *Jules Verne*, pp. 37–9.

7 For further comment on the culinary theme in Verne's writing, see Timothy Unwin, 'Eat my words: Verne and Flaubert, or the anxiety of the culinary', in John West-Sooby (ed.), *Consuming Culture: The Arts of the French Table* (Newark: University of Delaware Press, 2004), pp. 118–29.

8 Chelebourg, *Jules Verne*, p. 27.

9 Verne, *Michel Strogoff*, p. 332. The phrase, after making its first appearance at the end of chapter four in part two of the novel, then figures as the title of the following chapter and is repeated three times for emphasis in the next few pages.

10 It has often subsequently been used as a title, for example of the final chapter in Simone Vierne, *Jules Verne: mythe et modernité* (Paris: Presses Universitaires de France, 1989), or of the recent book by Jean-Yves Tadié, *Regarde de tous tes yeux, regarde!* (Paris: Gallimard, 2005), celebrating the Verne centenary. The phrase was also the title of an exhibition at the Musée des Beaux-arts de Nantes (June–October 2008) that celebrated the thirtieth anniversary of the publication of *La Vie mode d'emploi* through a Perecquian perspective on modern art.

11 Ghislain de Diesbach, while stressing the absence of God in the *Voyages extraordinaires*, argues for a more functional view of the cosmos on Verne's part than the one I am suggesting here: 'Il n'y a point . . . de dialogue entre le Créateur et sa créature, point d'effusion mystique . . . On y trouve seulement, à l'égard de Dieu, une sorte de déférence qui s'adresse au grand horloger de l'univers plutôt qu'au rédempteur du genre humain', in *Le Tour de Jules Verne en quatre-vingts livres* (Paris: Perrin, 2000 [1969]), p. 200.

12 Georges Perec, 'J'ai fait imploser le roman', *Galerie des arts*, 184 (1978), 73.

13 In his 'Avertissement de l'éditeur', in *Voyages et aventures du capitaine Hatteras* (Paris: Hetzel, 1866), pp. 1–2, Verne's editor Hetzel writes famously of the encyclopaedic task that the author has set out to accomplish: 'Son but est, en effet, de résumer toutes les connaissances *géographiques, géologiques, physiques, astronomiques*, amassées par la science moderne, et de refaire, sous la forme attrayante et pittoresque qui lui est propre, l'histoire de l'univers.'

14 See the *Ethics* (1677), Part I, Proposition 15: 'Since nature abhors a vacuum . . . and all parts must so concur as to prevent the formation of a vacuum, it follows that the parts of a corporeal substance cannot be really distinguished one from the

other, that is, a corporeal substance, in so far as it is substance, cannot be divided into parts' (Baruch Spinoza, *Ethics* (London: Dent, 1970), p. 14).

Affinities of Photography and Syntax in Proust's *À la recherche du temps perdu*

Áine Larkin

The mutual influence of literature and photography has been a subject of interest for practitioners of both arts since 1839. In the early years, literature and photography 'co-existed peaceably in an expanding aesthetic universe'.[1] This serene state did not endure, however, and literature quickly began to assimilate aspects of this new imaging system.[2] This chapter seeks to establish a link between photographic practice and Proustian syntax in several scenes from *À la recherche du temps perdu*. My aim is to underline affinities between photographic practice and Proust's crafting of his sentences, particularly in terms of rhythm, length of sentence and recurrent turns of phrase.[3]

Before embarking on the development of my own thesis, I shall outline the critical context and highlight the ways in which my own argument intersects with and is informed by the work of others. In recent years, Mieke Bal (1997), Michael Wood (2009), Katja Haustein (2009), Gabrielle Townsend (2007), Kathrin Yacavone (2012), and Dora Zhang (2012) have published insightful work on the links between Proust's work and photography.[4] Mieke Bal sees what she terms photographic 'effects of language' as serving to 'unify [Proust's] work under the auspices of "flatness"'.[5] Her argument is persuasive; however, it is predicated chiefly on an appreciation of photography in terms of its finished product, the photograph. In my research I have shown the importance of photographic practice, as well as the photograph, as a model for the representation of the protagonist's perception and memory in *À la recherche du temps perdu*.[6] Michael Wood's 'Other eyes: Proust and the myths of photography' examines the oddities of time and necromancy in the debate between cinema and photography, using Proust's ambivalent attitude to both systems of representation as a means to explore the nuances of their similarities and differences.[7] Wood draws attention to Proust's use of the photographic camera and photographic negative as metaphors for the development of the protagonist's awareness of the world. The state of 'inert perception, a knowledge of the world which is dead or sleeping until it is awakened by the mind' implies the stasis of habit-bound perception.[8] This point will be pertinent to my attempts later in this chapter to draw a parallel between photography and examples of what I take to be static Proustian syntax.

In 'Proust's emotional cavities: vision and affect in *À la recherche du temps perdu*', Katja Haustein examines some of the ways in which photography is used to elucidate the relationship between self and other, in two scenes from the novel.[9] She argues that photography serves to show absences or failures of emotion in the protagonist's interactions with the world and with his loved ones, and his consequent alienation. By pointing up the use of photography for the representation of 'emotional distance and difference', Haustein's work informs my analysis of other scenes where the protagonist is estranged – emotionally, perceptually – from the people and the places he contemplates or interacts with.[10]

The third chapter of Gabrielle Townsend's book, *Proust's Imaginary Museum: Reproductions and Reproduction in 'À la recherche du temps perdu'*, studies the ways in which photography informs the Proustian narrative in terms of the protagonist's manner of perceiving and gathering images of what fascinates him.[11] Like Katja Haustein, Gabrielle Townsend notes the relationship between death and photography; more pertinent in terms of my reading is her analysis of the 'photographic' narrative techniques Proust used, particularly with regard to the protagonist's framing of the encountered world, and the freezing and developing of slivers of space and time, that are juxtaposed or super-imposed in Proust's representation of passing time. The separateness of these *instantanés* 'destroys continuity between them' but they 'do not overlay and destroy each other sequentially' either.[12] Thus, for Townsend, the effect of such aspects of Proust's style is to make the description of time anything but an ever-flowing stream, and to deny his characters 'the possibility of smooth evolution and thus of any consistency'.[13] The uneven or abrupt temporal fragmentation that Townsend identifies in Proust's style will be relevant to my analysis of particular syntactical constructions in passages from Proust examined in detail later.

In 'A lens for an eye: Proust and photography', Dora Zhang explores instances of what she terms 'seeing photographically' in À *la recherche du temps perdu*, when there is a 'dispossession of selfhood' as the eye is turned briefly into an objective lens and thereby exposes the protagonist's habitual blindness.[14] Like Katja Haustein, Zhang identifies a temporary absence of affect in such scenes; she also underlines their effect of temporal discontinuity: 'seeing mechanically like a lens is to see ahistorically: it is to look without awareness of a past, and what it sees is a discrete instant segregated from its place within the continuous whole'.[15] In the third example of Proustian syntax explored later in this chapter, we find precisely this kind of ahistorical perception, though it is aural rather than visual in this case.

Some critics have suggested important links between Proust's syntax and the novel's major themes of time and memory.[16] Two works are particularly helpful to my reading: Walter Benjamin's 'The image of Proust' and Malcolm Bowie's *Proust Among the Stars*. Each acknowledges the halting or static quality of Proustian syntax, an aspect of Proust's work that is essential to the connection I wish to establish here between photographic practice and syntax. For Walter Benjamin, Proust's asthma is discernible in the syntax of his work, where it 'became part of his art – if indeed his art did not create it. Proust's syntax rhythmically and step by step reproduces his fear of suffocating. And his ironic, philosophical, didactic reflections invariably are the deep breath with which he shakes off the weight of memories'.[17] Certainly the rhythm of Proust's sentences, oscillating between long clauses and short ones, may be seen to reflect the uneven respiration of the bedridden writer. Despite being a writer of very long sentences, Proust is deftly concise when he wishes to come rapidly to the point, as Malcolm Bowie has affirmed.[18] That many of the passages where such deliberately ragged rhythms can be discerned include some reference to photography or the visual is suggestive of this other source of inspiration for the author, concerned as he is with the troublesome and, I would argue, disjointed and fragmented nature of perception and memory. Bowie views Proust's sentence construction as 'a form of retroactive play', and posits what he calls an 'eerie match between suspended syntax and being in love: both involve an incessant remaking of the past', says Bowie, 'and both allow [. . .] retroaction to be carried forward into a "free" future'.[19] It is precisely this 'suspended syntax' that Malcolm Bowie identifies that we see manifested in the passages examined in this chapter, and whose indebtedness to photography's immobilization of fragments of time and space merits consideration.

Writers since 1839 have exploited photographic motifs derived from their knowledge and understanding of photography, for the framing and composition of human experience in literature. My concern is with both thematic evocations of photography in *À la recherche du temps perdu* and stylistic uses of photography in relation to Proustian narration and the key themes of perception and memory. What I have found is a discernibly systematic exploitation of the *imaginaire* or popular imaginary of photography, especially photographic practice, in relation to these central concerns: photography is appropriated as a metaphor for the processes of perception and memory, and particularly as a model linking the ostensibly disparate processes of voluntary and involuntary memory in the novel. By delving more deeply into the matter of a few of Proust's sentences where photography is evoked stylistically, it is possible to argue for an affinity of syntax and perceptual practice informed by the model of photography. 'The photograph is a thin slice of space as well as time', affirms Susan Sontag, and key features of photography perceptible in Proustian syntax are visual discontinuity and temporal latency.[20] Perceiving objects of desire leaves the young protagonist Marcel perennially dissatisfied, aware of his inability to grasp the entirety of the thing or person he wants. It is in such situations that photography is frequently evoked, as when he learns of Albertine's death:

Pour que la mort d'Albertine eût pu supprimer mes souffrances, il eût fallu que le choc l'eût tuée non seulement en Touraine, mais en moi. Jamais elle n'y avait été plus vivante. Pour entrer en nous, un être a été obligé de prendre la forme, de se plier au cadre du temps; ne nous apparaissant que par minutes successives, il n'a jamais pu nous livrer de lui qu'un seul aspect à la fois, nous débiter de lui qu'une seule photographie. Grande faiblesse sans doute pour un être, de consister en une simple collection de moments; grande force aussi; il relève de la mémoire, et la mémoire d'un moment n'est pas instruite de tout ce qui s'est passé depuis; ce moment qu'elle a enregistré dure encore, vit encore, et avec lui l'être qui s'y profilait. Et puis cet émiettement ne fait pas seulement vivre la morte, il la multiplie. Pour me consoler, ce n'est pas une, c'est d'innombrables Albertine que j'aurais dû oublier. Quand j'étais arrivé à supporter le chagrin d'avoir perdu celle-ci, c'était à recommencer avec une autre, avec cent autres.[21]

This meticulous dissection of the nature of seeing and remembering the beloved fugitive woman now forever beyond tangible reach uses photography as a master metaphor for both these processes. According to Marcel, perception involves a condensing of the lived temporal continuum into discrete, discontinuous moments. Words like 'apparaissant', 'aspect' and 's'y profilait' reduce the process of multi-sensory perception to a predominantly visual mode, and photography is then explicitly referenced, together with 'enregistré', 'multiplie', and the evocation of framing in 'le cadre du temps'. In a conventional portrait photograph, time is spatialized; such an image represents a single aspect of the person. Proust's description of memory is predicated on the understanding that it is made up, not of a continuous series of images as in cinema or of an uncut photographic negative or contact sheet, but of free-standing, isolated fragments of the past, temporal crumbs (suggested by 'émiettement') of the beloved snatched from swift time by the hungry perceiver. Each discrete image, painstakingly recorded, is charged with the potential to revive one departed Albertine among many. The syntax of this passage is quite abrupt. The brevity of some of these sentences and the very terse juxtaposition of separate clauses within longer sentences, taken together with the incidences of asyndeton and anacoluthon, build to form a paragraph notable for its succinct exposition of the protagonist's emotional and mental anguish; striking here is the way photography, as well as being explicitly evoked, seems also to be written into the structure and rhythm of Proust's sentences, mirroring the qualities of memory that are being contemplated and discussed. The asyndetic 'mais en moi. Jamais elle n'y avait été plus vivante', 'nous livrer de lui [. . .], nous débiter de lui', 'Grande faiblesse [. . .]; grande force aussi' set up an unsettling rhythm, based on echoes ('nous [. . .] nous', 'de lui [. . .] de lui', 'grande [. . .] grande') which underline the disparities and inconsistencies in his thought. The anaphoric shift from first-person singular to first-person plural ('en moi [. . .] en nous') shows not only the multiplicity of Albertines to be mourned, but also the myriad selves of the protagonist, who must each grieve for her afresh. A sudden return to the first-person singular ('Pour me consoler') suggests the specificity of the protagonist's suffering, after his appeal to a universal experience of bereavement.

À la recherche du temps perdu is both a search for lost time and the tracing of a literary vocation. Photography may seem to have little relevance to such concerns. When explicitly referred to in the novel, it is indeed disparaged as a useless tool in the search for lost time, as when Marcel states: 'j'essayais maintenant de tirer de ma mémoire d'autres "instantanés", notamment des instantanés qu'elle avait pris à Venise, mais rien que ce mot me la rendait ennuyeuse comme une exposition de photographies'.[22] However, the explicitly anti-photographic aesthetics expounded in the novel are subverted by the underlying photographic poetology, which is detectable in the novel's narratological, temporal and syntactical structure. Its narratological structure comprises multiple voices.[23] Elsewhere I have explored how the representation of the spatio-temporal situation of these embodied narrative voices and their perceptual point of view in relation to the events they narrate is informed by photographic motifs, particularly the camera itself and photographic practice.[24] The contradictions between literal and stylistic evocations of photography make clear Proust's use – in thematic, narratological and syntactical structure and in description – of the medium his protagonist claims to scorn.

The stylistic representation of the Proustian protagonist's way of perceiving and remembering makes manifest the elaborate temporal relations inherent in photographic practice. The ways in which he conceives and represents his own perception and memory processes are profoundly informed by photographic practice, which is itself distinguished by a complex network of relations with time, numbering far more than the 'two moments in time' Michael Wood puts forward.[25] Preparing to take a photograph, developing it and printing it take time, and 'what enters a photograph by burning itself into the photographic plate is time itself *qua* time of exposure', so the result is a visual spatialisation of the time the camera shutter remained open.[26] Looking at the material photograph then sets up internal temporal links between elements of the image for the viewer: 'while wandering over the surface of the image', notes Vilem Flusser, 'one's gaze takes in one element after another and produces temporal relationships between them'.[27] Fixing and developing a photographic negative is a subjective, creative process requiring solitude and time. In *À la recherche du temps perdu*, Marcel expresses repeatedly the conviction that literary art needs production conditions mirroring those of photographs.[28]

Another sample of Proust's use of photography taken from the final volume shows how it informs (quite light-heartedly in this case) the representation of the complexities of lineage, which is such a prevalent theme – and a highly significant one where the idea of influence and the burden of family honour and duty are concerned. Witnessing the physical effects of age on old friends whom he has not seen for many years, the protagonist observes:

> Comparant ces images avec celles que j'avais sous les yeux de ma mémoire, j'aimais moins celles qui m'étaient montrées en dernier lieu. Comme souvent on trouve moins bonne et on refuse une des photographies entre lesquelles un ami vous a prié de choisir, à chaque personne et devant l'image qu'elle me montrait d'elle-même j'aurais voulu dire: 'Non, pas celle-ci, vous êtes moins bien, ce n'est pas vous.' Je n'aurais pas osé ajouter: 'Au lieu de votre beau nez droit on vous a fait le nez crochu de votre père que je ne vous ai jamais connu.' Et en effet c'était un nez nouveau et familial.[29]

Time is the artist acknowledged here for his work on the people who pass through his hands, but it is photography, both the image and the practices that surround it, which predominates in this passage, which appears after the protagonist has recognized his vocation in the library, and during the subsequent shocking reversal of realizing his own advanced age as well as everyone else's. In spite of its levity of tone, this evocation of photography ties together ideas about perception, memory, lineage, love and communication, which have been articulated in relation to photographic motifs throughout the novel. The anacoluthon in the passage takes the form of a pronominal shift between the first- and third-person singular, suggesting a distracted appeal to wider human experience, a wish to assert the banality of this experience of temporally and physiognomically dislocated perception of familiar faces. And yet the specificity of the description of a once elegantly straight, and now hooked, nose and the reporting of the exact words he has never dared to say, subvert this suggestion of universality and point rather to this bewildering, spatio-temporally specific and unique experience. The passive protagonist once again witnesses those around him as agents displaying themselves for him – he speaks of 'l'image qu'elle me montrait d'elle-même' – while he can merely look on as he gropes through his colossal mental photo album of memories to locate the most satisfactory image of them. Here the rhythm is much less hesitant and terse than in the previous passage, until the quotation of the first desired direct speech, where the protagonist's agitation comes through plainly in the reiterated negatives, and the short, one-, three- and four-syllable lines which make them up: together they constitute a gradual swelling of protest against the proliferating masks of age which are forcing themselves relentlessly on his defenceless optical nerves. But his distress has a very specific cause: the unique face before him has become overlaid with physical characteristics utterly foreign to the younger person he has known. In a process suggestive of close-up composite photography, that once blossoming young face has been buried by the coarser, thickened features of the father, and so now presents a face absurd in its simultaneous novelty and familiarity – 'un nez nouveau et familial'. There is nothing new about this nose, of course, except its appearance on this particular face. Marcel's alienation from his friends, suggestive of just the kind of 'emotional cavity' identified by Katja Haustein in other scenes, is coupled with the realization of their rootedness in the family, whose influence one may endeavour to flee as a youthful, straight-nosed 'être de fuite', to borrow Genette's term, and yet whose increasing facial rigidity and physiognomic conformity to family models is matched by the effacing of individual singularity, shown here through the disorienting perceptual zoom effect of Marcel's horrified eyes.[30] Like the 'vieillards dont les traits avaient changé, [qui] tâchaient pourtant de garder, fixée sur eux à l'état permanent, une de ces expressions fugitives qu'on prend pour une seconde de pose et avec lesquelles on essaye, soit de tirer parti d'un avantage extérieur, soit de pallier un défaut; ils avaient l'air d'être définitivement devenus d'immutables instantanés d'eux-mêmes', the influence of time will fix them in their family and in their friend's memory.[31] All that remains for the disabused Marcel to do after the Guermantes matinée is to fix his memories of these fleeting friends in words, thereby honouring their influence on his evolving understanding of perception, memory and the inexorable flow of time in whose 'chimie', as he refers to it, both he and his universe are bathed.[32]

The two passages explored above include explicit references to photography. As well as using photography as a means metaphorically to represent the complex web of temporal relations between past and present, both passages exploit photography's ambiguous relationship with futurity also. Roland Barthes articulates the uncanny power of the photograph with regard to the future when, looking at an 1865 photograph by Alexander Gardner of Lewis Payne, a handsome young man condemned to be hanged for an assassination attempt, he states that 'je lis en même temps: *cela sera* et *cela a été*; j'observe avec horreur un futur antérieur dont la mort est l'enjeu. En me donnant le passé absolu de la pose (aoriste), la photographie me dit la mort au futur.'[33] Death and family lineage undoubtedly preoccupy and exert a powerful influence on the protagonist in Proust's novel and inform the appropriation of photography with regard to these themes. This is particularly the case with Mlle Vinteuil's aberrant mourning for her recently deceased father, and Marcel's complex appreciation of the only photograph of his grandmother, taken by his friend Saint-Loup during her final illness.[34] However, it is the altogether less gloomy and more intriguing precariousness and stimulating suggestiveness of photographic practice and the photographic image, as they straddle past, present and future, which can also be seen to inform these and other passages in Proust's novel. In the first episode explored above, the multiple Albertines in Marcel's memory are each contained within a particular spatio-temporal fragment of memory, and each is charged with its own unique potential to enchant and to wound, but also to stimulate future speculation and even action: one pertinent though endlessly frustrating example being Marcel's fruitless attempts to discover details of Albertine's lesbian experience, even after her death.[35] In the second, the new appearance of family facial characteristics, attached to unique faces previously unmarked by any such signs of allegiance to the institution of the family, or by signs of temporal continuity and ageing, comically implies that there may have been some choice in the matter on the part of Marcel's old friends: a wry parallel is thereby drawn between the surprising wearing away of their physical specificity and their disappointing adherence to family tradition and social convention. The shock of time's impact on his former companions is thus all the more effectively conveyed, as the previously disregarded and unforeseen future has now left its tangible traces. Jean-Marie Schaeffer's *L'Image précaire: du dispositif photographique* points up in its title what Schaeffer considers photography's most distinctive characteristic: its precarious ambiguity. He notes 'le caractère protéïforme que prend l'acte de réception individuel' of the photograph, and affirms that the most irritating, but also stimulating, aspect of the photographic sign is its pragmatic flexibility:[36]

> Nous savons tous que l'image photographique est mise au service des stratégies de communication les plus diverses. Or, ces stratégies donnent lieu à [. . .] des normes communicationnelles, qui sont capables d'infléchir profondément son statut sémiotique [. . .] L'image photographique, loin de posséder un statut stable, est fondamentalement changeante et multiple.[37]

It is this fundamental protean instability of the photograph, as appropriated by Proust as a metaphor for the processes of perception and memory, which can be seen to inform its use with regard to the 'suspended syntax' of Marcel's repeated ruminations, caught between memory and action, and uncertain about the course to be taken in pursuit of knowledge or love or creative stimulus. While the two passages explored above both include explicit references to photography, it is possible to discern the same effects of temporal suspension and latency and, by extension, to read passages in the novel as photographic in style, even where no such mention of photography occurs. The particular quality of temporal latency or suspension that characterizes Marcel's pleasure on meeting Albertine at Balbec mirrors a feature of Proustian description which is his habit of depicting the effects of a particular, often pleasurable experience, before identifying its causes, in meandering sentences which Antoine Compagnon suggests are already postmodern.[38] Inherent in Proust's style therefore is a quality of temporal latency that defers the gratification of the curious reader who is repeatedly obliged to read on, and reread, in order to discover the source or cause of the recounted experience. Involuntary memory is a pertinent example of this inversion of cause and effect in Proust's style of description where joy is felt before the protagonist comes to recognize its cause; other such instances include the play of Charlus's predatory but initially misunderstood gaze at Balbec, and viewing Elstir's landscapes-as-seascapes and seascapes-as-landscapes.[39] A powerful stimulus towards creative action, such experiences are nonetheless all too frequently abandoned by the slothful protagonist; yet act he must, ultimately. At moments in the text where clarity is unexpectedly attained or decisions have been reached, Proust shows his mastery of the succinct turn of phrase. Such moments may strike the reader as decidedly abrupt in tone, and can be seen to have a photographic quality, as of a lens coming into sharp focus after a prolonged period of adjustment. Rapt perhaps rather than joyous, the description of rain on Tante Léonie's window follows the effect-before-cause pattern mentioned above, and provides a striking example of the complex interplay between past, present and future in Proust's writing of sensory experiences other than the visual:

> Un petit coup au carreau, comme si quelque chose l'avait heurté, suivi d'une ample chute légère comme de grains de sable qu'on eût laissés tomber d'une fenêtre au-dessus, puis la chute s'étendant, se réglant, adoptant un rythme, devenant fluide, sonore, musicale, innombrable, universelle: c'était la pluie.[40]

In this passage, photographic effects can be discerned in the syntactic play Proust makes of the dawning awareness that the sounds heard by the child are simply raindrops beginning to fall on the window. Past experience must come to the rescue and inform his understanding of what is happening in the present. His hesitation is apparent in the clipped rhythm of the first two clauses of the sentence, the second of which introduces the first simile, before the third confidently provides a striking simile of a decidedly earthy equivalent of the raindrops striking the glass in the form of 'grains de sable'. The sequence of events is carefully articulated through such words and phrases as 'suivi de' and 'puis', but no active verb is used until the 'c'était' of the boldly declarative final clause: all other verbs are in subordinate, speculative clauses ('l'avait heurté, 'qu'on eût laissés tomber'), or the present participle is used adjectivally to underline the immediacy of the changes in intensity of the rainfall ('s'étend-ant, se réglant, adoptant un rythme, devenant fluide'); and verbs become redundant in the ecstatic final clauses where the torrent of water is matched by the stream of increasingly grandiose adjectives ('fluide, sonore, musicale, innombrable, universelle'). The sudden appearance of a steadying colon stems the flow and clarifies the source of this reverie in four terse words (': c'était la pluie'). The affinity of photography and syntax in this sentence extends beyond the brevity of the final main clause, which turns so pithily on the subordinate clauses layered one over the other in the preceding lines, and so swiftly explains the origin of the rapturous extemporisation on the experience of listening to the rain; it includes also the way grammatical tenses are used to emphasize both the specificity of an experience, and its repetition throughout the annual Easter holidays spent at Combray. Proust's manipulation of grammatical tenses throughout 'Combray' and particularly after the tea-and-madeleine episode results in what Gérard Genette defines as an essentially iterative narrative:

> Ce type de récit, où une seule émission narrative assume ensemble plusieurs occurrences du même événement (c'est-à-dire, encore une fois, plusieurs évén-ements considérés dans leur seule analogie), nous le nommerons récit *itératif* [...] Aucune œuvre romanesque, apparemment, n'a jamais fait de l'itératif un usage comparable – par l'extension textuelle, par l'importance thématique, par le degré d'élaboration technique – à celui qu'en fait Proust dans la *Recherche du temps perdu*.[41]

The effect of the iterative is to underline the repetitive nature of experience. Using the iterative in 'Combray' effectively superimposes the routine rituals the child experienced in that village. In this passage, there is the suggestion that this experience of rain on the window is a fresh and exciting one for the child, contrasting with life indoors where he is caught up in Tante Léonie's strict observance of village protocols, religious services and dietary regimes.

In conclusion, it is possible to see 'photographic' effects in the syntax of Proust's novel, even where no explicit reference to photography is made. Whilst scenes where photography is openly called upon as a metaphor for perceptual experience and memory may more easily be argued to display some syntactical effects of the temporally and spatially complex imaging system that is photography, affinities of syntax and photography in Proust's novel are also to be found in scenes where cause and effect refuse to follow one another in a neatly ordered sequence. Philippe Ortel asserts that, within the context of the relationship between literature and photography, there is significant scope for future research on elements of Proust's style, particularly on rhythm, turns of phrase, and sentence length in his work.[42]

The structure and rhythm of Proust's sentences in the three passages explored here show how photographic practice informs Proust's style more profoundly than the protagonist's dismissive comments about this system of visual representation might suggest. Long sentences do characterize Proust's style, but the effect of their hesitant multiple clauses is more suggestive of an uncertain stumbling towards meaning than a smooth, confident representation of perceived and remembered experience. Photography can suspend a moment of time and space, releasing it from the flow of time and enabling it to develop an intricate network of links with past, present and future. In his lengthy sentences, Proust's complex syntax frequently suspends meaning, holding it at bay while it enables individual clauses to build into dense signifying units. Such sentences can be seen as collections of juxtaposed spatio-temporal 'snapshots' of multi-sensory impressions received and stored until their development – in inked words on paper – into legible signs for the reader to unravel.

Notes

1   Jane M. Rabb, *Literature and Photography: Interactions 1840–1990* (Albuquerque: University of New Mexico Press, 1995), p. xxxv.

2   Philippe Hamon notes that the nineteenth century ought to be seen as a battlefield where multiple systems of representation competed and influenced each other: 'Images à lire et images à voir: "images américaines" et crise de l'image au XIXe siècle', in Stéphane Michaud, Jean-Yves Mollier and Nicole Savy (eds), *Usages de l'image au XIXe siècle* (Paris: Éditions Créaphis, 1992), p. 235.

3   Philippe Ortel states that 'la métaphore photographique a […] une valeur heuristique bien réelle, qu'une étude stylistique de la phrase proustienne menée en termes

d'indicialité manifesterait certainement'. *La Littérature à l'ère de la photographie: enquête sur une révolution invisible* (Nîmes: Éditions Jacqueline Chambon, 2002), p. 311.

[4] Kathrin Yacavone's book *Benjamin, Barthes, and the Singularity of Photography* (London and New York: Continuum, 2012) is a comparative analysis of Benjamin's and Bathes's engagement with photography; however, Yacavone explores the significance of Proust for Barthes in the sixth chapter, 'Photography and memory: Barthes's Proustian quest'. Frank Wegner's unpublished doctoral thesis is another valuable addition to this field of research.

[5] Mieke Bal, *The Mottled Screen: Reading Proust Visually* (Stanford, CA: Stanford University Press, 1997), p. 201.

[6] Áine Larkin, *Proust Writing Photography: Fixing the Fugitive in 'À la recherche du temps perdu'* (Oxford: Legenda, 2011).

[7] Michael Wood, 'Other eyes: Proust and the myths of photography', in André Benhaïm (ed.), *The Strange M. Proust* (London: Legenda, 2009).

[8] Wood, 'Other eyes', p. 104.

[9] Katja Haustein, 'Proust's emotional cavities: vision and affect in *À la recherche du temps perdu*', *French Studies*, LXIII/2 (spring 2009), 161–73.

[10] Haustein, p. 162.

[11] Gabrielle Townsend, *Proust's Imaginary Museum: Reproductions and Reproduction in 'À la recherche du temps perdu'* (Oxford: Peter Lang, 2007).

[12] Townsend, *Proust's Imaginary Museum*, p. 145.

[13] Townsend, *Proust's Imaginary Museum*, p. 146.

[14] Dora Zhang, 'A lens for an eye: Proust and photography', *Representations*, 118/1 (spring 2012), 103–25 (109).

[15] Zhang, 'A lens for an eye', 110.

[16] Important studies of Proust's style and syntax include Gérard Genette's 'Métonymie chez Proust' and 'Discours du récit', both in *Figures III* (Paris: Seuil, 1972), pp. 41–63 and pp. 65–282 respectively; Jean-Yves Tadié's *Proust et le roman* (Paris: Gallimard, 1971); B. G. Rogers's *Proust's Narrative Techniques* (Geneva: Droz, 1965); Jean Milly's *Proust et le style* (Paris: Lettres Modernes, 1970), and V. E. Graham's *The Imagery of Proust* (Oxford: Blackwell, 1966).

[17] Walter Benjamin, 'The image of Proust', in *Illuminations* (London: Pimlico, 1999), p. 209.

[18] Malcolm Bowie, 'Postlude: Proust and the art of brevity', in *The Cambridge Companion to Proust* (Cambridge: Cambridge University Press, 2001), pp. 216–29.

[19] Malcolm Bowie, *Proust Among the Stars* (London: Harper Collins, 1998), pp. 56–7.

[20] Susan Sontag, *On Photography* (London: Penguin, 1977), p. 22.

21 Marcel Proust, *À la recherche du temps perdu*, IV, p. 60. All references to Proust's work are taken from the Pléiade edition published in four volumes and edited by Jean-Yves Tadié (Paris: Gallimard, 1987–9).

22 Proust, *À la recherche*, IV, p. 444.

23 Gérard Genette confirms the 'pluralités de focalisation' resulting from the many voices speaking in the novel in *Figures III* (Paris: Seuil, 1972), p. 258.

24 Notably in 'Narrative focalization and image juxtaposition' in Larkin, *Proust Writing Photography*, chapter 2, pp. 94–132.

25 While Michael Wood does acknowledge that 'photography [. . .] belongs to two moments in time [. . .] There is the time of the shot and the time of the image', the time of image making between these two points must also be considered. Michael Wood, 'Other eyes', p. 102.

26 Frank Wegner, 'Photography in Proust's *À la recherche du temps perdu*', unpublished doctoral thesis (University of Cambridge, 2004), 80.

27 Vilem Flusser, *Towards a Philosophy of Photography* (London: Reaktion, 2000), p. 8.

28 Proust, *À la recherche*, IV, p. 461; IV, p. 475; IV, p. 485; IV, p. 563–4.

29 Proust, *À la recherche*, IV, p. 513.

30 Genette, *Figures III*, p. 216.

31 Proust, *À la recherche*, IV, p. 520.

32 Proust, *À la recherche*, IV, p. 534.

33 Roland Barthes, *La Chambre claire: note sur la photographie* (Paris: Seuil, 1980), p. 150.

34 Mlle Vinteuil acts out the frustration and grief of her mourning in a seemingly sadistic sexual role play involving a photographic portrait of her late father (Proust, *À la recherché*, I, pp. 157–63); Marcel's grandmother's session of posing for the photographer Saint-Loup constitutes one of the few occasions where she and her grandson do not communicate honestly or kindly, and Françoise's unwitting disclosures years later compound his grief (Proust, II, 144–5; III, 172–6).

35 Proust, *À la recherche*, III, pp. 504–5.

36 Jean-Marie Schaeffer, *L'Image précaire: du dispositif photographique* (Paris: Seuil, 1987), p. 105.

37 Ibid., p. 10.

38 Antoine Compagnon, *Les Cinq Paradoxes de la modernité* (Paris: Seuil, 1990), p. 160. In *À l'ombre des jeunes filles en fleurs*, the protagonist Marcel reflects on the pleasure of being introduced to the desired Albertine by using an explicitly photographic metaphor of perceiving and subsequently remembering her (Proust, *À la recherche*, II, pp. 226–7).

39 Proust, *À la recherche*, II, pp. 110–12; II, pp. 191–6.

[40] Proust, *À la recherche*, I, p. 100.

[41] Genette, *Figures III*, pp. 148–9.

[42] Philippe Ortel, *La Littérature à l'ère de la photographie: enquête sur une révolution invisible* (Nîmes: Éditions Jacqueline Chambon 2002), p. 311.

Portraits and Neologisms: Understanding the Visual in Henri Michaux's 'Voyage en Grande Garabagne'[1]

Nina Parish

Henri Michaux composed many different types of travel narratives during his lifetime and the idea of travel is central to his creative concerns. He writes in 'Observations': 'J'écris pour me parcourir. Peindre, composer, écrire: me parcourir. Là est l'aventure d'être en vie.'[2] The first of his imaginary journeys, 'Voyage en Grande Garabagne', was published in 1936, at around the same time as this poet-artist was beginning to publish books including his own texts and images and when the visual was becoming established as an important part of his output. 'Voyage en Grande Garabagne' contains no visual elements, however. There had been plans for an atlas including maps, sketches and portraits to accompany the text, but these projects never came to fruition. In this chapter, I shall examine the place of this text in Michaux's visual and verbal production, its publishing history and its relationship to the traditional travel narrative in order to demonstrate that the absence of images in this work is telling for the representation of Michaux's fictional stay in Garabagne. Although there are no physical images in 'Voyage en Grande Garabagne', the visual is still very much present. Using Mieke Bal's visual analysis of Marcel Proust's À la recherche du temps perdu as a starting point, I shall explore her questions in relation to Michaux: 'So where is the visual situated in a literary text? How can we read "visually"?[3] It seems that in 'Voyage en Grande Garabagne' portraits and neologisms pre-empt the emergence of the visual in Michaux's works and add to the sense of otherness created in this depiction of exotic lands. Studying the absence of conspicuous visual elements in 'Voyage en Grande Garabagne' helps us to understand the creative process and how representation works.

'Voyage en Grande Garabagne' was published for the second time alongside two other accounts of invented countries, *Au pays de la magie* and *Ici Poddema* in *Ailleurs* in 1948.[4] These texts participate in an extensive cycle of travel narratives in Michaux's œuvre, which range from his so-called real journeys evoked in *Ecuador* (1929) and *Un barbare en Asie* (1933) to the imaginary journeys related in books such as *Ailleurs*, to the drug narratives published in the 1950s and 1960s, which can arguably be referred to as metaphorical spiritual or inner journeys across mescaline country. Michaux travelled widely throughout his life and visited various countries in Latin America and Asia, as the titles of these early writings imply. He comments on his reasons for travelling in *Quelques renseignements sur cinquante-neuf années d'existence*:

> Il voyage *contre*.
>   Pour expulser de lui sa patrie, ses attaches de toutes sortes et ce qui s'est en lui et malgré lui attaché de culture grecque ou romaine ou germanique ou d'habitudes belges.
> Voyages d'expatriation.[5]

Michaux travelled in order to escape the constraints imposed on him by the Western world and to start anew. But, rather than experiencing some type of liberation or revelation offered by faraway places, in the writing of his first travel narratives, Michaux finds himself instead confronted with an uneasy and sometimes confusing relationship between the real and the imaginary. Michel Butor has categorized these first travel narratives as 'livres de pérégrination', adding: 'C'est d'abord le voyage réel qui sert de modèle à l'imaginaire'.[6] They will in turn give rise to the creation of the imaginary countries and peoples evoked in texts such as 'Voyage en Grande Garabagne'.

Ecuador, with its purposely misleading subtitle 'journal de voyage', sup-posedly relates the actual journey that Michaux undertook with the Ecuadorian poet Alfredo Gangotena at the end of 1927. Its preface immediately throws the reader off track with the following words: '*Un homme qui ne sait ni voyager ni tenir un journal a composé ce journal de voyage.*'[7] According to Raymond Bellour, editor of Michaux's complete works in the Pléiade edition, this journey into the unknown and the exotic, inscribed in the authentic native spelling of the place name in the title, is transformed into a 'lieu d'écriture' through its very subtitle.[8] Michaux's initial travel writings are, therefore, less to do with the experience of travelling itself than with the writer's own efforts to represent this experience. In these travel works, the real journeys are as imaginary as the imaginary journeys are real. The preface to *Ailleurs* underlines this friction: 'Il traduit le Monde, celui qui voulait s'en échapper, qui pourrait échapper? Le vase est clos.'[9]

Some critics have identified allusions to real events – such as the German occupation of France or South African apartheid – in the evocations of imaginary countries in *Ailleurs*.[10] Indeed, recent research on 'Voyage en Grande Garabagne' has explored its extra-literary relevance and underlined its intertextual links with other travel narratives, whether literary or scientific, countering claims by writers such as André Gide that this text's interest lies in its actual 'inactualité'.[11] These extratextual and intertextual links confirm that all texts are woven out of existing structures and other texts. No text is ever completely original or contained in a cultural and linguistic vacuum because of the need to use a conventional signifying system. Indeed, it could be argued that this impossibility of total originality leads Michaux to disrupt textual conventions and to experiment with other expressive forms. But, to return to Gide, the inactuality of Michaux's writing is ultimately liberating because it points to the role of literature as a means of subtracting the factual and of opening up possibilities for reimagining the world.

In his travel narratives Michaux interweaves reflections on different journeys and the creative process (both verbal and visual) itself, which in turn produce tensions between the real and the imaginary. From an early stage, Michaux argues that through leaving language and expressing himself using visual means, he will be able to render the real in a more direct way. In *Ecuador* he writes:

Le nom. Je cherchais des noms et j'étais malheureux. Le nom: valeur d'après coup, et de longue expérience.

 Il n'y a que pour les peintres dans le premier contact avec l'étranger; le dessin, la couleur, quel tout et qui se présente d'emblée![12]

Michaux is attracted to the representational possibilities offered to him by the visual, in this case, painting. But his conscious and written fictionalisations of his various journeys represent the condition of all travel writing or writing in general. Michaux is well aware that any textual representation can only ever be figurative; it can never be real, thus highlighting how language constructs and shapes the world rather than the world determining language. This is why Roland Barthes makes reference to Michaux's 'Voyage en Grande Garabagne' in the opening pages of *L'Empire des signes*, his visual and verbal exploration of Japan:

> Si je veux imaginer un peuple fictif, je puis lui donner un nom inventé, le traiter déclarativement comme un objet romanesque, fonder une nouvelle Garabagne, de façon à ne compromettre aucun pays réel dans ma fantaisie (mais alors c'est cette fantaisie même que je compromets dans les signes de la littérature).[13]

L'Empire des signes and 'Voyage en Grande Garabagne' remind us powerfully that the creative process does not depend on some pre-given reality, but can transcend the empirical and intimate the new.

 Michaux started work on a first version of 'Voyage en Grande Garabagne', entitled 'Mœurs et coutumes des tribus et des peuples de Grande Garabagne', in 1934. A turbulent publishing history ensued and the book appeared two years later, the first volume of Jean Paulhan's 'Métamorphoses' collection with Gallimard.[14] In the introduction to this first edition, Michaux alluded to a parallel project, an *Atlas de Grande Garabagne (cartes, portraits, croquis)*, which was also mentioned amongst the works that he was said to be preparing at the time: 'Il a paru intéressant à l'éditeur de publier séparément, en un atlas de grand format, les belles cartes de Fitzgerald, et les croquis et portraits que j'ai faits des différentes races observées. Cet ouvrage sera bientôt terminé.'[15] A work containing both visual and verbal elements was planned, reminding us of the importance for Michaux of the visual as well as the interaction between these two expressive forms at that time. Bellour elaborates on this point:

> C'est la première des trois tentatives avortées par lesquelles Michaux tenta de lier l'écriture de ses voyages imaginaires à sa création de dessinateur et de peintre, qui commence alors à prendre forme: *Entre centre et absence*, son premier recueil illustré, paraît deux mois à peine après *Voyage en Grande Garabagne*, et le jour victorieux de son 'Eurêka' en peinture, annoncé à Paulhan, date du 6 janvier 1936.[16]

In this quotation, Bellour places this visual project in the context of Michaux's contemporary interdisciplinary production. Why would Michaux bring together text and image for the first time in *Entre centre et absence*, published in the same year as 'Voyage en Grande Garabagne', yet not provide a visual accompaniment to the latter?[17]

It can be argued that the genre of the traditional travel narrative where the image serves an illustrative function so that the non-traveller is able to glimpse little-known regions of the world from the comfort of their armchairs would not be what Michaux had in mind when combining text and image in book form. He would have been familiar with this type of travel book from his own journeys. Bellour even suggests that his choice of the name Fitzgerald for his travelling companion in the first drafts of 'Voyage en Grande Garabagne' was influenced by this type of publication; three different Fitzgeralds produced publications on South America, Australia and Africa at the turn of the twentieth century.[18] But Michaux's own publications including text and image indicate that he had little interest in replicating the form of the traditional travel narrative in which the image is subordinate to the text. Indeed, the relationship between word and image in Michaux's books varies immensely. *Peintures et dessins* (1946), for example, follows the ekphrastic tradition with images accompanying the text whilst other works reverse this practice, the text providing a commentary on the image, such as in *Mouvements* (1951). Some works contain images by Michaux; others include works by other artists, for example, *Lecture de huit lithographies de Zao Wou-Ki* (1950) and *Tranches de savoir, suivi de la situation politique* (1950) in which the only visual contribution is a frontispiece, an etching by Max Ernst. Michaux's travel narratives, both real and imaginary, generally do not contain visual images, let alone images with a straightforward illustrative function.[19] It is unsurprising then that the atlas for 'Voyage en Grande Garabagne' was never to see the light of day.

For many, these imaginary worlds are recreated visually in Michaux's series of gouaches and alphabets produced around the same time. Adrienne Monnier recalls her experience of the series:

> En les regardant, j'ai tout de suite vu qu'on était en Grande Garabagne: voici des arrivées de Rocodis et de Nijidus à notre rencontre, sur celle-là on voit une violente mêlée d'Arpèdres, et sur cette autre une galopade de Vibres le long d'une plage.[20]

However, as Jérôme Roger has pointed out in a recent article exploring Michaux's visual output, although there are some salient analogies, 'correspondances' even, to be made between certain aspects of his visual and verbal works, this is ultimately not the point.[21] Michaux rather scathingly relates in *Ecuador*:

> Il faut écouter le public dans un salon de peinture. Soudain, après avoir longuement cherché, quelqu'un, montrant du doigt sur le tableau: 'C'est un pommier', dit-il, et on le sent soulagé.
> Il en a détaché un pommier! Voilà un homme heureux.[22]

The viewer of any visual work will naturally seek some type of equivalence in their own reality. The absence of visual portraits of lands and peoples in 'Voyage en Grande Garabagne' allows readers to imagine their own world and to alter this image as they please. This absence in fact reinforces the creative powers of language. It emphasizes the liberation of languages from what can be seen or observed, its lack of a need to be rooted in reference, its abstraction, and this gives verbal language the potential to move into a new dimension not bound by the empirical or lived reality.

In 'Voyage en Grande Garabagne', Michaux constructs verbal portraits of various peoples and tribes. The portrait adds a visual dimension to the text through the cultural knowledge of readers (Da Vinci's iconic *Mona Lisa*, Rembrandt's self-portraits, the harrowed and haggard heads painted by Fautrier, to name but a few) and through their desire to be able to visualize what they are reading. But who delivers these portraits to the reader in Michaux's text? It is a type of hybrid narrator-author-traveller, whose identity is unstable, who divulges very few details about himself, and who can be identified by the use of the first-person masculine singular in twelve of the thirty-one chapters of 'Voyage en Grande Garabagne', for example, in the opening sentence, 'Chez les Hacs': 'Comme j'entrais dans ce village, je fus conduit par un bruit étrange.'[23] Very quickly this 'je' implicates the reader in the narrative. For example, in 'Chez les Hacs': 'Ces grimaces hideuses vous mordent [...]'[24] This narrative technique develops a form of complicity between the narrator and the reader; again in 'Chez les Hacs': 'On devine tout de suite quels sont les combats les plus appréciés.'[25] The narrator figure remains in charge until the last chapter when he suddenly disappears and Dovobo, the Emperor of Grande Garabagne, takes his place and signs the last chapter: 'Maison maudite!' Bellour writes about the first narrator: 'C'est un homme sans âge et sans visage. Sa nature d'Européen s'affirme grâce à quelques rappels disséminés.'[26] And indeed, at a given moment, the anonymous narrator mentions 'ces petites mêlées comme en Europe', thus creating links with a familiar environment (rugby) for a European reader.[27]

The narrator of 'Voyage en Grande Garabagne', therefore, remains practically unknown to the reader both mentally and physically, and he often appears indifferent to what is going on around him. In many ways, this is typical of Michaux's fictional characters, for example, Plume, who cannot avoid coming up against social order and convention in Chaplinesque adventures which signify the hostility and absurdity of the outside world for the poet-artist.[28] It is, however, through the narrator that the reader accesses various portraits that are anchored in the visual in 'Voyage en Grande Garabagne'. The narrator is the voyeur, who invites the reader to see what he sees and yet like the reader is never seen. The strangeness of this project is further emphasized because the reader will ultimately never visit these imaginary lands. Indeed, it seems as if these texts will always remain foreign to us.[29] Michaux's construction and destruction of faces and his introduction of neologisms in 'Voyage en Grande Garabagne' further reinforce this foreignness.

In the first chapters of 'Voyage en Grande Garabagne', faces are often evoked, for example, 'Chez les Hacs':

Alors que dans la journée, la fureur elle-même ruse et se dissimule, jamais démoniaque, la nuit au contraire, elle congestionne ou blêmit le visage aussitôt, s'y colle en une expression infernale. Il est dommage qu'on ne puisse saisir cette expression que dans une demi-obscurité. Néanmoins, ce moment d'envahissement du visage est un spectacle inoubliable [...] Les spectateurs de la haute société Hac ne manquent jamais de vous expliquer que ce n'est pas le combat qui les attire, mais les révélations qui sortent du visage.[30]

Likewise, in the description of the customs of the Emanglons:

C'est le matin après le sommeil épais et lourd de la nuit, que l'expression du visage de l'Emanglon est la plus étrange, et comme hors de l'humanité; avec ce regard sombre et parlant, quoique pour ne rien dire d'intelligible, qu'ont parfois de vieux chiens malades et rhumatisants près d'un maître méchant mais auquel ils sont attachés.[31]

Every house constructed by the Emanglons even includes an image of a face carved above the front door: 'Au-dessus de la porte d'entrée de sa maison est gravée en relief dans la pierre ou le bois une grosse tête d'homme. Cette figure exprime une tranquillité en route vers la colère.'[32] This face participates in a complex and humorous set of codes regarding visits that ultimately leads to a cold reception by the Emanglon host of anyone daring to visit.

So, what is in fact revealed by these faces in 'Voyage en Grande Garabagne'? If we consider that in the Western world the head is assumed to be the seat of reason, of identity, of personality, and of civilisation even, it is fitting that the narrator attempts to capture and render these peoples by describing this part of the body. There exist many allusions to faces and heads in other contemporary texts by Michaux, such as *Un certain Plume* and 'Mon roi'.[33] Switching expressive forms, Michaux admits that faces appear on paper as soon as he begins drawing or painting:

Dessinez sans intention particulière, griffonnez machinalement, il apparaît presque toujours sur le papier des visages.

Menant une excessive vie faciale, on est aussi dans une perpétuelle fièvre de visages.

> Dès que je prends un crayon, un pinceau, il m'en vient sur le papier l'un après l'autre dix, quinze, vingt. Et sauvages la plupart.[34]

Michaux battles with these faces, as he also does with the written word, for they are a corporeal constraint because of their social and identifying capacity. With this in mind, the first reference to faces in 'Voyage en Grande Garabagne' takes on another layer of significance:

> Et ce qui arrive toujours arriva: un sabot dur et bête frappant une tête. Les nobles traits, comme sont même les plus ignobles, les traits de cette face étaient piétinés comme betterave sans importance. La langue à paroles tombe, tandis que le cerveau à l'intérieur ne mijote plus une pensée, et le cœur, faible marteau, à son tour reçoit des coups, mais quels coups![35]

It is unsurprising that Michaux presents his/her reader with the spectacle of the destruction of this first head, when its frequently constraining role in Western society is considered.

In this respect, Michaux's portraits, verbal as well as visual, could be interpreted as being somewhere between an emergence and a destruction of the human form, as Claire Stoullig writes, 'entre figuration et défiguration'.[36] In a similar way to Bataille's understanding of dust explored in *Documents*, the mud in the fights between family members in 'Chez les Hacs' contributes to a spectacle of the formless:[37]

> La boue gluante est la seule animatrice du combat, impartiale, mais perfide, tantôt exagérant jusqu'au tonnerre une simple claque, tantôt dérobant presque entièrement un coup tragique au bas-ventre, basse, rampante, toujours ouverte à l'homme qui s'abandonne. Les buffles luisants aux membres d'homme, la tête ruisselante de boue, soufflent, luttent, à moitié asphyxiés, aveuglés, assourdis par cette boue traîtresse qui entre partout et reste et obstrue.

Here, Bataille's concept of doing violence to representation as the basis of any representational act finds an echo in Michaux's own mud-filled images of annihilation and obliteration.

This form rendered other is also present on a lexical level in 'Voyage en Grande Garabagne' in the neologisms introduced by Michaux. These invented words can be found in several contemporary texts to 'Voyage en Grande Garabagne' such as 'Le Grand Combat' (1927) and the controversial 'Rencontre dans la forêt' (1935).[38] Both of these texts use neologisms which connote physical violence to carry the meaning of the text but also to inflict violence on the textual form itself. Bellour comments on Michaux's neologisms, using the metaphor of battle:

> Ce langage informel, ou déformé ('déformel' ferait bien l'affaire), est le langage d'un combat entre vie et mort: c'est accepter ou non – avoir depuis l'origine accepté ou non – de manger, de parler, puis de lire et d'écrire, et retrouver chaque fois le théâtre entier du drame du corps, de l'accès douloureux que toute altérité ouvre à la sensation comme à la pensée.[39]

Michaux's invented words attempt to transcribe the physical, visceral nature of language and the writing or creative process. They attract inevitable comparisons with the 'nonsense' languages playfully developed by Edward Lear and Lewis Carroll, the *zaoum* language composed by the Russian formalists, and various phonetic and lexical innovations created and often performed by poets and artists linked to the Dada tendency. They also bear witness to the presence of another language, which, in Michaux's case, recalls his Belgian childhood and that nation's other language, Flemish. Barthes writes of the opportunities afforded by a 'langue inconnue' in *L'Empire des signes*:

> Le rêve: connaître une langue étrangère (étrange) et cependant ne pas la comprendre: percevoir en elle la différence, sans que cette différence soit jamais récupérée par la socialité superficielle du langage, communication ou vulgarité; connaître, réfractées positivement dans une autre langue nouvelle, les impossibilités de la nôtre; apprendre la systématique de l'inconcevable; défaire notre 'réel' sous l'effet d'autres découpages, d'autres syntaxes; découvrir des positions inouïes du sujet dans l'énonciation, déplacer sa topologie; en un mot, descendre dans l'intraduisible.[40]

Michaux's neologisms can be understood in the light of Barthes's descent into the untranslatable. Through their incomprehensibility and strangeness, they refuse habitual communicational conventions and open the text up to the idea of being foreign relative to one's own language.

In 'Voyage en Grande Garabagne', the names of different peoples and tribes are often composed of neologisms: 'les Hacs' and 'les Emanglons' have already been mentioned, but there are many others, for example, 'les Ecarissins', 'les Aravis' and 'les Halalas'. Furthermore, neologisms form part of the sentences employed to construct portraits of these peoples. They trouble the reading process, for francophone and non-francophone readers alike, as they follow the basic grammatical, orthographic and phonetic rules of the French language, but have little or no semantic value, for example, in 'Les Ossopets':

Les Ematrus sont lichinés ou bien ils sont bohanés. C'est l'un ou l'autre. Ils cousent les rats avec des arzettes, et sans les tuer, les relâchent ainsi cousus, voués aux mouvements d'ensemble, à la misère, et à la faim qui en résulte.

Les Ematrus s'enivrent avec de la clouille. Mais d'abord ils se terrent dans un tonneau ou dans un fossé, où ils sont trois ou quatre jours avant de reprendre connaissance.

Naturellement imbéciles, amateurs de grosses plaisanteries, ils finissent parfaits narcindons.[41]

These neologisms ('lichinés', 'bohanés', 'arzettes', 'clouille', 'narcindons') are surrounded by words that have specific meanings. The invented words 'contaminate' the authentic words by taking them out of their usual context and placing them in new linguistic situations where their conventional meaning no longer prevails. The statement 'C'est l'un ou l'autre' is ultimately unhelpful when trying to build an image of 'Les Ematrus', but the invented adjectives 'lichinés' and 'bohanés' take on their own levels of signification in this context by association and connotation. The referential makes way for the self-reflexive: the neologisms in 'Voyage en Grande Garabagne' signify the emptiness of linguistic conventions and bring more alterity to the written text.

These neologisms can be seen as forerunners to the introduction of images and signs in Michaux's books. Indeed, the first question in the third book incorporating signs, *Saisir* (1979), refers to this neologistic and onomatopoeic experimentation and bears witness to the signifying possibilities of the graphic sign: 'Qui n'a voulu saisir plus, saisir mieux, saisir autrement, et les êtres et les choses, pas avec des mots, ni avec des phonèmes, ni des onomatopées, mais avec des signes graphiques?'[42] The poet-artist appears to have stopped his experimentation with invented words after 'Rencontre dans la forêt'. Neologisms do exist in Michaux's drug narratives.[43] However, these operate in a different fashion to the earlier 'espéranto lyrique'.[44] It is around this time, in the mid-1930s, that visual production and particularly painting becomes more dominant in his creative output. His first individual exhibition of gouaches took place at the Paul Magné Ancienne Pléiade Gallery in Paris in 1937.

The evocation of faces and the use of neologisms in 'Voyage en Grande Garabagne' accentuate Michaux's approach to the inhabitants of Garabagne and their various societies. On the one hand, he directly depicts destructive authoritarian structures which deprive individuals of freedom, for example, in 'Les Nonais et les Oliabaires':

> Depuis une éternité, les Nonais sont les esclaves des Oliabaires. Les Oliabaires les font travailler plus que de raison, car ils ont peur que les Nonais, s'ils reprennent quelque force, n'en profitent pour regagner leur pays, à peu près inculte actuell-ement, il est vrai, et en partie inondé.[45]

On the other hand, Michaux creates subversive phenomena, figures and attitudes which resist these structures as in the strange logic introduced by a neologism in the portrait of the Emanglons: 'En somme, les Emanglons sont des Yoffes.'[46] Hence, the poet-artist attacks the hierarchical signifying systems established in our society from both inside and out and his decision not to include images in a genre that would traditionally include them, his description and destruction of faces and his neologisms all participate in this process of subversion.

The various evocations of faces and the neologisms in 'Voyage en Grande Garabagne' do not give us the *essence* of the inhabitants of Garabagne, or provide a clear visual image of them. Instead they subvert the textual status quo and make the reader sensitive to something else, something different creeping into the text. As Barthes writes in *L'Empire des signes*:

> L'auteur n'a jamais, en aucun sens, photographié le Japon. Ce serait plutôt le contraire: le Japon l'a étoilé d'éclairs multiples; ou mieux encore: le Japon l'a mis

en situation d'écriture. Cette situation est celle-là même où s'opère un certain ébranlement de la personne, un renversement des anciennes lectures, une secousse du sens, déchiré, exténué jusqu'à son vide insubstituable, sans que l'objet cesse jamais d'être signifiant, désirable.[47]

Although *L'Empire des signes* does contain photographs, including several by the Swiss travel writer, Nicolas Bouvier, Barthes chose not to give a precise account or to provide a photographic image of Japan in his verbal text so that a space could be opened for another type of creation. Garabagne appears to provoke a similar reaction in Michaux: '[elle] l'a mis[e] en situation d'écriture'. *L'Empire des signes* is concerned with an experience of the textual character of reality, its mediate nature and the impossibility of direct access to the real. Michaux's travel narratives probe similar ideas. His quest to disrupt textual conventions and show how those conventions can be re-imagined within the text itself, through the foregrounding of textual otherness in *Voyage en Grande Garabagne*, ultimately reinforces the power of language and signs to create worlds beyond reference.

Notes

[1] This chapter develops some of the ideas explored in 'Lire le visuel dans "Voyage en Grande Garabagne": une approche interdisciplinaire', in Ruggero Campagnoli, Eric Lysoe and Anna Soncini (eds), *'Voyage en GrandeGarabagne' de Henri Michaux*, Proceedings of the Séminaires d'analyse textuelle Pasquali, Lucelle (Bologna: Clueb, 2012), pp. 7–25.

[2] Henri Michaux, 'Observations', in *Passages*, in Henri Michaux, *Œuvres complètes*, vol. II, ed. Raymond Bellour, with Ysé Tran (Paris: Gallimard, Collection 'Bibliothèque de la Pléiade', 2001), pp. 344–52 (p. 345). This edition will henceforth be referred to as *OC* II.

[3] Mieke Bal, *The Mottled Screen: Reading Proust Visually*, translated by Anna-Louise Milne (Stanford: Stanford University Press, 1997), p. 91.

[4] *Ailleurs* was first entitled 'Voyages imaginaires' and then 'Le Livre du voyageur'. See Raymond Bellour, 'Notice' to *Ailleurs*, in *OC* II, pp. 1035–51 (p. 1035).

[5] Michaux, *Quelques renseignements*, in *Œuvres complètes*, vol. I, ed. Raymond Bellour, with Ysé Tran (Paris: Gallimard, Collection Bibliothèque de la Pléiade, 1998), p. CXXXIII (Michaux's italics). This edition will henceforth be referred to as *OC* I.

[6] Michel Butor, *Improvisations sur Henri Michaux* (Fontfroide-le-Haut: fata morgana, 1985), p. 59.

[7] Michaux, *Ecuador*, in *OC* I, pp. 137–243 (p. 139) (Michaux's italics).

[8] Bellour, 'Notice' to *Ailleurs*, *OC* II, p. 1035.

[9] Michaux, 'Préface' to *Ailleurs*, *OC* II, p. 3.

[10] Bellour discusses links to contemporary historical events in 'Notice' to *Ailleurs*, *OC* II, pp.1048–9.

[11] In her doctoral thesis, Maria Wennerström Wohrne argues that the texts contained in 'Voyage en Grande Garabagne' are inextricably linked to a sociocultural reality and to a specific literary and scientific tradition. She makes reference to works by Linnaeus, Swift, Diderot, Malraux and Abraham Hyacinthe Anquetil-Dupperon. See Maria Wennerström Wohrne, 'Att översätta världen: Kommunikation och subversivt ärende i Henri Michaux "Voyage en Grande Garabagne"' (unpublished doctoral thesis, University of Uppsala, Sweden, 2003). André Gide speaks of 'sa gratuité totale, parfaite', in 'Découvrons Henri Michaux', *Essais critiques*, ed. Pierre Masson (Paris: Gallimard, Collection Bibliothèque de la Pléiade, 1999), pp. 733–49 (p. 744).

[12] Michaux, *Ecuador*, *OC* I, p. 151 (Michaux's italics).

[13] Roland Barthes, *L'Empire des signes* (Paris: Seuil, Collection Points Essais, 2005), p. 11.

[14] See Bellour, 'Notes et variantes' to *Ailleurs*, *OC* II, pp. 1053–93 (p. 1054).

[15] Michaux, 'En marge d'*Ailleurs*', *OC* II, pp. 133–45 (p.133). This introduction was not included in the 1948 publication of *Ailleurs*. James Fitzgerald was the Englishman who, with his anonymous wife, supposedly accompanied the narrator on the first versions of this journey.

[16] Bellour, 'Notes et variantes', to 'Voyage en Grande Garabagne', *OC* II, p. 1056.

[17] 'Le livre est annoncé "avec sept dessins et un frontispièce de l'Auteur"'. Quoted in Bellour, 'Notes et variantes' to *Plume précédé de Lointain intérieur*, *OC* I, pp. 1262–90 (p. 1262).

[18] Bellour, 'Notes et variantes' to *Ailleurs*, *OC* II, p. 1091.

[19] The exceptions are *Meidosems* (1948), which contains twelve lithographs by Michaux of this strange imaginary race, constantly undergoing metamorphoses, and *Vigies sur cibles* (1959), which includes nine etched engravings by Matta.

[20] See Adrienne Monnier, 'Les Peintures d'Henri Michaux', *Les Lettres nouvelles*, 2 (April 1953). Quoted in *Correspondance Adrienne Monnier & Henri Michaux 1939–1955*, ed. Maurice Imbert (Paris: la hune, 1995), unpaginated.

[21] Jérôme Roger, '"Le phrasé même de la vie" ou la vie plastique d'Henri Michaux', in Pierre Vilar, Françoise Nicol and Guénaël Boutouillet (eds), *Conversations avec Henri Michaux* (Nantes: Cécile Défaut, 2008), pp. 75–98 (pp. 81–2).

22 Michaux, *Ecuador*, *OC* I, p. 151.

23 Michaux, 'Voyage en Grande Garabagne', in *Ailleurs*, *OC* II, pp. 5–65 (p. 5).

24 Michaux, 'Voyage en Grande Garabagne', *OC* II, p. 7.

25 Ibid., p. 6.

26 Bellour, 'Notice' to *Ailleurs*, *OC* II, p. 1039.

27 Michaux, 'Voyage en Grande Garabagne', *OC* II, p. 61.

28 The opening passage of 'Un certain Plume' describes Plume asleep as his house is stolen, his wife is run over by a train in bed next to him, and he is condemned to death. Michaux, 'Un homme paisible', in *Plume précédé de Lointain intérieur*, *OC* II, pp. 557–665 (pp. 622–3).

29 Maurice Blanchot writes : 'Ces fictions que nous comprenons ne sont pas écrites pour nous'. Blanchot, 'L'Ange du bizarre', in *Henri Michaux ou le refus de l'enfermement* (Tours: farrago, 1999), pp. 11–25 (p. 25).

30 Michaux, 'Voyage en Grande Garabagne', *OC* II, p. 7.

31 Ibid., p. 13.

32 Ibid., p. 14.

33 Michaux, *Un certain Plume*, *OC* I, pp. 622–42; Michaux, 'Mon roi', in *La Nuit remue*, *OC* I, pp. 422–5.

34 Michaux, 'En pensant au phénomène de la peinture', *Passages*, *OC* II, pp. 320–31 (p. 320).

35 Michaux, 'Voyage en Grande Garabagne', *OC* II, p. 5.

36 *Henri Michaux: Œuvres complètes choisies, 1927–1984* (Musées de Marseille, Seuil, 1997), p. 24. Quoted in Jérôme Roger, '"Le Phrasé même de la vie" ou la vie plastique d'Henri Michaux', in *Conversations avec Henri Michaux*, p. 76.

37 See *Documents*, no. 5, October 1929, reprinted in *Documents année 1929*, vol. I (Paris: Éditions Jean-Michel Place, 1991), p. 278. Briony Fer dedicates a chapter, '"Poussière/Peinture": Bataille on Painting', to this subject in *On Abstract Art* (New Haven and London: Yale University Press, 1997), pp. 77–91.

38 Michaux, 'Le Grand combat', *Qui je fus*, *OC* I, pp. 118–19; Michaux, 'Rencontre dans la forêt', *OC* I, p. 416.

39 Bellour, 'Notice' to 'Rencontre dans la forêt', *OC* I, pp. 1156–66 (p. 1158).

40 Barthes, *L'Empire des signes*, p. 15.

41 Michaux, 'Voyage en Grande Garabagne', *OC* II, pp. 41–2.

42 Michaux, *Saisir*, in Michaux, *Œuvres complètes*, Vol. III, ed. Raymond Bellour, with Ysé Tran and the collaboration of Mireille Cardot (Paris: Gallimard, Collection Bibliothèque de la Pléiade, 2004), pp. 933–83, (p. 936).

43 Malcolm Bowie states on this subject: 'The neologisms which frequently occur in Michaux's reports on mescaline [. . .] represent attempts to accommodate within

language sensations and concepts for which words do not already exist; for example: *infinisation, fagocité, encharnellement, imagification, bilogé, omnirelié, infiniverti* [. . .] In short, the neologisms to be found in poems such as "Le Grand Combat" allow the poet, by means of connotation, to approach new varieties of experience, whereas those in the drug narratives allow him, by means of exact denotation, to withdraw.' Malcolm Bowie, *Henri Michaux: A Study of his Literary Works* (Oxford: Clarendon Press, 1973), pp. 159–60.

[44]   See René Bertelé, *Henri Michaux* (Paris: Seghers, Collection 'Poètes d'aujourd'hui', 1975, 1st edn, 1946), p. 12.

[45]   Michaux, 'Voyage en Grande Garabagne', *OC* II, p. 55.

[46]   Michaux, 'Voyage en Grande Garabagne', *OC* II, p. 29.

[47]   Barthes, *L'Empire des signes*, p. 14.

The 'trou noir': Visualizations of Nihilism in Nietzsche and Modiano

Jenny Devine

In his 1997 publication *Chien de printemps,* Patrick Modiano describes a descent into what he terms a 'trou noir'. The visual metaphor of a 'black hole' is addressed in Modiano studies in a range of theoretical contexts where it has been aligned with, for example, the death of Modiano's brother;[1] collective memory and the Occupation;[2] and personal memory loss or amnesia.[3] In this chapter, I consider Modiano's evocation of a 'trou noir' in the context of nihilism and a loss of values, and explore some of the visual properties and processes that the author engages with in his portrayal of a 'perte progressive d'identité'.[4]

The 'trou noir' evoked in Modiano's writings acts as visual metaphor for the disturbing and disorienting existential state entered after our value system has disintegrated; this evocation of darkness and empty space communicates the removal of limits after our values have dissolved and the blindness experienced when the world as we have previously perceived it has unravelled. Informed by Nietzschean theory, I demonstrate that Modiano relies on visual properties and processes to communicate the immediacy of this experience of dissolution and disorientation, employing the visual devices of perspective, light and shade to convey the vivid impression of a descent into the 'trou noir'.

My reading of Modiano's accounts of dissolution is underpinned by Nietzsche's philosophical project of overcoming nihilism. A co-reading of Nietzsche and Modiano may at first appear unusual; the abrasive and assured rhetoric of the philosopher seems at odds with Modiano's nebulous and oneiric writings. Modiano claims that he lacks any 'culture philosophique'.[5] However, despite this, his writings are steeped in Nietzschean thinking and the eternal return is a recurring motif in his novels.[6] Modiano has explicitly introduced the philosopher's thought in his recent novels, whilst also referring to him in corresponding interviews.[7] In both *Dans le café de la jeunesse perdue* (2007) and *L'Horizon* (2010), narrators experience the eternal return in an intense and fleeting moment. Furthermore, in the former novel, one of the multiple narrators, Roland, is engrossed by Nietzschean thought and particularly by his concept of the eternal return.[8]

Despite their stylistic disparity, both Nietzsche and Modiano create narratives which explore nihilism and self-overcoming. Indeed, Nietzsche's accounts of the stages involved in a reappraisal of values provide an enlightening framework for understanding the descent into and emergence from a 'trou noir' in Modiano's texts. More importantly in the context of this chapter, I will focus on the visual as a point of commonality between Nietzsche and Modiano, interrogating how and why the writers engage with visual properties and processes in their attempts to communicate the experience of nihilism.

The disparity between the writing styles of Nietzsche and Modiano is in itself of interest. As a philosopher, Nietzsche writes from the perspective of one who understands *theoretically* the ultimate benefit of dissolution and disorientation, regarding these processes as necessary stages in the broader narrative of overcoming nihilism. Although his texts note the potential angst and displeasure that may be felt by the subject who is lost in a 'trou noir', they do not dwell on this. Nietzsche thus broadly describes the separation from society and the dissolution of values and disorientation in positivistic tones, regarding them as stages of liberation. However, Modiano's texts offer a very different perspective, relating feelings of confusion, anxiety and even horror. Modiano's literary accounts of the descent into nihilism communicate something that does not feature with regularity in Nietzsche's theoretical discourse; what they offer is an insight into the frightening and sometimes pleasurable *experience* of nihilism and of nihilistic disorientation.

Nietzsche is conscious of the failures of theoretical language to com-municate and translate experience and perception, and he appears to value aesthetics as a space in which the immediacy of experience might be explored. Nietzsche draws from literary, visual and musical sources throughout his oeuvre. In *Ecce Homo: How One Becomes What One Is* (1888) he expresses his preference for his most literary text *Thus Spoke Zarathustra*, which he feels best communicates his philosophy. As a theorist, Nietzsche works with con-cepts, yet he often advocates an approach in which the immediacy of experi-ence takes precedence over detached theoretical discourse. In *The Use and Abuse of History for Life*, for example, he discusses historiography, expressing his abhorrence of the sober detachment that historians assume and the distanced language used in historical discourse. Contrary to the general idea that temporal and psychological distance is necessary for the objective recording of the past, Nietzsche suggests that it is precisely our proximity to and experience of the past that allows for a greater understanding leading to true objectivity.

If Nietzsche recognizes the value of aesthetics in the exploration and communication of existential experience, he goes further by suggesting that the specifically *visual* will take us as close as possible to the immediacy of perception. In his essay *On Truth and Lies in an Extra-Moral Sense* (1873) Nietzsche examines the roles of language, concept and image in the explor-ation and communication of what he calls the 'nerve stimulus'. Discussing the 'binding designation' or the 'legislation' of language, he implies that it limits freedom, sets in stone and imposes rigid rule over perceptions and impulses. In Nietzsche's words, language locks [man] within a proud, deceptive consciousness, 'aloof from the coils of the intestines, the quick current of the bloodstream, and the involved tremors of the fibres'.[9] Furthermore, he identifies a certain falsehood with which man wilfully surrounds himself; essentially man believes that language is an equivalent of truth when it is in fact only a metaphor for things that are difficult to express. Stressing the arbitrariness of language, Nietzsche posits that man's conception of reality is in fact:

> a mobile army of metaphors, metonyms, and anthropomorphisms, in short, a sum
> of human relations which have been enhanced, transposed and embellished

poetically and rhetorically, and which after long use seem firm, canonical and obligatory to a people: truths are illusions about which one has forgotten that this is what they are.[10]

Aligning language with concept, Nietzsche claims that words are removed from the vivid first impressions of perception, placing language at the end of the process that converts experience into concept. To begin with, the nerve stimulus is transferred into an image. This image represents the first metaphor for reality. Next, the image is imitated in sound, which constitutes the second metaphor. Finally, Nietzsche equates words with concepts since they must be applicable in many simultaneous contexts. What is interesting here is Nietzsche's suggestion that image, whilst never escaping its metaphorical status, is at least in a better position to take us close to our vivid first impressions.

Nietzsche thus places himself in a contradictory and awkward position. As a writer and philosopher, words and ideas are his tools, yet he sees in them the 'strength and coolness' of 'the great edifice of concepts' and recognizes that theoretical discourse effectively distances him from the immediacy of experience. Nonetheless, Nietzsche often employs visual metaphors in order to convey ideas sensually. Sunlight and darkness often feature in Nietzschean texts as visual metaphors for nihilism and self-overcoming. In *The Wanderer and his Shadow*, the shadow struggles to come to terms with his nihilism whilst the wanderer stands in full sunlight having found the means for self-overcoming. Like Modiano's 'trou noir', Nietzsche's evocation of darkness acts a useful device for communicating the experience of nihilistic despair and the disorientation felt by those who are unsure as to where they should turn after the dissolution of their values. However, Nietzsche's depiction of the wanderer and his shadow has a still more subtle significance. The philosopher does not conceive of light and darkness as forming a distinct dichotomy; rather, he is interested in the potential of the metaphor to convey the very relatedness of nihilism and self-overcoming. As such, his wanderer and shadow do not present us with binary opposites; on the contrary, one cannot exist without the other, they are inextricably linked and, as Nietzsche writes, the two 'stand lovingly hand in hand'.[11] The wanderer cannot *permanently* master self-overcoming, and his nihilism will always exist within him. At times the wanderer will be drawn back into the depths of nihilistic despair, and thus his shadow may outsize him. Conversely, Nietzsche aligns the experience of self-overcoming and the affirmation of the Eternal Return with the midday sun, under which shadows are at their shortest.

Thus, while Nietzsche primarily employs theoretical language, he nevertheless recognizes the potential for visuality within this rhetoric to communicate ideas to the reader. However, Nietzsche's visual evocations serve to support his theoretical discourse in which the communication of experience remains subordinate to that of ideas. Conversely, Modiano's texts take us much closer to the 'nerve stimulus'. Like Nietzsche, Modiano relies on visual properties and processes to evoke the sensation of a descent into nihilism. I will examine two pivotal visual devices employed by Modiano in his depictions of the dissolution of identity and nihilistic disorientation. Examining an episode of dissolution in *Chien de printemps*, I will discuss the role that sunlight and shadow play in triggering the onset of the 'trou noir' whilst *Vestiaire de l'enfance* will allow us to consider the author's references to perspective as a means of communicating disorientation.

Sunlight and dissolution in *Chien de printemps*

In an interview with Jérôme Garcin, Modiano states that the summer is for him a 'saison brutale, oppressante et métaphysique'.[12] It is a sentiment observed by Lecaudé who, in his essay on the subject of 'disparition', notices 'l'influence de l'été sur le psychisme du narrateur'.[13] He also quotes the narrator's assertion in *Voyage de noces* that 'l'été est une saison qui provoque chez moi une sensation de vide et d'absence [. . .] Est-ce la lumière trop brutale [. . .], ces contrastes d'ombre et de soleil couchant?'[14] Whilst Lecaudé identifies the fundamental role that sunlight and shadow play in the process of dissolution, he does not proffer an explanation for this. A close reading of *Chien de printemps*, however, enables us to establish the relationship between light and shadow and the breakdown of one's sense of reality. As the strong sunlight reduces three-dimensional forms to flat surfaces, the narrator's world appears to him as an artifice, causing him to question the validity of his constructed world.

In discussing dissolution in Modiano's texts, it is important to identify what actually dissolves. In *Dans le café de la jeunesse perdue* one of Modiano's narrators expresses his interest in Nietzschean philosophy and borrows from his friend and mentor a copy of Karl Löwith's treatise *Nietzsche: philosophie de l'éternel retour du même*. Löwith proposes in his interpretation that three stages of liberation exist within Nietzsche's philosophy: *le Dieu chrétien mort*, *l'homme face au néant* and *la volonté de l'éternel retour*.[15] Nietzsche's 'first liberation' involves the separation from the herd and the dissolution of what he calls 'received ties'. These are the inherited values to which a particular society adheres. One who questions such 'received ties' is, in Nietzschean terms, already on a path to liberation.

In the final and dramatic account of dissolution in Modiano's *Chien de printemps*, we witness the unravelling of the narrator's 'received ties', and thus the narrator's first liberation. To begin with he loses his memory and then his knowledge of the French language begins to dissolve. The narrator remarks:

> Les efforts que j'avais fournis depuis trente ans pour exercer un métier, donner une cohérence à ma vie, tâcher de parler et d'écrire une langue le mieux possible afin d'être bien sûr de ma nationalité, toute cette tension se relâchait brusquement. Je n'étais plus rien.[16]

This revealing passage provides an idea of what constituted the narrator's goals *prior* to this moment of dissolution and consequently allows us to establish his values. The reader learns that the narrator wishes to carry out his 'métier' effectively, to speak and write a language (French) as best he can, to give his life coherence and to be sure of his nationality. We might conclude from this that prior to their dissolution, the narrator's values involved being *certain* of one's identity, having a *fixed* or *stable* nationality, obeying *limits* and *boundaries*, and having a discernible *function* or *role* in society. But what causes the dissolution of a protagonist's values? In *The Affirmation of Life: Nietzsche on Overcoming Nihilism*, Bernard Reginster underlines a crucial assumption in Nietzsche's understanding of nihilism:

> A goal makes life worth living only if it inspires the agent to go on living [. . .] A goal's ability to inspire depends on two conditions: first, it depends on the agent's

estimation of the *value* of the goal; second, it also depends on the agent's estimation of the *realisability* of this goal [. . .] Nihilism, then, may have two sources: a devaluation of the goals in the realisation of which our life has hitherto found its meaning, or the conviction that these goals are unrealisable.[17]

For the purposes of this chapter, we will consider Reginster's first condition and the suggestion in Modiano's texts that dissolution takes place after the *devaluation* of the values to which protagonists have previously adhered. In *Chien de printemps*, the narrator appears to recognize the constructed nature of his value system, and he acknowledges that adhering to it has required significant exertion. During his moment of dissolution he implies that striving to attain his goals has required 'effort' and, as his world dissolves, he remarks that 'toute cette tension se relâchait brusquement', suggesting that it has hitherto been held together by sheer will.[18] The difficulty with which Modiano's narrators comply with their received value system and the fact that the fulfilment of their goals does not make them happy cause them to question the validity of their values.

In a Nietzschean context, this devaluation of existing values is generally recognized to be the result of the realisation that there is no objective value, that the 'received values' are nothing more than false projections. The implication of Nietzsche's proposal is potentially drastic and the philosopher summarizes the idea in *The Will to Power*, in which he states that 'all belief – all assumption of truth – is false: because no real world is at hand'.[19] The 'dead God' phase to which Löwith refers not only involves the discrediting of the Christian ethical code, with its emphasis on asceticism and a metaphysical 'beyond', but equally the discrediting of the notion of objective value. As Reginster writes, 'it is not that we [now] lack reliable guidance to the good life, it is rather that there is really no good life to be had'.[20]

Löwith's proposals thus provide a useful conceptual framework for understanding why dissolution takes place and what exactly dissolves. During these moments of dissolution, we witness the narrator's first liberation, his separation from the herd and the devaluation of his values. However, Modiano does not offer theoretical accounts of dissolution; rather, his literary texts provide experiential descriptions of the onset of the 'trou noir'. Sunlight and the casting of shadow act as important triggers for dissolution in *Chien de printemps*. As the narrator's world unravels outside the Café de la Paix, for example, he wonders whether or not his dissolution has been caused by the June sunshine and the contrast created between light and shadow. The narrator has arranged to meet his friend, the photographer Jansen. Awaiting Jansen's arrival, he sits alone and recalls that he had frequented this cafe with his father when he was a boy. The narrator remembers a machine which, when coins were inserted, distributed a pink ticket displaying his weight, and is surprised to find that it is still in situ. He weighs himself and sits down with his pink piece of paper. At this point, his world begins to dissolve. The narrator experiences the blurring of temporal boundaries and this leads to the dissolution of other 'points fixes' which had hitherto rendered his life meaningful. He gradually descends into a 'trou noir', becoming increasingly estranged from the surrounding, chromatically varied world:

> J'éprouvais une drôle de sensation, assis tout seul à la terrasse du café de la Paix où les clients se pressaient autour des tables. Était-ce le soleil de juin, le vacarme de la circulation, les feuillages des arbres dont le vert formait un si frappant contraste avec le noir des façades, et ces voix étrangères que j'entendais aux tables voisines? Il me semblait être moi aussi un touriste égaré dans une ville que je ne connaissais pas [. . .] Un engourdissement, une amnésie me gagnaient peu à peu, comme le sommeil le jour où j'avais été renversé par une camionnette et où l'on m'avait appliqué un tampon d'éther sur le visage. D'ici un moment je ne saurais même plus qui j'étais et aucun des ces étrangers autour de moi ne pourrait me renseigner. J'essayais de lutter contre cet engourdissement, les yeux fixés sur le ticket rose où il était écrit que je pesais soixante-seize kilos.
> Quelqu'un m'a tapé sur l'épaule. J'ai levé la tête mais j'avais le soleil dans les yeux [. . .] Je voyais Jansen en ombres chinoises.[21]

Sitting alone in a crowded cafe, Modiano's narrator finds himself estranged in his surroundings and separated from the herd. This isolation is made all the more acute as those at neighbouring tables communicate in a language foreign to him. Not comprehending the meaning of the words being spoken around him, the narrator feels himself to be 'un touriste égaré dans une ville qu'[il] ne connaissait pas' (p. 96). Modiano's message is thus unambiguous: what makes sense and has meaning for the narrator's neighbours, who happily chat together, safe in one another's company, *does not have meaning for him.* Isolated in this cafe, the narrator now describes the stark contrast between light and shadow caused by the sun, a contrast that appears to cause deep anxiety within him. The overpowering light does not allow him to perceive the three-dimensional qualities of objects and people, and as his friend approaches the table he sees him in 'ombres chinoises'. The narrator's surroundings appear to him as a theatre of shadows; he perceives the world as artifice. This realisation that the world as he has hitherto perceived it is potentially false renders the narrator uneasy and calls to mind Nietzsche's evocation in *Human all too Human* of the free spirit, who in horror asks: 'is everything perhaps in the last resort false?'[22]

Modiano offers in this scene a Nietzschean reworking of Plato's allegory of the cave. Plato recounts the story of prisoners shackled in a cave who observe shadows on the wall, projected by firelight, and mistakenly believe they are observing reality. Only on freeing themselves from their fetters, exiting the cave and encountering the sun will they perceive true reality. For Plato the sun is the arbiter of truth, it 'produces the changing seasons and years and controls everything in the visible world'.[23] Modiano's account of dissolution shares Plato's message; like Plato, Modiano describes his protagonist's realisation that what he hitherto perceived as reality is in fact artificial. However, there exists a crucial difference between the Platonic and Nietzschean versions of events. In *Chien de printemps*, Modiano's narrator perceives his surroundings in 'ombres chinoises', but these shadows are produced by the sun itself and not by an artificial or man-made light. In this account, then, the sunlight reveals not the truth, but the complete and devastating absence of truth. Nietzschean sunlight thus reminds us that all realities are nothing more than shadows and false projections.

Similar to Plato's protagonist, who is 'dazzled by the glare' of the sun, Modiano's narrator in *Chien de printemps* is blinded by the overwhelming sunlight. In both accounts, the writers describe the necessity of focusing vision and growing 'accustomed to the light' (pp. 242-3). When his friend joins him at the cafe, the narrator is lifted out of the 'trou noir' and his doubts about the reality of his world are temporarily dispelled. 'Peu à peu, le monde autour de moi', the narrator recalls, 'reprenait ses formes et ses couleurs, comme si je réglais une paire de jumelles pour que la vision devienne de plus en plus nette' (p. 98). The overcoming of the 'trou noir' is visually communicated, the flat monochrome shapes gradually filling out into three-dimensional, colourful forms. Referring to a pair of binoculars which, through focusing, enable the narrator to restore clarity to his world, Modiano suggests that we must choose what we wish to focus upon and adjust our vision accordingly. In Plato's allegory, the prisoner's eyes will gradually become accustomed to the ultimate and objective truth, as embodied in the sun, but for Nietzsche the subject must choose which reality he wishes to see. Modiano's binoculars thus act as a useful device for communicating the impossibility of objective value. Although we might attain a focused vision of the world by adjusting the lens of the binoculars, we will nevertheless lose this clarity if we alter our position. With myriad realities upon which we might focus, we can no longer establish fixed dichotomies between blurring and distinction, certainty and uncertainty, truth and untruth. In *Beyond Good and Evil* Nietzsche exhorts us to reject black-and-white formulations (such as good and evil), and promotes the blurring of boundaries:

> Indeed, what forces us at all to assume that there is an essential opposition of 'true' and 'false'? Is it not sufficient to assume degrees of apparentness and, as it were, lighter and darker shadows and shades of appearance – different 'values' to use the language of painters?[24]

Perspective and disorientation in *Vestiaire de l'enfance*

Nietzsche's discrediting of the concept of objective value is further encapsulated in the visual function of perspective giving rise to the philosophical theory of *perspectivism*. In his 'Attempt at self criticism', Nietzsche vehemently claims that 'life rests on semblance, art, deception, prismatic effects, and the necessity of perspectives and error'.[25] Referring to the prism, Nietzsche suggests that the refraction of light that takes place in such an object affects our perception of reality and demonstrates that our vision of truth is determined by the lens or medium through which it is viewed. Truth, then, is a construct which changes according to our circumstances and given that multiple circumstances might exist, it follows that there might thus exist a multiplicity of truths.

While Nietzsche draws parallels between the rejection of absolute or objective value and perspective, this visual construct equally plays a role in communicating the experience of nihilistic disorientation. If Löwith's 'dead God' phase of liberation results in the devaluation and dissolution of existing values, this gives rise to the second stage of liberation, which he describes as 'the man before the nothing'. Without objective values we are no longer guided by external forces and must, therefore, become masters of ourselves: we should not be doing or avoiding anything because, as Zarathustra's shadow exclaims, 'nothing is true [and] all is permitted'.[26] While the prospect that 'all is permitted' may appear enticing, Nietzsche admits that it can be terrifying because man cannot live without goals. Rather than finding pleasure in their now goalless existence then, nihilists are horrified by the loss of something to will. Nietzsche communicates this terrible disorientation through the voice of the madman in *The Gay Science*, who enters the market place crying:

> 'Whither is God'? [. . .] 'I will tell you. *We have killed him*, you and I! [. . .] Who gave us the sponge to wipe away the entire horizon? What were we doing when we unchained this earth from its sun? Whither is it moving to now? Whither are we moving? Away from all suns? Are we not plunging continuously? Backward, sideways, foreword, in all directions? Is there still any up or down? Are we not straying as through an infinite nothing? Do we not feel the breath of empty space?'[27]

Nietzsche thus describes the sensation of goallessness as something distinctly disorientating. Entering nihilism, he suggests, we lose the fixed points which have anchored us in our world and, lacking such anchors, our perspectives shift leaving us unable to establish a direction in which to travel.

This allegory from *The Gay Science* describing nihilistic disorientation is mirrored in a pivotal scene in Modiano's *Vestiaire de l'enfance*, which similarly takes place in the *place du marché*. Set in an unnamed Mediterranean town, Modiano creates a sense of deep solitude by evoking empty sunlit squares and constructing a narrative in which much of the action takes place during the hours of siesta. The narrator's status as an outsider is marked by the antisocial hours he keeps. Writing episodes of a radio serial, he is available to go swimming when the pool is empty, and equally wanders the town when most are taking an afternoon break. Typically, then, we encounter a narrator who lives in solitude, who is not in sync with the rest of society, and who feels 'détaché de tout'.[28] As is the case in *Chien de printemps*, the most detailed and lengthy episode of dissolution in *Vestiaire de l'enfance* takes place on a hot and sunny day. The narrator experiences a sudden and unpleasant encounter with his past, a past which he has assiduously attempted to forget. Once again it is the resurgence of passed times which acts as a catalyst for dissolution and the narrator's world begins to unravel as he stands alone in the blazing sunlight under the statue of a certain Cruz-Valer. Readers will have encountered this statue earlier in the narrative and the bronze figure plays a crucial role in the portrayal of disorientation. In its earlier evocation, the statue of Cruz-Valer has a protective function. He is a 'bienfaiteur' of the town, and the narrator stands beneath him with a girl with whom he is falling in love. In this scene, the narrator contemplates the statue, whose bronze finger signals a point on the horizon, offering us a hint as to the role it will play in his nihilistic disorientation. 'J'ai levé mon index', Modiano writes, 'vers l'index bronze de Cruz-Valer indiquant pour l'éternité un chemin à suivre, mais lequel?' (p. 65).

As the narrator stands beneath this statue once more, this time experiencing the dissolution of his world, the figure becomes increasingly ominous:

> Le soleil tapait si fort que je sentais la pierre brûlante, malgré la semelle des mes espadrilles, en traversant la place du marché. Je me suis abrité à l'ombre de la statue de Javier Cruz-Valer [. . .] Ainsi, j'étais revenu dans l'ombre protectrice de Cruz-Valer, à cet endroit même où, l'autre nuit, je m'étais arrêté avec cette Marie de l'hôtel Alvear [. . .] Une sorte de complicité me liait à Cruz-Valer, dont l'index était pointé – me semblait-il – en direction de la plage [. . .] J'étais seul, par quarante degrés à l'ombre, au pied d'une statue de bronze. Devant moi, l'esplanade du Fort, déserte. Pas une seule table à la terrasse du café Lusignan. Personne. Pas un bruit. Une ville morte sous le soleil [. . .] La sensation de vide m'a envahi, encore plus violente que d'habitude [. . .] Je ne quittais pas du regard l'index de bronze de Cruz-Valer pointé maintenant vers une autre direction que celle de la plage. Un mauvais rêve où les doigts des statues bougent et indiquent chaque fois une direction différente? Ou bien, simplement, cet index m'apparaissait-il sous un autre angle de vue? (pp.100–3)

While the usual signals of dissolution are present in this passage (isolation, sunlight and shadow, the blurring of perception), the evocation of dissolution focuses less on the *process* of a 'perte progressive d'identité', offering instead an insight into the confusion and disorientation felt after dissolution has taken place.[29] Being liberated from all received ties, and as masters of themselves, free spirits may not know which direction to follow. Modiano's narrator looks to Cruz-Valer to provide him with external guidance, but the bronze index finger points at first in one direction and then another so that the narrator must now choose and command himself.

Like Nietzsche's madman, Modiano's narrator can no longer establish a single perspective: he appears to perceive the statue from differing viewpoints each time he sets his eyes upon it. Modiano refers in this passage to 'points de repère' but he more frequently employs the term 'points fixes' to indicate solid elements which punctuate and give structure to a world which would otherwise be 'flou'.[30] The narrator's 'points fixes' have dissolved, rendering it impossible to determine the fixity required for the establishment of a single perspective. To counteract this, the narrator attempts to restore these 'points fixes':

> Il faut que je me répète doucement à moi-même mon nouveau nom: Jimmy Sarano, ma date de naissance, mon emploi du temps, le nom des collègues [. . .], le résumé du chapitre des *Aventures de Louis XVII* que j'écrirai, mon adresse, 33, Mercedes Terrace, bref, que je m'agrippe à tous ces points de repère pour ne pas me laisser aspirer par ce que je ne peux nommer autrement que: le vide [. . .] J'avais beau répéter cela de plus en plus fort, ma voix, mes activités quotidiennes, ma vie se diluaient dans le silence et le soleil de cette ville morte. (pp.101–2)

If the kindly statue once indicated a 'point fixe' on the horizon, it has now become a malevolent figure which one might encounter in a nightmare. As we have seen, man cannot remain goalless and longs for something to will, but without his 'points de repère' he cannot delineate a path to follow. Thus, after the dissolution of 'points fixes', the narrator feels as though he is standing in 'du sable mouvant', his perspective is constantly shifting and like Modiano's madman he experiences the sensation of 'plunging continuously', 'backward, sideways, forward, in all directions'.[31] In a desperate attempt to avoid being overcome by the 'vide' or the 'infinite nothing', Modiano's narrator grasps at fixed points hoping thereby to rebuild his perspectival coordinates.

Despite employing a variety of literary devices, Nietzsche remains broadly faithful to the language of theory throughout his oeuvre. Although he provides the reader with some insights into the experience of nihilism, as we have encountered in his allegory of the madman, these act as supportive aids to his philosophical narrative. Modiano's texts, on the other hand, are not theoretically engaged, offering instead an aesthetic account of the experience of nihilism. His novels recount the sensation of descending into a nihilistic void and describe the anxiety invoked when one lacks the ability to perceive such experiences as necessary events in a larger narrative of liberation.

However, Nietzsche and Modiano share a similar problematic: words are their tools, tools which, if we are to conform to Nietzsche's model set out in *On Truth and Lies in an Extra-Moral Sense,* necessarily entail a distancing from the 'nerve stimulus'. We might conclude, then, that the visual has a crucial function in Nietzsche's but more particularly in Modiano's texts as it acts as a bridge between ideas and physical and sensual reality. It is Modiano's engagement with perspective and light which enables him to portray the vivid first impressions experienced by his narrators as they struggle with the 'trou noir'. Literature thus provides Modiano with a space in which to explore and translate perception, enabling him to communicate those fundamental states and sensations on which traditional philosophical discourse often focuses, but for which it struggles to find adequate linguistic and conceptual expression. Aesthetics, through the textual visuality of shadow and monochrome, form an enriching, even necessary, counterpart to philosophical discourse and have a crucial role to play in the communication of ideas.

Notes

[1] For example, see chapter on 'Rudy' in Thierry Laurent, *L'Œuvre de Patrick Modiano: Une autofiction* (Lyon: Presses Universitaires de Lyon, 1997).

[2] Anna Bitton, 'Patrick Modiano ôte le masque', *L'Histoire*, 299 (2005), *www.histoire. presse.fr/content/2_portraits/article?id=365#titre*, accessed 9 September 2011.

[3] Jacques Lecarme, 'Variations de Modiano: (autour d'*Accident nocturne*)', in Roger-Yves Roche (ed.), *Lectures de Modiano*, p. 33.

[4] Patrick Modiano, *Chien de printemps* (Paris: Seuil, 1993), p. 117.

[5] MK2 Diffusion, '[Rencontre] Patrick Modiano: à l'occasion de la sortie de *Dans le café de la jeunesse perdu*', in 'Au Temps', *Le Dictionnaire Patrick Modiano* (24 January 2008), *www.litt-and-co.org/au_temps/autemps_t.htm*, accessed 1 October 2011.

[6] The subject of the eternal return is addressed in five of the eighteen essays in Roger-Yves Roche's critical volume on Modiano. See Roger-Yves Roche (ed.) *Lectures de Modiano* (Nantes: Éditions Cécile Defaut, 2009).

[7] In his interview with MK2 Diffusion, Modiano insists that, despite the public's tendency to view his writings as primarily retrospective, he has in fact been more interested in the concept of time itself rather than the past, adding that 'cette notion d'"Eternel Retour" m'a frappé'.

[8] In this novel, Modiano goes beyond a mere nod to Nietzsche when he refers to a specific interpretation of Nietzsche's philosophy, that of Karl Löwith, whose 1935 treatise, *Nietzsche et la philosophie de l'éternel retour*, Roland borrows from his friend and mentor Guy de Vere. Modiano is thus aware of Löwith's book, and we might go further and speculate on its presence in the author's own library.

[9] Frederich Nietzsche, 'On truth and lies in an extra-moral sense', in *The Portable Nietzsche*, ed. and trans. Walter Kaufmann (England and U.S.A: Viking Penguin, 1982), p. 44.

[10] Ibid., pp. 46–7.

[11] Frederich Nietzsche, *Human, All Too Human: A Book for Free Spirits* (Cambridge: Cambridge University Press, 1996), p. 301.

[12] Patrick Modiano, interview with Jérôme Garcin, *Le Nouvel Observateur*, no. 2238, September 2007, *http://hebdo.nouvelobs.com/hebdo/parution/p2238/articles/a355309.html*, accessed 6 December 2009.

[13] Jean-Marc Lecaudé, 'Patrick Modiano: Le narrateur et sa disparition ou qu'y a-t-il derrière le miroir?' in John Flower (ed.), *Patrick Modiano* (Amsterdam and New York: Rodopi, 2007), p. 246.

[14] Patrick Modiano, *Voyage de noces* (Paris: Gallimard/Folio, 1992), p. 26.

[15] Karl Löwith, *Nietzsche: philosophie de l'éternel retour du même* (Hamburg: Calmann-Lévy, 1991), p. 50.

[16] Modiano, *Chien de printemps*, p. 117.

[17] Bernard Reginster, *The Affirmation of Life: Nietzsche on Overcoming Nihilism* (Cambridge, Mass. and London: Harvard University Press, 2008), p. 24.

[18]   Modiano, *Chien de printemps*, p. 117.

[19]   Oscar Levy (ed.), *The Complete Works of Friedrich Nietzsche*, 18 vols (Edinburgh: T. N. Foulis, 1909), XIV, p. 16.

[20]   Reginster, *The Affirmation of Life*, pp. 26–7.

[21]   Modiano, *Chien de printemps*, pp. 96–7.

[22]   Nietzsche, *Human, All Too Human*, p. 7.

[23]   Plato, 'The simile of the cave', in *The Republic* (London: Penguin Books 2003), pp. 242–3.

[24]   Frederich Nietzsche, *Beyond Good and Evil; Prelude to a Philosophy of the Future*, trans. Walter Kaufmann (New York: Vintage Books, 1989), pp. 46–7.

[25]   Frederich Nietzsche, 'Attempt at self criticism', in Raymond Geuss and Ronald Spiers (eds), *The Birth of Tragedy* (Cambridge: Cambridge University Press, 1999), p. 9.

[26]   Frederich Nietzsche, *Thus Spoke Zarathustra* (Cambridge: Cambridge University Press, 2006), p. 221.

[27]   Frederich Nietzsche, *The Gay Science: with a prelude in German Rhymes and an Appendix of Songs*, trans. Walter Kaufmann (New York: Random House, 1974), p. 181.

[28]   Patrick Modiano, *Vestiaire de l'enfance* (Paris: Gallimard/Folio, 1989), p. 48.

[29]   Modiano, *Chien de printemps*, p. 117.

[30]   The term 'flou' features regularly in Modiano's texts and in interviews with the author.

[31]   Modiano frequently refers to 'moving sand' in his literature and in interviews.

II

Intermedial migrations in the 1920s

Painting and Cinema in Aragon's *Anicet*

Katherine Shingler

Louis Aragon's first novel, *Anicet ou le panorama, roman* (1921), combines in its very title the notion of visual spectacle with that of literary narrative. In his 1964 preface to the novel, Aragon indicated that he considered the generic marker 'roman' to be very much part of the title, but added that it had been included primarily 'par la consonance avec le mot *panorama*'.[1] Thus, one might wish to read the novel, if not as a straightforwardly ironic reflection of the surrealist generation's anti-literary stance – 'un défi aux conceptions mêmes de mes plus proches amis de ce temps', as Aragon put it (p. 14) – then as an indication of the inseparability of literary and visual impulses in this 'panorama-roman'. If, however, we examine what Mieke Bal calls the 'subter- fuges' through which the visual domain is allowed to be present in the text, we discover that these subterfuges do not give rise to a unified, global vision.[2] The relatively outmoded visual technology of the panorama is marginalized as a visual model for writing in favour of two alternatives whose expressive resources Aragon explores in *Anicet*: painting and cinema. Thus, while the novel's title may suggest that it offers a panoramic vision of early twentieth- century artistic culture, this vision turns out to be composed of a series of partial, subjective views – or, alternatively, a series of *ciné-feuilleton* episodes.

This chapter aims to explore the relative roles of painting and cinema in *Anicet*, and especially the strategies Aragon uses to link writing to painted and cinematic images. The research presented here is part of a broader project examining the development of the French art novel in the early twentieth century – a project itself inspired by the conference 'French Art in Narrative and Drama', held in February 2005 under the aegis of the University of Bristol Centre for the Study of Visual and Literary Cultures in France, and which gave rise to a special issue of *French Studies*, on the nineteenth-century art novel.[3] Moving on from the Frenhofers and the Lantiers of nineteenth-century fiction, this new project considers the extent to which it remains appropriate to talk about the art novel as a coherent genre after 1900. To what extent do early twentieth-century representations of painting and painters share or reject the concerns of their nineteenth-century precedents? My working hypothesis is that writers of fiction remain interested in the visual arts, and certainly still tend towards modes of writing that encourage us to 'see' or to visualize; however, the art novel undergoes a transformation in the period 1900–30, as the emergent art of the cinema competes with painting as the principal visual reference point for writers. From the opening of the Lumières' first *cinématographe* in Paris in 1895 to the advent of the 'talkies' in 1929, writers were inspired by the new technologies, effects, techniques and perceptual dynamics of the cinema. At the same time they felt keenly the threat posed to literature by this new popular form of visual art, both in terms of its economic viability and its status within the field of cultural production. Their response, very often, was to incorporate 'cinematic' techniques into their writing, and one key area of investigation in this project will be the ways in which such techniques competed, interacted with, or displaced formal strategies linking writing to painting, and literary experience to picture perception.

Anicet is a crucial point of departure for the investigation of tensions between these two visual models for writing. As Aragon's first novel, it is an aesthetic testing-ground, a space in which the writer reflects on the properties of his medium and its current position within the field of cultural production, situating it in relation to alternative genres and art forms. The novel's plot, indeed, is structured around a competition between different art forms, each struggling to innovate and to attain 'la beauté moderne' – represented in the form of a woman, Mirabelle, whose favours the artist must seek to win. Through a chance encounter at an inn, the young Anicet, who aspires to be a poet, is witness to a strange ritual whereby Mirabelle is presented with gifts by seven masked men. These men are members of a secret society devoted to the cult of Mirabelle and are all artists or creators of one sort or another, seeking literally to conquer Mirabelle and symbolically to conquer modern beauty by innovating in their respective artistic domains. All, moreover, have real-life referents, or at least models: Bleu is 'indiscutablement Picasso', while Chipre is based on Max Jacob, Omme on Valéry, Baptiste on Breton, and Pol represents Charlie Chaplin (pp.14–16). Agreeing to join their organization, Anicet finds himself in competition with these other artists, and especially with the painter Bleu, quickly identified as his strongest rival: 'Anicet pensa tendrement à Mire. Quelle œuvre créerait-il pour mériter son amour? Il songea à l'attrait de la robe du faisan, et craignit que le peintre, maître des couleurs, ne gagnât avant lui le prix qu'il enviait' (p. 112).

The painter's resources are perceived to be more powerful and seductive than those of the poet, and there is a sense that literature is in crisis, under pressure from the stunning innovations of modern painting. This is reflected in the fact that Anicet, as the principal representative of modern literature in the novel, is singularly inactive: he has produced only one rather inferior poem, and harbours vague plans for 'un article sur la peinture moderne' (p. 179), a project which is ironically dependent on the endeavours of his rivals in the visual arts. The rivalry between literature and painting comes to a head in Bleu's studio, where Anicet, who has been recruited into a gang of art thieves, finds himself one night. Overcome with admiration and jealousy, Anicet is tempted to destroy Bleu's work, but resists this temptation in the hope that he may one day 'inventer des charmes plus puissants' by literary means. He seeks to channel 'des cris qui viennent de plus loin dans les cœurs des hommes que de cette zone facilement atteinte où règne l'amour des formes colorées', releasing unconscious currents of thought in a creative process that clearly recalls Breton and Soupault's early experiments in automatic writing. These attempts end in failure, however, and Anicet remains acutely aware of the limitations of verbal language relative to the immediate visual appeal of coloured forms, lamenting, 'Pauvre poète qui cherche à lutter avec tes malheureuses images verbales!' (pp. 200–1).

Anicet may resist the impulse to destroy Bleu's work, but earlier in the novel his first act in the pursuit of Mirabelle is one of vandalism: raiding Paris's museums, he burns their most celebrated examples of academic art on top of the Arc de Triomphe. This daring feat is motivated not so much by the need to eliminate a competitor for Mirabelle's affections – the works in question, 'les Greuze, les Boucher, les Meissonnier, les Millet' (p. 93), are seen as obsolete and irrelevant – as by a desire to topple revered artistic monuments, and to create a spectacle whose beauty is grounded in violent destruction. Bleu's painting is aligned with these iconoclastic desires, and thus distanced from the stale forms of the past. Conceiving of artistic creation as the ability to conjure beauty from worthless materials, 'Bleu, le génie de cette époque, se sert pour ses tableaux de papiers peints, de journaux, de sable, d'étiquettes' (p. 103). In his fictionalized portrait of Picasso and his work, Aragon highlights the way in which the artist's collage aesthetic called into question the values of uniqueness, authenticity and the well-made object that are traditionally attached to high art, alongside the idea that the dual aesthetic and monetary value of an artwork derived partly from the materials used in its creation. The value of Bleu–Picasso's work lies instead in the process by which those materials are transformed, a process which combines creative and destructive impulses. Indeed, in the ritual where Anicet first encounters the masked men, Bleu's gift to Mirabelle is, significantly, a railway signal whose removal will cause a collision between two trains. This found object, apparently devoid of aesthetic value, is transformed into a potential art object through its causal relationship to an act of destruction, and this is suggestive of Picasso's dissection of objects and their contours, as well as of the more general iconoclasm of the cubist aesthetic, as Anna Balakian notes: 'Here the conquest of modern Beauty demands the sacrifice of order and risks terrible destruction. Had not Picasso caused, indeed, the collision and explosion of long-established and orderly systems, the break-down of standardization and of accepted relationships?'[4] Equally, the signal's value may be seen to derive from its multivalency, as Anicet compares it successively 'à une tache de sang, à un œil, à un sexe, à un chapeau de conte de fée' (p. 81). This signal or 'sign' which, once removed from its original context, is able to take on a variety of alternative, coexisting meanings, calls to mind the punning substitutions of Picasso's cubist works and the multiple readings they generate, and suggests that their power lies in this semiotic proliferation.

If we are to read Aragon's representation of Bleu as a fictionalized form of art criticism – and this interpretation is certainly invited by the writer's provision of various 'clés' inviting the reader to identify Bleu with Picasso – then this critical account is equally attentive to the perceived failings of Picasso's art at the beginning of the 1920s as it is to the successes of the earlier cubist period. While his collages may have playfully highlighted and mocked the market forces governing the production of art, their market value has ironically increased, and the once-revolutionary Bleu is incorporated into the bourgeoisie as 'l'Homme arrivé', standing in contrast to Chipre, or Max Jacob's ascetic 'Homme pauvre'. Now that he has 'arrived', his primary interest is 'circulaire et dorée' (p. 106), and his art begins to slip into the clichés of academic painting. Having admired many of the works in Bleu's studio, Anicet comes across his much-trumpeted new work, entitled *La Louange du corps humain*, and discovers it to be:

> Une parfaite académie, une figure de proportions avec ses cotes en chiffres connus. Anicet saisit subitement que Bleu en atteignant la perfection avait passé du domaine de l'amour à celui de la mort et de la gloire. Il prononça plusieurs noms de grands hommes, et sourit. (p. 202)

At the conclusion of this episode – related within a chapter whose title, 'Décès', seems to signal the demise of modern painting – Anicet is finally able to breathe a sigh of relief. Bleu is no longer a contender in the pursuit of modern beauty, and his name joins the ranks of those salon painters whose works were destroyed earlier in the novel.

Aragon's representation of Bleu culminates, then, in a thinly veiled attack on Picasso's return to classicism, suggesting that such a move leaves the painter in an aesthetic dead end, unable to respond adequately to modernity.[5] The moment of the painting's unveiling and Anicet's discovery of its failure explicitly recall similar episodes in nineteenth-century art novels such as *Le Chef-d'œuvre inconnu*, and this intertextual echo further consigns Bleu–Picasso's art – and, by implication, painting in general – to the past. The failure of painting is also reflected in the withheld visuality of Aragon's writing.

Aragon refrains, in particular, from detailed ekphrastic description, giving only rough, deliberately enigmatic sketches of the works encountered in the studio. Anicet sees, in turn, 'une maison schématique qui fidèlement figurait la *Maison*, celle qu'on ne désigne que par ce nom tendre sans le nantir d'un possessif', 'un adolescent grand et maigre dont les mains souffrent d'être vides, un garçon qui n'a pas encore appris la beauté du corps, ni quel secret cache ce maillot trop large' and 'une nature morte qui laissa voir au jeune homme dans le jeu ambigu de la guitare et des bouteilles au centre du guéridon les formes jointes d'un couple amoureux que le monde ne pouvait plus troubler ni le charme des objets usuels' (pp.196–7). These poetic descriptions are extremely evocative, but they are very much focused upon what Anicet reads into the paintings – on their affect, which is not literally visible on the surface – rather than on the arrangement of painted elements on the canvas. Thus, while readers familiar with Picasso's work will certainly draw on their knowledge in order to visualize the paintings, Aragon does not fully expose them through his writing, providing only an enigmatic starting point for imaginative visualization. By focusing on the viewing subject, he places the painted image itself on the sidelines. Furthermore, Aragon's sketched indications dwindle to almost nothing as Anicet approaches *La Louange du corps humain*. We can guess from the painting's title that it is a nude, but are given no further details: visualization is rendered all but impossible.

Since painting is ultimately revealed to fail in its attempt to capture modern beauty, it ceases to be either a rival in Anicet's quest, or a potential model for Aragon's own writing in the novel.[6] There is a single instance in *Anicet* where the fragmentation of narrative perspective might be compared to the multiple viewpoints of cubist painting – but Aragon quickly cancels this association by making it clear that the effect is a 'photographic' one:

> Les quatre interlocuteurs n'envisagèrent plus le paysage du même point de vue, de telle façon qu'un spectateur impartial qui n'aurait pas su choisir entre leurs quatre visions, n'eût plus obtenu de la scène qu'une photographie brouillée par la superposition des clichés. (p. 109)

What is 'seen' here is conceived in terms of an effect of superimposition used in still photography, but particularly common in early twentieth-century film, especially the trick-films of Georges Méliès. Indeed, allusions to such special effects are, as we shall see, one means by which Aragon places the novel's action within a specifically filmic universe. More generally, *Anicet* is peppered with references to film, tapping directly into the cinematic culture of the period.[7] Pol is involved in a series of Chaplinesque chase scenes; Nick Carter, the fictional detective to whom a series of films had been devoted, features as a character; and many episodes within the novel (the antics of the art thieves, for instance) inescapably call to mind Feuillade's *Fantômas* and *Les Vampires*.[8] The aesthetic potential of the seventh art is also explicitly discussed during Baptiste's and Anicet's visit to the cinema, an episode in which the unusual spectatorial behaviour of the characters looks forward to Breton's description of his cinema-going habits in *Nadja*:

> Sans se préoccuper des voisins, ils parlaient à voix haute et mêlaient à leurs discours des jugements sur les films. Ainsi vous regardez passer la vie, vous y intéressez votre sensibilité, vous vous en détournez pour explorer votre esprit et vous reportez de nouveau les yeux sur les spectacles quotidiens. (p.137)

Just as Breton enters screenings at random and never fully follows the film, Aragon places emphasis on the possibility of engaging and disengaging one's attention from the film at will, and treats the cinema as a social space, the setting for a new type of collective experience which Anicet and Baptiste happily disrupt as they pursue their discussions.[9] *Anicet* moves beyond these elements common to both Aragon's and Breton's representations of cinema-going – beyond the surrealist 'bravo pour les salles obscures'.[10] It suggests that the status of film as the modern art form par excellence is closely bound up with the formal qualities of the medium itself.[11] Watching a film starring Pearl White (probably the extremely popular *Mystères de New-York*), Anicet notes that it is fundamentally non-literary in that its fast-moving action eliminates the need, and indeed the opportunity, for verbal discourse or analysis. He concludes, 'Voilà bien le spectacle qui convient à ce siècle' (p. 138). A similar view is expressed in Aragon's 1918 article on film, 'Du décor', where he argues that cinema 'doit être dépouillé de tout ce qui est verbal', and that it must hence liberate itself from the example of theatre.[12] It may be precisely because film was, prior to the advent of the sound film, an essentially visual medium, and because it was, therefore, opposed to literary forms (such as the *roman d'analyse*) which emphasised discourse at the expense of pure action, that it seemed to Aragon to supply a viable model for a new form of writing – a visual form of writing appealing to the sensibilities of the cinema-going public.[13]

Anna Balakian has contested the influence of film on *Anicet*, reading it as an overwhelmingly pessimistic novel within which cinema, like painting, is seen to be incapable of meeting the demands of modern beauty – and, by extension, incapable of providing new impetus for literary experimentation. Balakian cites as evidence of this the gift given by Pol, an avatar for Charlie Chaplin, to Mirabelle. The gift in question is a mandarin, which Pol steals from a cinema usherette, triggering the first of many comical chases. Balakian interprets the gift as follows:

> Much valor is displayed, and stunningly succulent is the fruit, but rapidly consumed. Aragon gives a succinct indictment of the value of cinema to aesthetics: brilliant, gilded, savory but ephemeral – so much effort for so short a satisfaction. We are here very far from the high hopes that Apollinaire had entertained for film as an eventual replacement for the word in the making of poetry, i.e. the Beautiful.[14]

It is true that Pol's gift is not enough to win Mirabelle – but none of the other artists' gifts are either, and it is the businessman Gonzalès whom she marries, beauty ending up 'aux mains des marchands' (p. 166). It is also true that the novel does express some reservations about cinema, as Anicet's glowing assessment of its aesthetic potential is countered by Baptiste's complaints about the passivity of the film spectator. Nevertheless, it remains the case that filmic references permeate Aragon's writing, and that these go beyond superficial nods to popular film at the level of plot and discussions between characters of the aesthetic merits of cinema. The properties of the filmic medium are incorporated into the very techniques of Aragon's writing, and the experience of reading the novel is brought into close contact with the experience of the filmgoer.

Aragon achieves this primarily by identifying narrative perspective with the camera's gaze, which in turn invites the reader to conceive of the narrative as a cinematic sequence, projected onto a screen for us to 'see'. Often this effect is achieved by quite subtle means, as in the following sentence, where it hinges on the reference of the pronoun 'on': 'À ce moment-là, on s'aperçut que les interlocuteurs se trouvaient dans un Biard près de Saint-Philippe-du-Roule' (p. 97). Since we know from the context of this sentence that 'on' does not refer to observers located within the frame of the narrative, the reader is obliged to posit an audience whose presence is exterior to and does not affect the action, and who are not omniscient or privy to all the facts about the fictional world that is represented: they discover the location in which the conversation is taking place only as the camera zooms out or cuts to a long shot revealing the cafe setting.[15] When Anicet realizes that it is in fact Bleu's studio he has broken into, we are told 'il y avait un siècle que tout le monde le savait' (p. 197). Here it is 'tout le monde' that introduces the idea of an audience observing the action, and once more the reference is not to a solitary 'lecteur', but to a collective spectatorship whose privileged position of knowledge contrasts with the obliviousness of the observed character, creating suspense characteristic of the *film policier*.[16]

Aragon also draws attention to the way in which the action is visually presented to the reader/spectator – to the composition of his 'shots'. During a scene at Mirabelle's mansion, 'tout à coup les valeurs se renversèrent':

> Les protagonistes devinrent les spectateurs, le sens de la chambre changea. Le haut de la page se trouva vers le seuil. D'en bas, Anicet et Mirabelle virent se dresser, la main gauche sur le battant ouvert, un grand personnage masqué de velours, coiffé d'un haut-de-forme et drapé dans une cape à collet. (pp. 165–6)

The equation between 'page' and screen explicitly invites us to visualize the action as if it were being projected in front of us as we read, as we cut from one shot to another. Anicet and Mirabelle, who had been the protagonists – the focus of the camera's gaze – become spectators. From the bottom of the page/screen, or the foreground of the space that is now viewed from a different angle, they observe the dramatic entrance of Omme (another of the seven masked men), whose costume recalls Fantômas as he figures in the famous Gaumont posters. This initially appears to render Omme as dashing and mysterious as Feuillade's criminal mastermind, but this implication is quickly undermined and the filmic reference takes on a parodic aspect as

Mirabelle mockingly comments, 'Mon Dieu, qu'est-ce que cette mascarade? Mon cher Omme, vous faites vos entrées sans grand art. Mais vous devez étouffer, un après-midi d'été, sous un tel accoutrement' (p.166).

The most important filmic sequences in the novel, however, occur when two films are projected for the characters to see. The first of these is a newsreel entitled 'Paris: Un grand mariage', which Anicet and Baptiste see during the cinema excursion mentioned earlier, and from which they learn of Mirabelle's marriage to Gonzalès. Aragon is once again attentive to framing and describes the camera singling out Omme, who has observed Mirabelle's wedding, broken-hearted. The camera follows Omme as he leaves the church, enters a cafe and plots to get Mirabelle away from her new husband: observing this lengthy sequence of actions, the reader is likely to forget that it is presented via the cinema screen, which Anicet and Baptiste are watching. At the end of the chapter, Anicet and Baptiste also enter the action; but, although they have left the cinema, we (as readers/spectators) have not. Aragon reminds us of this by concluding the chapter with the following image: 'En haut, dans un coin de la toile, le sourire énigmatique, Baptiste semblait le génie directeur de l'aventure' (pp.152–3). We are still observing the action via the cinema screen and this is brought to our attention through the use of a special effect of superimposition which allows multiple shots representing simultaneous events to be shown at once (and which once again draws on the vocabulary of adventure and mystery films, with Baptiste being cast as the dastardly genius presiding over the action). The fantastic effects obtainable by the manipulation of the cinematic medium are even more stunning in the film screening at the Gonzalès house, which tells the assembled guests of Mirabelle's and her new husband's respective life stories. Here, one of Mirabelle's former lovers performs the Méliès-esque feats of lighting his cigarette on the sun and catching a cloud that he attaches to his buttonhole (p. 210).

Such special effects are also present in scenes which are not explicitly framed as film – that is, they are not films the characters themselves watch – but which are, as Gindine notes, 'prêts à être enregistrés tels quels par une caméra, grâce à leurs indications précises de mouvements et d'éclairages'.[17] This is the case in the following passage, in which Anicet dreams of seeing Mirabelle perform in a music hall:

La rampe bleuâtre permet de voir le rideau se fendre comme un cœur. Il s'ouvre sur un autre rideau sombre, uni, lourd, aux plis droits. Un cercle lumineux apparaît tout en haut à gauche, et dans ce cercle une tête de femme. Sans étonnement Anicet reconnaît Mirabelle: il l'attendait. Elle a l'air d'une jolie réclame pour dentifrice. Elle chante en anglais, il ne peut la comprendre parce qu'elle ne va pas assez lentement. Cependant au passage, il accroche le mot *Darling* pareil à une clochette d'argent. Tout à coup, la tête s'éteint. Mais elle se rallume plus bas, à droite; la chanson continue et Anicet s'émeut de saisir le mot *lèvre*. Après une nouvelle éclipse, la tête reparaît plus bas encore et à gauche [. . .]

Maintenant la tête est au milieu de la scène au ras du sol comme si Mirabelle s'était couchée à plat ventre. (p.186)

As Gindine's comment suggests, the passage is eminently visual, Aragon's attention to *mise en scène* and lighting allowing us to imagine the action unfolding before our eyes. What links the passage to cinema – what makes us conceive of the action as taking place not simply on a music hall stage, but a filmed music hall stage – is the trick effect of Mirabelle's head disappearing in one location, only to reappear suddenly in another. The lack of *vraisemblance* may be explained by the fact that the scene is taking place within a dream; but, equally, the effect is one that could be realized in a film, through the use of straight cuts. Contemporary readers would have been extremely familiar with this, given its use in a number of films of the period (alongside the many examples from Méliès, the apparition of Fantômas before Juve in the first episode of Feuillade's serial is one that Aragon would certainly have known). It is in 'filmic' sequences such as this that Aragon's writing attains visuality, giving the reader full access to visual experience, while withholding it in the passages relating to painting.

Aragon's *Anicet* relates an allegorized quest for modern beauty and asks how the novel might attain this, looking to the visual arts for inspiration. Painting, as we have seen, fails in this quest and is displaced as a model for writing by cinema. The latter, meanwhile, is not conceived as a rival to literature that must be defeated or dispatched but, rather, as a complementary resource that may be appropriated and adapted to the needs of the narrative text. Of course, the question remains: why cinema? The glamour and excitement of the new cinematic medium, combined with literature's need to look beyond itself for inspiration, arguably provide sufficient explanation for Aragon's *rapprochement* between novel and film. In one of the novel's most self-conscious filmic episodes, we find Anicet imagining his break-in at Bleu's studio as if it were being filmed, and indeed as if he were the star, his exploits calling to mind images of 'Belles affiches des films américains!' (p. 194). Anicet has been seduced by the cinema to the extent that it mediates his own experience, and the episode demonstrates an awareness of the powerful hold of the seventh art over the popular imagination – something that Aragon was clearly keen to exploit through a literary incursion into cinematic culture.

A rather more nuanced response, however, might be gained by reconsidering Aragon's attention to special effects, or more generally to the manipulations that may be performed on the filmic image. David Trotter, in his book *Cinema and Modernism*, has claimed that modernist writers in early twentieth-century Britain were interested in the cinema as pure mechanism – as a non-art, consisting in the recording of reality rather than its representation.[18] For the surrealists, in contrast, the filmed image is already potentially 'truqué'. As Aragon commented in 'Du décor', film is 'maître de toutes ses déformations', and this is certainly borne out by *Anicet*, where the reader is frequently made aware of techniques used to distort the filmed image so as to create visual experiences not possible in reality.[19] Nevertheless, the conception of cinema as a mechanical, entirely neutral form of representation remains present in the novel – although it only reveals itself fleetingly, in 'slips' such as Baptiste's dismissive branding of cinema as 'cette mécanique' (p. 139), and the representation of Pol/Chaplin as a robotic 'marionette' (p. 75).[20] And what is crucial to understanding the appeal of cinema, both to Aragon and to the surrealist movement as it was to develop later in the 1920s is that these two conceptions of cinema are only apparently at odds with one another. Cinematic tricks and illusions of the type frequently mobilized in *Anicet* rely for their power and effect on the unconsciously accepted idea that film constitutes a neutral, undistorted record of reality. Like surrealist photography, which, as Rosalind Krauss has observed, 'exploits the special connection to reality with which all photography is endowed', Aragon's text plays on the fact that the filmed image gives a seamless and convincing impression of reality. The illusion of Mirabelle's head moving around the stage, of a suitor catching a cloud and attaching it to his buttonhole: these derive their aesthetic value from their combination of, on the one hand, the creation of marvellous feats, and, on the other, the status of the filmed image as an unproblematic, unmediated 'deposit of the real'.[21] Putting this in rather crude terms, one may say that the spectator knows that what he is seeing is impossible, and yet the idea that film is not *representation* (mediated by a subjectivity) but, rather, direct, neutral *recording*, works against this, encouraging the spectator to accept the marvellous as part of reality – or at least as part of the reality of the film. This paradoxical quality was particularly appealing to the nascent surrealist aesthetic, which hinged on a conception of the surreal not as detached from but as very much rooted in the real. It is from this perspective – taking into account these implications of Aragon's use of filmic representation as a model for literary representation – that *Anicet* may be read as a proto-surrealist text, anticipating the movement's central principles (although this is not to overlook its Dadaist leanings, which are evident notably in the writer's lack of deference towards his filmic references). The 'cinematic' aspects of Aragon's novel might in addition provide grounds for a reassessment of the role of film in the development of the surrealist aesthetic, suggesting that its influence was profound, and indeed that it might be placed alongside still photography as what Krauss calls a 'condition of Surrealism'.

Notes

1 Louis Aragon, *Anicet ou le panorama, roman* (Paris: Gallimard/Folio, 2001), pp. 9 and 14. Further page references will be included in parentheses in the main text.

2 Mieke Bal, *The Mottled Screen: Reading Proust Visually*, trans. Anna-Louise Milne (Stanford: Stanford University Press, 1997), p. 3.

3 Paul Smith (ed.), 'The Nineteenth Century Art Novel', special issue, *French Studies*, 59/1 (2007).

4 Anna Balakian, '*Anicet*, or the search for beauty', in *The Snowflake on the Belfry: Dogma and Disquietude in the Critical Arena* (Bloomington: Indiana University Press, 1994), pp.199–213 (p. 204).

5 Jean Arrouye proposes this reading in 'Bleu et *La Louange du corps humain*', in Jean Arrouye (ed.), *Écrire et voir: Aragon, Elsa Triolet et les arts visuels* (Aix-en-Provence: Publications de l'Université de Provence, 1991), pp. 23–37. Aragon's view of Picasso's work of course changed as the latter moved away from classicism; on the range

of Aragon's art-critical responses to Picasso, see André Daspre, 'Écrits d'Aragon sur Picasso', in *Hommage à Claude Digeon* (Paris: Les Belles Lettres, 1987), pp. 233–47. The fact that Picasso illustrated *Anicet* for its republication in Aragon and Elsa Triolet's *Œuvres romanesques croisées* (Paris: Robert Laffont, 1964) is also evidence of a subsequent turnaround in attitude.

[6]   On the role of painting in the later *monde réel* cycle of novels, see Marc Chiassaï, *Aragon/Peinture/Écriture. La Peinture dans l'écriture des 'Cloches de Bâle' à 'La Semaine Sainte'* (Paris: Kimé, 1999).

[7]   For a general analysis of the role of cinema in *Anicet*, see Yvette Gindine, *Aragon: prosateur surréaliste* (Geneva: Droz, 1966), pp. 18–22.

[8]   Aragon expressed his admiration for the latter in 'Les Vampires', in Marc Dachy (ed.), *Projet d'histoire littéraire contemporaine* (Paris: Gallimard, 1994), pp. 7–9.

[9]   André Breton, *Nadja* (Paris: Gallimard, 1964), p. 40.

[10]   André Breton, 'Manifeste du surréalisme' (1924), in *Manifestes du surréalisme* (Paris: Gallimard, 1972), pp. 11–64 (p. 62).

[11]   Aragon's attention to the formal qualities of the filmic medium contradicts Michael Richardson's suggestion that the surrealists were not interested in film *per se*, so much as the collective experience of cinema-going, or seeing a film in a darkened hall. See his *Surrealism and Cinema* (Oxford and New York: Berg, 2006), p. 8.

[12]   Aragon, 'Du décor', *Le Film*, 16 September 1918, repr. in *Écrits sur l'art moderne*, ed. Jean Ristat (Paris: Flammarion, 1981), pp. 5–9 (p. 9).

[13]   On Aragon's distaste for literary forms, see Gindine, *Aragon: prosateur surréaliste*, p. 16.

[14]   Balakian, '*Anicet*, or the Search for Beauty', p. 203.

[15]   'On' is used in a number of other instances to refer to an audience: cf. p. 115 ('on comprit'), and pp.191–2 ('on n'entend pas les légers crissements').

[16]   Cf. also p. 201: 'personne n'avait envie d'en rire'.

[17]   Gindine, *Aragon: prosateur surréaliste*, p. 20.

[18]   David Trotter, *Cinema and Modernism* (Oxford: Blackwell, 2007).

[19]   Aragon, 'Du décor', p. 9.

[20]   Aragon also insists on 'la découverte de la mécanique et de ses lois' in Charlot's films, in 'Du décor', p. 8.

[21]   Rosalind Krauss, 'The photographic conditions of surrealism', *October*, 19 (1981), 3–34 (26 for both quotations).

Isotypes and Elephants: Picture-Language as Visual Writing in the Work and Correspondence of Otto Neurath

Michelle Henning

In 1920s Vienna, as part of the larger socialist experiment that earned the city the nickname 'Red Vienna', the picture language of Isotype was born. It was the invention of the Vienna Circle philosopher and sociologist Otto Neurath, working with a team of artists and researchers at his Gesellschafts- und Wirtschaftsmuseum (museum of society and economy, hereafter GWM). Isotype began as the Vienna method of pictorial statistics, a means of making statistical information and comparison legible to non-expert and even semi-literate audiences through the use of pictures. Later, it became Isotype, an acronym for International System of Typographic Picture Education. Individual symbols or pictograms were made as ink drawings, then as linocuts (later metal letter-press blocks). These were printed, cut out and pasted onto charts for display in exhibitions or for publication. A key innovation of Isotype was in the way it represented quantities as repeated pictograms of identical size, not as differences in size or volume. In this way Isotype made visual statistics measurable, because the number of pictograms could be counted and com-pared to the given numerical figures, but it was also far less dependent on written labels and contextual information than previous methods. Isotype was among the first standardized systems for representing social facts

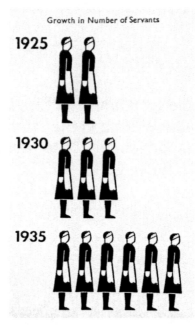

Fig. 6.1: Simple example of an Isotype chart. From Otto Neurath, *International Picture Language: The First Rules of Isotype*, Psyche Miniatures (London: Kegan Paul, 1936)

in pictures, and the elegance of its visual solutions arguably remains unsurpassed (see fig. 6.1).[1]

Though it had this specialized use, Isotype is sometimes described as the precursor of contemporary visual icon systems (used on toilet doors, and as road and airport signage). This claim is not entirely accurate insofar as Isotype symbols were always part of larger charts, maps and illustrations. Nevertheless, in his 1936 book, *International Picture Language: The First Rules of Isotype*, Neurath did connect Isotype with the emergent sign systems that were appearing in instruction manuals, on the street, and on the road.[2] Here Neurath explicitly presented Isotype as a language, comparing it to other artificial (and 'semi-artificial') languages such as Esperanto and Basic English. He was keen to emphasize its limitations, such as its inability to deal with emotional content, and suggested Isotype be considered as a supplement to, rather than replacement for, 'natural' languages. Until his death in 1945 he continued to stress that Isotype was not intended to be a 'quasi-language in full-dress'.[3]

In 1920s and 1930s Vienna, the primary use of Isotype charts was in specially designed exhibitions, alongside architectural models, maps and photographs. In The Hague, in the late 1930s, Isotype work for exhibition and public information continued, but commissions were rarer. In Britain, the Isotype Institute, established in 1942, gained much of its work through the company Adprint, a 'book-packaging' firm which designed illustrated books on behalf of publishers such as Penguin and Collins. The institute produced charts for these books, but also made public-information leaflets and animated sequences for wartime propaganda films, as well as exhibition charts. If in Vienna Isotype had been primarily part of exhibitionary and statistical techniques, now, through its use in a wide variety of books, and through Neurath's explicit promotion of it as a 'picture language', it began to be more connected with linguistics and literature.

Isotype's increased involvement in publishing and literature must have suited Neurath, who was a prolific writer and a keen reader. He wrote philosophical and sociological books and journal articles and an extraordinary number of letters, as well as a popular book *Modern Man in the Making*, published in 1939 and illustrated by Isotype. Though never entirely fluent in English, he wrote in English and Basic English as well as his native German. He had no artistic training and his role in the production of Isotype was as the director of the various institutes and organizations. He negotiated commissions, instigated new projects and gave public talks promoting and explaining Isotype. He also had a strong influence on the execution of projects and on establishing the basic principles and conventions they deployed. Several artists were responsible for the visual appearance of Isotype, but the one who had the greatest impact on its development was Gerd Arntz, who worked closely with Neurath from 1928 in Vienna and then in The Hague. Arntz's ability to condense the details of everyday objects into simple recognizable shapes and to convey social types through silhouette and line was evident in his own political prints of the 1920s. He gave to Isotype clarity and a modern style, but it was up to 'transformers' such as Marie Neurath (née Reidemeister) to mediate between researchers and artists, planning

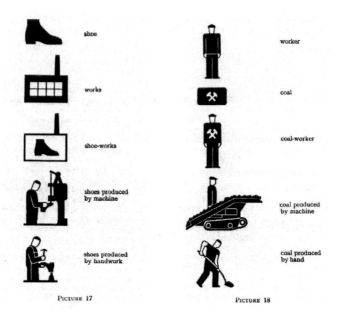

Fig 6.2: Illustrations demonstrating how Isotype symbols combine to produce
specific meanings. From Otto Neurath, *International Picture Language:
The First Rules of Isotype*, Psyche Miniatures (London: Kegan Paul, 1936)

the layout of charts in order to ensure they communicated information clearly
and consistently (see fig. 6.2).[4]

Although he did not consider himself an artist, Neurath commonly signed
his letters with a cartoon of an elephant. These signatures were so distinctive that one obituary for Neurath, by Waldemar Kaempffert, was titled
'Appreciation of an elephant' and began, 'Otto Neurath signed his letters to
friends with the drawing of an elephant, usually cheerful, sometimes subdued.
Now those brilliant letters have ceased.'[5] These signature drawings might be
seen to constitute another picture language, insofar as Neurath uses them
to communicate with his correspondents. Stylistically they differ very much
from Isotype, not least in being rapidly hand drawn. Recent studies have
made much of the distinction between the flowing, expressive, hand-drawn
line and the straight, unmodulated, mechanical line, associating the latter

with Enlightenment notions of rationalization and progress.[6] This opposition may be complicated by comparing Isotype and Neurath's elephant, and by considering what, exactly, a picture language might entail.

Neurath set out some of his thoughts on picture languages in a book written in the last two years of his life. It was finally published in 2010 as *From Hieroglyphics to Isotypes: A Visual Autobiography*.[7] Here, Neurath describes Isotype as a system of modern hieroglyphics inspired by eighteenth-century military illustrations, pictorial atlases and encyclopaedia such as the Orbus Pictus and ancient Egyptian wall paintings. He was fascinated by the potential of pictures to communicate with clarity and affect, and interested in language and writing systems. This is evident in Neurath's philosophical work, especially in his logical empiricist opposition to metaphysical claims and his early practice of prohibiting himself from using certain words that he saw as obscurantist or quasi-theological. Like many of his contemporaries, Neurath was also interested in attempts to produce new artificial languages. He wrote *International Picture Language* in C. K. Ogden's Basic English: not an entirely artificial language but a radically simplified English. Neurath's interest in pictographic writing extended to Chinese writing, and this was part of his broader interest in contemporary Chinese culture, including philosophy and cuisine, and involvement in the China Campaign committee.[8]

Though Isotype's first context had been the social projects of Vienna's socialist city government, it is evident that Neurath saw Isotype as having a role in the context of the growing internationalist planning movements of the 1930s. On its migration to Britain in the early 1940s, Isotype was adopted by various groups that were adapting the pre-war vision of a planned society for the purposes of British social reconstruction, but also for a post-war, post-Empire Commonwealth of nations.[9] *The Loom of Language* (1943) gives some clues as to the stakes for thinking about language in this period in Britain. This best-selling book was written by an acquaintance of Neurath's, the Swiss/South-African linguist Frederick Bodmer, and edited by Lancelot Hogben, who worked with Neurath on other publications. Commissioned for Hogben's series, *Primers for the Age of Plenty*, it was aimed at the 'home-student' and members of the Adult Education movement. It sets out to demystify language learning by showing the common roots of different languages and by explaining how traditional approaches to learning languages derive from an elite, academic approach rooted in 'the Latin scholarship of the humanists, and in the teaching of Greek in schools of the Reformation'.[10] The book demonstrates how the residues of past linguistic habits exist in contemporary writing and speech and can provide clues to the commonalities between languages, but Bodmer and Hogben make it clear that their sympathies lie with a standardization of spelling and the pursuit of an artificial language for international communication. Their sympathies are clearly socialist; their vision is for a self-educating working class to play a central role in the construction of a democratic, rational and international post-war 'age of plenty'.

Neurath's political sympathies and ideas about language had much in common with this. So it is worth looking at what Bodmer tells us about picture languages. Bodmer writes of ideographic and logographic languages (such as Chinese writing and Egyptian hieroglyphics) in which symbols that began as pictures had then 'lost their explicit pictorial meaning' and become logograms and ideograms that require a key to be interpreted. In Bodmer's view, the ancient picture languages probably became obscure and difficult to interpret because 'picture-writing was necessarily the secret lore of a priestly caste'.[11] Neither Ancient Egyptian hieroglyphics nor Chinese writing initially had any connection with the sounds of speech, although Egyptian hieroglyphics eventually incorporated phonograms and the Japanese adapted Chinese logograms and transformed them into a syllabic script. One of Bodmer's claims is that Chinese people who speak different languages may read exactly the same scripts. This understanding of Chinese writing is one of the reasons it was of particular interest for internationalists in the period. Another reason can be found in Bodmer's claim that English is coming increasingly to resemble Chinese because there is a 'large and growing group of words which can be verbs, nouns or adjectives'.[12] This linguistic simplification was seen as significant in the search for new means of international communication and a tool in the democratization of knowledge.[13]

If Bodmer's text points to how hieroglyphic and logographic scripts might lend themselves to this political effort, it also suggests their inappropriateness by arguing that this was a secret code, intended to keep knowledge, and therefore power, within the circle of priests. The difficulty of deciphering ancient hieroglyphics in the modern period is perhaps testimony to the success of this strategy. Yet Neurath was not the only person to connect hieroglyphs with a modern, popular visual education. His acquaintances Theodor Adorno and Max Horkheimer made the same connection, but with very different conclusions. In the early 1940s, at the same time as Neurath was writing about Isotype as hieroglyphics in Britain, Adorno and Horkheimer were in the US, completing *Dialectic of Enlightenment* (1944). Hieroglyphics are discussed in the first chapter of this work, which is in part an indirect critique of Neurath and the Vienna Circle, and in another chapter, not included in the published version, entitled 'The schema of mass culture'.[14]

In Adorno's and Horkheimer's argument, mass culture takes the form of images that parade themselves as natural, immediate and obvious, but that are an encoded means of domination: 'in the rulers' dream of the mummification of the world, mass culture serves as the priestly hieroglyphic script which addresses its images to those subjugated, not to be relished, but to be read'.[15] In the picture language of mass culture, images appear as 'neutral counters' to be read unreflectively, as mere signs: yet what they conceal is reification (described here as 'mummification') and domination. In other words, for Adorno and Horkheimer, mass culture communicates with images: these are hieroglyphics both because they make language pictorial, and because they operate as hieroglyphics did, not to disseminate knowledge and power, but to consolidate and preserve the social position of a few 'priests'.

In Bodmer's account, picture language becomes logographic as the priests increasingly attempt to maintain secrecy. Pictograms are accessible, because they resemble the things and ideas they represent, but logograms and ideograms are cryptic, maintaining only traces of visual resemblance. Neurath recognised that the Ancient Egyptian hieroglyphs worked in combination with wall paintings to form a complex picture-writing system. Some of the little hieroglyphic symbols derived directly from the wall paintings, and these were the ones that particularly interested Neurath. He was influenced less by the mysterious hieroglyphic script than by the communicative clarity and vividness of these images derived from everyday experience. Adorno and Horkheimer, on the other hand, relate the very clarity of the picture language of mass culture to the rule of a modern, capitalist 'priestly caste'. Adorno and Horkheimer generalize mass culture, discerning little difference between

Fig. 6.3: Example of Neurath's signature. The cat represents Marie Neurath. From a carbon copy of a letter to Helen Coppen, Otto and Marie Neurath Isotype Collection, Department of Typography & Graphic Communication, University of Reading, Isotype 1/10–11

advertising, comic strips and pictograms like Isotype. In a brief essay of 1944, entitled 'Picture book without pictures', Adorno referred to 'little silhouettes of men and houses that pervade statistics like hieroglyphics', and that, like the newspaper 'funnies' in his view, replaced aesthetic contemplation with the training of people in a mode of visual reading that is instant and un-reflective.[16]

Neurath emphasized the distinctive qualities and value of different media which 'ought not to be lumped together in one category'.[17] He too saw a connection between newspaper comic strips and Isotype, and on several occasions expressed interest in producing Isotype strips for newspapers. Yet it was in his correspondence, not in Isotype, that Neurath constructed a form of pictorial communication that shared the hand-drawn, fluid cartoon style of the popular comic strips. The signatures are informal, playful and closely associated with handwriting, and contrast vividly with the rigid elegance of Isotype. The elephant is an expressive character that changes according to the content of the letter, for instance, growing thin and surrounded by cactuses if the writer is in a tight spot, or using its trunk to offer flowers in love or gratitude, usually smiling with a raised trunk, but very occasionally with drooping ears and trunk and a tear in its eye. By the 1940s, the drawings are quickly and confidently executed. The elephant always faces to the left, usually with an open smiling mouth, large cartoon eyes, two simple curves for the ears and three toenails on each foot. Although the position of his trunk varies, and he becomes fatter or thinner in different drawings, the elephant's pose and the way it is drawn remain consistent. The drawing works successfully as a handwritten signature: repeatable, quickly executed and instantly recognisable (see fig. 6.3).

This character was arrived at over the course of Neurath's correspondence.[18] It is used frequently in letters dating from after his arrival in Britain in 1940. Photographs and drawings of elephants appear in a collection of love letters written by Otto to Marie, during their internment on the Isle of Man in 1940–1 (they married on their release). The camp authorities appear to have imposed a word limit on these letters, which would have passed through the British censors, and it seems Neurath used the pictures to compensate for the restrictions on written expression. Though Neurath did have a 'proper' written signature which appears on some letters, much of his correspondence after 1940 is signed with the elephant and carries no written name at all. After leaving Onchan camp, he returned to the long-established habit of typing all his letters. In this context, the signature drawings add a personal touch. However, there was no mechanical means of making images as cheaply and swiftly as a typewriter prints text, and hand-drawn images also illustrate the typed newsletters that were mimeographed and circulated by internees at Onchan camp. Printed images appeared on business letters in the form of elaborate letter headings, but these are fixed and unresponsive. Cartoon auto-graphs are not rare, as many autograph books will testify, but the responses of Neurath's correspondents indicate that they were not usual or conventional. The elephant often attracted commentary. When one correspondent enquired why he depicted himself as an elephant, Neurath replied that he had gained that reputation 'because I am so capacious' – perhaps not referring to the fact that he was physically big, but to his reputation as a polymath.[19]

Neurath's German-speaking peers also used informal and affectionate animal symbolism. In his private written correspondence, Theodor Adorno referred to himself and his mother as hippopotamuses, and to Horkheimer as a 'mammoth'.[20] The common use of animal symbolism and personification in modern culture has been understood in various ways: as symptomatic of the modern marginalization of actual animals, as evidence of the enormous importance of animals to the ways in which we imagine ourselves, and as a means of negotiating the 'otherness' of animals and other human beings.[21]

Animal drawings are also, of course, associated with children's literature and with 'light' culture and frivolity: in Neurath's correspondence the hand-drawn elephant lends a playful informality, and he used it to set a friendly tone in business correspondence as well as in correspondence with close friends. It is evident just how effective this is as a form of visual communication as other writers, sometimes hesitantly, begin to draw in response.

For example, a letter written to a printing company, Hall the Printer, in February 1944, requests 3,000 sheets of notepaper to be printed with Neurath's Oxford address as the heading. In the same brief letter he asks for tissue paper sheets to be used to cover the Isotype charts in transportation, saying 'We want to paste it on the upper edge of the card boards we got from you'. He ends the letter 'yours sincerely' and below that is a drawing of an elephant lifting a sheet of tissue to reveal an Isotype board beside it. Next to the board is a cat, his symbol for Marie Neurath. Here the signature works as a joint signature, indicating that the request is written by Otto on behalf of himself and Marie. It also illustrates and explains the tissue paper request. In another letter to Hall the Printer written two weeks later, Neurath reminds the company of his other request for 'the paper with my name and address on' and ends 'what can I do, without a "head"? Yours sincerely', and here is the elephant again, smiling as usual, and holding out a flower in his trunk. The sun is shining, but the elephant's head floats free of its body, which stands below it, in its usual pose, but with flesh and bones revealed in the cross-section of its severed neck. The sun, the proffered flower and the elephant's smile, all indicate Neurath's good will and good humour, even in this decapitated state.

The printing company wrote back to say that they were working on the notepaper. Nothing in this letter is particularly unusual or informal except the signature. In place of a signature is a drawing of a man, in hat, raincoat and pinstripe trousers, replacing the head on an elephant. The correspondence continued for some time: on 16 March, Neurath, still without his headed notepaper, asks 'How may I appear in society, without my letter head?' and an entirely headless elephant stands on its hind legs, with its front legs raised as if beseeching the printer.[22]

This example is not entirely unusual. Repeatedly, correspondents felt the need to comment on, or engage in, Neurath's practice of signing his letters with a drawing. Dorothy Woodman, author and secretary of the China Campaign and the Union for Democratic Control, writes: 'I can't draw elephants so I only send by substitute what I think is a very delightful card to you both.'[23] Here the elephant is seen as a picture-gift, which must be reciprocated. On 12 March 1941, the photographer Lucia Moholy writes to Neurath thanking him for a letter and expressing delight that he has survived the war in Europe: 'I hoped you may have been able to escape but not having heard from you all this time I had almost given you up.' She ends with a postscript: 'I do not know which animal would be the one to replace my signature – can you tell?! I enjoyed your two.' A month later she decides, and signs a letter to Neurath with her own animal picture, a long-eared cat seen from the back. Adapting his convention for the expression of good will, Moholy gives her cat a red flower, which it holds with its tail.[24] Helen Coppen, a South African student at the Institute of Education, signs one of her earliest letters: 'Being a Westerner I must leave picture writing to the Chinese and sign myself very sincerely yours, Helen Coppen.' In their subsequent correspondence, she signs herself first 'Table Mountain', in writing, with an outline of the mountain over the words, and then eventually with a drawing of the mountain and no words. Neurath responds by omitting her name from his letters and addressing her with his own drawing of Table Mountain, elaborating her simple line by adding trees on one side and waves beneath.[25]

What is the relationship of this with the practice of Isotype? The signature appears on letters relating to the business of the Oxford-based Isotype Institute, which Otto and Marie ran together, as well as on Neurath's correspondence with friends and students such as Coppen. Since the content of these letters has often to do with Isotype, it is not surprising that many of the drawings incorporate Isotype-like figures. One example is a brief letter to Peggy Volkov, the editor of *The New Era in Home and School*, the London-based journal of the New Education Fellowship. Writing on 15 April 1944, Neurath expresses regret that Volkov had not advised him of the difficulties she had reproducing an Isotype chart in colour. He sets out some of the colour rules of Isotype: 'Blue is always used as a "speaking" colour and never used as a "text" colour in our charts ... Black is text colour and symbol colour.' He ends the letter: 'Of course, I know there is a war on and everything goes

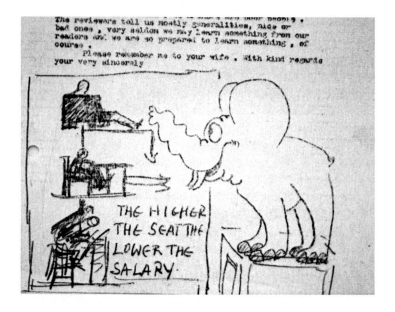

The reviewers tell us mostly generalities, nice or
bad ones , very seldom we may learn something from our
readers are we are so prepared to learn something , of
course .
      Please remember me to your wife . With kind regards
your very sincerely

THE HIGHER
THE SEAT THE
LOWER THE
SALARY.

Fig 6.4: Letter from Otto Neurath to Lancelot Hogben, Otto and Marie Neurath
Isotype Collection, Department of Typography & Graphic Communication,
University of Reading, Isotype 1/35–37

on in a hurry, where periodicals are concerned. I hope all this strain is not
endangering your recovery. With kind regards, yours sincerely,' and beneath,
the elephant on the right, and on the left, a family of Isotype figures: a woman
with her arm stretched out to the left, a girl and two young children.[26]

The New Education Fellowship was concerned with child-centred education,
so it is possible that the cartoon Isotype figures represent Volkov's or the
fellowship's protective role in relation to children. But perhaps most interesting
about this example is the contrast between the emphasis on the rules governing colour in Isotype charts, and the improvisational signature. In another
letter to Volkov Neurath speaks of her recent appendix operation and his
own childhood appendicitis, and then depicts the elephant, smiling at a
floating appendix in a jar, and below, Isotype-style infants sit on grass, with
flowers growing between them.[27] Some of the most elaborate signatures
appear in letters to the author and biologist Lancelot Hogben, the editor of

the series of *Primers for the Age of Plenty* who later authored an Isotype-illustrated history of visual communication entitled *From Cave Painting to Comic Strip* (1949). In the letters to Hogben, Isotype figures appear as circus tumblers, balancing on one another's shoulders, helped by the friendly elephant; Isotype diagrams of the workings of the ear are discussed, and then an anthropomorphized inner ear is drawn, as if singing to the elephant; political or social commentaries are thus made. One letter includes Isotype-style figures at desks, with the slogan 'the higher the seat, the lower the salary'. Often, the elephant is an instructor or guide, using his trunk to point (see fig. 6.4).

In the signatures, then, Isotype symbols are allowed to do things which they were not allowed to in the context of the charts: to illustrate personal opinions, to tumble around playfully, and to symbolize in ways that were outside the possibilities of the charts. An Isotype symbol of a child always represents a given number of children; figures are always equal size and arranged in rows; they do not hold hands like paper-chain people; and they stand for verifiable 'facts' not personal observations (however insightful) about things like the relationship of furniture to social position. The signatures have qualities in common with speech and writing that the picture language of Isotype does not have: the improvisational and inventive quality, the ability to deviate from and within a given formula, as discursive, dialogic and intimate. This picture language is *scriptible* (writerly) in Roland Barthes's sense, in that it invites and elicits responses in kind; it is participatory.[28] Anyone can do this, Neurath's signature seems to suggest, and perhaps the fact that his drawing is not particularly accomplished helps to encourage his correspondents to draw too. Isotype, by contrast, is an expert practice. As Marie Neurath wrote after Neurath's death, 'the writing of it was a very responsible and difficult job which can only be carried out by a group of experienced persons'.[29] The two approaches to a visual language could be seen to embody two opposing perspectives on language: one that holds that language is primarily creative and generative, produced 'from the grass roots up', and another that emphasizes its rule-bound, systematic nature.[30]

Retrospectively, it may be tempting to read the signifying differences between the picture language of Isotype and the picture language Neurath uses in his correspondence in terms of fundamental differences in meaning between the mechanically produced and uniform, and the hand made, uneven and expressive. After the war, several modernist designers and artists, including Neurath's close friend Josef Frank and the typographer Jan Tschichold, repudiated the modernist insistence on a uniform style, associating this with totalitarianism.[31] Isotype's standardized appearance has been linked with the popularization of Henry Ford's assembly line and F. W. Taylor's scientific management.[32] While Neurath himself had emphasized diversity and pluralism in early critiques of modernist design and Taylorist planning, Isotype was necessarily uniform.[33] As Neurath argued, a picture language sets out to be understood by everyone and, therefore, needs to be standardized, systematic, coherent and unified. Isotype grew from a particular cultural context in which to side with mass reproduction over individual expression was to commit to democratization, social renewal and to socialism.

The GWM in particular, grew out of social activism and avant-garde experimentation. It employed successful artist-printmakers working as part of the modernist avant-garde. The GWM had connections with the con- structivist and Dada movements, and had exhorted the artist to be more like an engineer or factory worker, closing the gap between artistic production and mass reproduction. It had connections with the Bauhaus and with the Soviet avant-garde, who were putting this aim into practice by placing art in the service of mass design. 1920s photographs of Arntz and his colleagues working at the GWM, in their white laboratory coats, bear strong resemblance to photographs of constructivists at work in the same period.

Yet the institutes and museums that produced Isotype were small con- cerns, never factories mass-reproducing images. While individual symbols were hand drawn then reproduced in multiples through linocut and letter- press, the exhibition charts made by the various institutes were assembled and pasted by hand. In these production contexts it is difficult to make a sharp distinction between manual and mechanical forms of production: the history of picture making is a history of the use of technical aids, including pen and ink, rulers and scissors.

That Isotype charts can be read more easily than they can be produced has to do with the range of techniques deployed and the expertise required for signifying clearly and coherently in Isotype. This is underscored by a 1942 correspondence between Neurath and George Stevenson, medical director of the US National Committee for Mental Hygiene. Stevenson had suggested communicating mental disorders such as 'gross distortion of ideas' by using wavy and dotted lines around a central figure, a symbolism that is completely incoherent within the context of the 'picture language'.[34]

Yet Isotype and the signature cartoon drawings are not as far apart as they might seem. Neurath maintained that, while the making of Isotype charts may have been a difficult expert business, learning to read picture statistics meant getting involved in practices of communicating through pictures: to read we must also learn to write. His archive includes photographs of charts hand drawn by Viennese school children, and in Britain he carried out similar experiments at Dartington Hall. His approach to this was informed by an understanding of child-centred education practices of Montessori and others. These had shaped the education delivered at the civic kindergartens of Red Vienna, and also possibly informed the practice of Isotype. Maria Montessori's approach to kindergarten education emphasized the early acquisition of literacy. Reading is learnt through writing and in visual and tactile ways: using cut-out sandpaper letters, children gradually form their own words, and through this begin to identify the words they see elsewhere.

Moreover, cartoons are not unrepeatable forms of individual expression, free from social convention. Like Isotype, Neurath's drawings follow a standardized format, with the same conventionalized symbolism used to communicate certain things (such as cactuses for 'prickly' situations and flowers for love and affection), even if they are more improvised than Isotype charts. The GWM itself experimented with using cartoon-like drawings, as shown by a chart prepared in the early months of the museum, 'Police action in Vienna in February 1925'. The chart resembles later Isotype charts in its linear layout but, instead of neatly separated and countable figures, the hand-drawn figures are brawling. Neurath's archive includes prints by George Grosz, which suggests he had an interest in Grosz's caricatures. However, Arntz reportedly criticized Grosz's use of caricature for conflating social types with physical types, by imposing a certain physiognomy on figures like bankers, army officers and workers.[35] Neurath's own drawings never caricature people, but either render them as Isotype-style silhouettes and figures or represent them as animals.

In *International Picture Language*, Neurath contrasted Isotype with advertising, trademarks and corporate logos. In advertising and corporate identity, pictures do not form a language, but mark distinction, competing with and outdoing one another: each picture 'has the tendency to put all such other pictures out of the memory of the onlooker'.[36] The picture language of the free market is chaotic and incoherent, yet it all functions in the same way, to impress itself on the viewer. If it repeatedly uses the same devices and techniques, it attempts to conceal this through novelty (as Adorno and Horkheimer noted).[37] Trademarks are recognizable and repeatable because they are acting as authentication, as a guarantee of the authorship of the product and (increasingly) as an assertion of property rights.[38]

Signatures also authenticate, and monograms, which usually originate as names or initials given pictorial form, have close association with the trademark and logos of corporations, which are also often based on the initial letters of the company's name. In his obituary, Kaempffert compared Neurath's signature to James McNeill Whistler's butterfly monogram.[39] As Kaempffert pointed out, the monogram does not have the expressive variety of Neurath's elephant. Although the butterfly changed over time, and may have had some expressive features (developing a sting, for instance), it remained a means to authenticate Whistler's work. Neurath's elephant does more by communicating his feelings, mood and character. Graphology might claim that a signature can also communicate character, a contentious claim, but even if it does, it does so in an unconscious and coded way, which only the expert graphologist can decode. Even this code, though supposedly directly expressive of character, can be learnt, as initiates adapt their handwriting to the character they want to project. Neurath's own interest in symbolism had to do with the explicit, convention-bound and conscious ways in which societies communicate. If a picture language was to communicate feelings (something he acknowledged Isotype could not do), it could not do so in a direct way, but through analogy (the elephant is sad, the elephant is Otto, therefore Otto is sad) or conventional symbols (such as the flower and the cactus). If the elephant signature communicates something of Otto's character, if ,for instance, it suggests to us that he was an optimist, original, irrepressible and playful, this assumption also has to do with our interpretations of the cultural conventions surrounding letter writing, signatures and the practice of drawing.

While his work brought him into close contact with both avant-garde experimentation and artificial language movements, Neurath's own drawings are very different from attempts to explore the potential of language and mark making for expressing inner psychic states, and far removed from the idea of producing an entirely new, entirely rational international language. Nevertheless, and despite evident differences, the picture language that Neurath develops in his correspondence and the picture language of Isotype do share some common features. Both reject the reduction of pictures and writing to stamps of authentication or property, and instead emphasize their communicative function. Both avoid encouraging a physiognomic reading that might reduce people to visual types. Both aim to be easily legible by using recognizable and established symbols where possible.

When Neurath died suddenly in December 1945, Isotype continued. Out of financial necessity Marie Neurath was back at work in January, and over the next thirty years she ran the Isotype Institute, successfully adapting the method to the production of non-fiction children's books. But when Neurath died, 'those brilliant letters [. . .] ceased' and the elephant died too. Far more dependent on one man than Isotype was, this picture communication ended, because Neurath's friends also gave up drawing on their letters. Affection was expressed in different ways, in writing. But a trace of the picture language remains in the nickname Helen Coppen continued to use for Marie Neurath: 'Dear brr brr', she wrote, a reference to the cat that Neurath had so often drawn to accompany his elephant.

Notes

[1] On the importance of Isotype see Robin Kinross, 'On the influence of Isotype', *Information Design Journal*, 2/11 (1981), 122–30; Michael Twyman, 'The Significance of Isotype' in *Graphic Communication through ISOTYPE* (Reading: Reading University 1975), pp. 7–17. For a history of the Vienna period, see Nancy Cartwright, Jordi Cat, Lola Fleck and Thomas E. Uebel, *Otto Neurath: Philosophy between Science and Politics* (Cambridge: Cambridge University Press, 1996).

[2] Otto Neurath, *International Picture Language: The First Rules of Isotype, Psyche Miniatures* (London: Kegan Paul, 1936).

[3] Otto Neurath letter to R. W. Moore, 23 May 1944. Otto and Marie Neurath Isotype Collection, Department of Typography & Graphic Communication, University of Reading, Isotype 1/10–11.

[4] For more on Gerd Arntz's work see Ed Annink and Max Bruinsma (eds), *Gerd Arntz: Graphic Designer* (Rotterdam: 010 publishers, 2010). For Marie Neurath's role as a 'transformer' see Marie Neurath and Robin Kinross, *The Transformer: Principles of Making Isotype Charts* (London: Hyphen Press, 2009).

[5] Waldemar Kaempffert, 'Appreciation of an elephant', *Survey Graphic*, February 1946.

[6] See for example, Tim Ingold, *Lines: A Brief History* (London and New York: Routledge, 2007). In a conference paper on technical drawing, Frances Robertson argued that this view of the straight line originated in mid-twentieth-century modernist theory. Frances Robertson, 'Marking the line: discourses of mechanical drawing in British culture around 1790–1830', paper given at Orientations, Inaugural Conference of the International Society for Cultural History, Ghent University, Belgium, August 27–31, 2008.

[7] Otto Neurath, *From Hieroglyphics to Isotypes: A Visual Autobiography*, ed. Matthew Eve and Christopher Burke (London: Hyphen Press, 2010).

[8] Neurath's involvement and interest in things Chinese is evident in much of his correspondence, especially in 1942–3. See the Otto and Marie Neurath Isotype Collection at the University of Reading, Isotype 1/1–5.

[9] Robin Kinross writes: 'The Isotype Institute fitted well into the project of social and political reconstruction in Britain, which got underway from about the time of its foundation.' Kinross points out that one of their early commissions was for a 1943 pamphlet publicizing the Beveridge report. See Robin Kinross, 'Emigré graphic designers in Britain: around the Second World War and afterwards', *Journal of Design History*, 1/3 (1990), 35–57 (44).

[10] Frederick Bodmer, *The Loom of Language: A Guide to Foreign Languages for the Home Student*, ed. Lancelot Hogben (London: George Allen and Unwin, 1943), p. 36.

[11] Ibid., pp. 57–8.

[12] Ibid., p. 125.

[13] For a discussion of European uses of, and assumptions about, Chinese characters and script in relation to Orientalism, see Nina Parish, *Henri Michaux: Experimentation with Signs* (Amsterdam: Rodopi, 2007), chapter 3.

[14] This chapter was eventually published in 1981. It appears in English translation in Theodor W. Adorno, *The Culture Industry: Selected Essays on Mass Culture*, ed. J. M. Bernstein (London: Routledge, 1991), pp. 53–84.

[15] Miriam Hansen, 'Mass Culture as Hieroglyphic Writing: Adorno, Derrida, Kracauer', *New German Critique*, 56, special issue on Theodor W. Adorno (spring–summer, 1992), 43–73 (48–9).

[16] Theodor Adorno, 'Picture book without pictures', in *Minima Moralia: Reflections from Damaged Life*, trans. E. F. N. Jephcott (London: NLB, 1974 [1951]), pp.140–1.

[17] Neurath, *From Hieroglyphics to Isotypes*, p. 99.

[18] Marie Neurath possessed one drawing, a souvenir of the 1928 Press Exhibition in Cologne, that may be by Neurath. This rather distorted elephant is seen from the rear, a pile of books upon his back, his trunk raised as if he is trumpeting. The drawing shows some attempt at realism that is not present in the signatures: there is laboured shading and modelling, and the air snorted from the trunk is drawn using nineteenth-century conventions (source: the Otto Neurath Nachlass, Vienna Circle Archive, Haarlem).

[19] Neurath to Coppen, Otto and Marie Neurath Isotype Collection, University of Reading, Isotype 1/1–5.

[20] See Detlev Claussen, *Theodor W. Adorno. Ein letztes Genie* (Frankfurt am Main: S. Fischer, 2003), and Stefan Müller-Doohm, *Adorno. Eine Biographie* (Berlin: Suhrkamp, 2003). Adorno's use of animal metaphors is discussed in a review of both books: Robert, 'Adorno's family and other animals', *Thesis Eleven*, 78 (August 2004), 102–12.

[21] See, for example, John Berger, 'Why look at animals?', in *About Looking* (London: Writers and Readers, 1980), pp. 1–26, and Margaret Blount, *Animal Land: The Creatures of Children's Fiction* (London: Hutchinson, 1974).

[22] Otto and Marie Neurath Isotype Collection, University of Reading, Isotype 1/6–9.

[23] Otto and Marie Neurath Isotype Collection, University of Reading, Isotype 1/1–5.

[24] Otto and Marie Neurath Isotype Collection, University of Reading, Isotype 1/1–5.

[25] Ibid.

[26] Otto and Marie Neurath Isotype Collection, University of Reading, Isotype 1/6–9.

[27] Ibid.

[28] Roland Barthes, *S/Z* (Paris: Seuil, 1970).

[29] Marie Neurath to Philip Dingle, town clerk of Manchester, 27 March 1947, Otto and Marie Neurath Isotype Collection, University of Reading, Isotype 1/1–5.

[30] This was politicized in V. N. Vološinov's 1927 critique of Ferdinand de Saussure's linguistics for placing too much emphasis on the system of language over living speech. Vološinov instead emphasized the competing meanings produced by different social classes in class struggle. See V. N. Vološinov, *Marxism and the Philosophy of Language* (Cambridge, MA: Harvard University Press, 1973).

[31] See Christopher Burke's epilogue to his book on the typographer Jan Tschichold for a discussion of Tschichold's repudiation of his earlier work in *Active Literature: Jan Tschichold and New Typography* (London: Hyphen Press, 2007). See also Christopher Long's discussion of Frank's post-war anti-style of 'accidentalism' in Christopher Long, *Josef Frank: Life and Work* (Chicago: University of Chicago Press, 2002).

[32] See Peter Wollen, 'Modern times: cinema, Americanism, the robot' in *Raiding the Icebox: Reflections on Twentieth-Century Culture* (London: Verso, 1993).

[33] See, for instance, Otto Neurath 'The converse Taylor system: reflections on the selection of the fittest', in Marie Neurath and Robert S. Cohen (eds), *Otto Neurath: Empiricism and Sociology* (Dordrecht: D. Reidel, 1973), p. 133. Originally published as 'Das umgekehrte Taylorsystem', in *Kunstwart und Kulturwart* (Dresden, 1917).

[34] George Stevenson to Otto Neurath, Otto and Marie Neurath Isotype Collection, University of Reading, Isotype 1/6–9.

[35] Gerd Arntz quoted in Martyn Everett, 'Art as a weapon: Frans Seiwert and the Cologne Progressives', online at *http://martyn.everett.googlepages.com/ artasaweapon*. Originally published in *The Raven*, 12 (October/December 1990).

[36] Neurath, *International Picture Language*, p. 28.

[37] Adorno and Horkheimer, *Dialectic of Enlightenment*, p. 123.

[38] See Jane Gaines, *Contested Culture: The Image, the Voice and the Law* (Durham, NC: University of North Carolina Press, 1991).

[39] Kaempffert, 'Appreciation of an elephant'.

Colette: An Eye For Textiles

Anne Freadman

Je touche, je regarde, ces soieries modernes...[1]

A major part of Colette's writing career was devoted to *les arts du spectacle*, musical performances and the cinema in the period before the First World War, the theatre for decades after that, public gatherings and events in the streets of Paris and, importantly during the 1920s, vestimentary fashion. It is to this last category that I attend here. In exploring fashion Colette brings all her observational talents to bear on the transformation of women in modernity. Many people have pointed out over the years that Colette was not a 'feminist', in the sense of being militant, or even particularly sympathetic to the access of women to professional and other roles in public life. But she herself was primarily a journalist, and she used this position to pursue her interest in women in their daily engagement with the conditions of modern urban life. Most significantly, it is in Colette's journalistic writing, far more than in her novels, that we find her examining the evolution of femininity and revealing for us one of the deep paradoxes of modernism: at the same time as women were laying claim to various forms of emancipation, they were lending themselves to the role of visual object in new, informal though not unstated, sumptuary laws. They had been used in this way throughout the nineteenth century when the sobriety of men's dress asserted equality and the display of women's dress its opposite. A similar paradox is evident in the early twentieth century, but within the feminine realm: here the form of the dress appears to assert freedom, but its materiality – how it is worn and what it is made of – have other things to say. I have written elsewhere about how the dress is worn.[2] In this chapter I am concerned with what the dress is made of. In an era remarkable for its conspicuous consumption, the inventiveness of the textile arts, their sumptuous richness in all senses and the luxury of their use in ephemera good for a single season are the components of an assertion of social dominion. This assertion is made by the women who display them and who are displayed by them.

These art textiles of the 1920s are familiar to us through their likenesses in picture books, whether catalogues of exhibitions or academic studies.[3] Such books purvey splendid, deeply pleasurable images, but they cannot give us the feel of these precious stuffs. Indeed, even outside the books, the textiles are seldom available to the touch. Rare indeed is the museum that would authorize a laying-on of hands. So it has interested me to ask whether, in her descriptions, Colette gives a place to tactility, or whether her writing is primarily a writing of the visual. I shall argue that, in general, the latter is the case, but that the restriction to visuality is no mere oversight on her part. It is a significant aspect of her analysis of fashion, and of that special dimension of fashion which is the art of textiles, that she shows why it matters to understand it as an art of spectacle.

I write 'analysis' – Colette's 'analysis' of the art of textiles – for two reasons, of which the first is polemical. In general, Colette should, but does not, count as a major figure in French literary modernism. This is partly because much of her journalism is devoted to fleeting moments, to ephemera and to women's business. Yet surely we should be suspicious of such dismissals. Like a latter-day Baudelaire, Colette's attention to the momentary is devoted to recording the everyday and to capturing the non-monumental, but it is the feminine everyday – 'girls' talk' – made remarkable. She finds, or makes, art from subjects and materials, that do not have the status of high art. To dismiss her for doing so is to remain within a certain canon (that is, a rule concerning what counts as Art); it is to fail utterly to understand the extent to which Colette contributes to the contesting of that canon.

My second reason consists in asking the 'speech act' question: what is she doing by writing what she writes? This is a question about genre. Colette's attention to textiles is the work of a cultural critic. She is interested in the temporality of fashion; she is interested in modes of production and consumption and their commercial conditions; she is interested in the relation between handwork and machine work; she is interested in the luxury market and in the moulding of women and of femininity by industrial modernity. Granted, she develops no theory of such things; my point is that what she sees, what she makes us see, is far more ramified than a simple image. But, on reflection, 'analysis' is inappropriately used for Colette's modes of writing and engaging with her materials: she reads the moment, she reads the desires and the fears and the playthings of that moment; she reads its arts and its crafts, its self-delusions and its hypocrisies. Colette's writing is not cast in the analytical mode: it is satirical and it is ekphrastic.

Ekphrasis has many places or functions in literature, and we are most often drawn to its use as a *mise en abyme*. But another crucial function is in criticism of the visual arts; the critic is expected to bring to the gaze of her readers the visible object in all its vividness. In Colette's writing, this function is associated with a second tradition inherited from the ancient world: this is satire, a genre that serves in Roman letters as the setting for literary criticism. Only on the basis of a pointed description could the critic ground his judgements of a work, or of an author. We find something of this sort at the beginning of the *Ars Poetica* of Horace, when the poet invites his reader to 'Imagine a painter who wanted to combine a horse's neck with a human head, and then clothe the miscellaneous collection of limbs with various kinds of feathers, so that what started out at the top as a beautiful woman ended in a hideously ugly fish' (Horace, *On the Art of Poetry*, 1–10), going on to draw his lessons from this failed attempt at creative ingenuity. Roman literary criticism was satirical because it made didactic use of exempla, and the passage from Horace shows the potential for this practice to extend into the arena of the visual arts. When description goes beyond itself to ask questions of its objects and their social conditions, to investigate them as behaviours encapsulating values, it blends scopic pleasure with satire. Colette, I shall argue, is writing criticism in this rather lofty sense.

However, it is important not to confuse criticism with the aesthetic gaze. In the following description, Colette discerns two quite different responses to the rhetoric of the fashion parade. One is from the women whose desire to possess the dresses is solicited by the spectacle; the other is from their male companions:

> Seul l'homme goûte aux défilés de modèles un plaisir complet, qui n'est pas gâté par la convoitise. Pendant que sa compagne, secrètement frénétique, renonce, le cœur en lambeaux, à une petite «création» de six mille francs, l'homme s'épanouit, se renseigne, note la taille basse de chez X . . ., le drapé de chez Z . . ., comme il retient les caractéristiques d'une école de peinture. ('Mannequins', p. 1117)

Colette's interest in this piece is with the mannequin. The aesthetic gaze of the men disguises – as it always has done – a far more predatory attitude: 'Parmi les formes modernisées de la plus luxueuse industrie, le mannequin, vestige d'une barbarie voluptueuse, est comme une proie chargée de butin' (ibid., p. 1118). Furthermore, the mannequin is merely the instrument of the designer:

> Elle est la conquête des regards, sans frein, le vivant appât, la passive réalisation d'une idée. [. . .] Une mission démoralisante la tient à égale distance du patron et des ouvrières normales. [. . .] Aucun autre métier féminin ne contient d'aussi puissants facteurs de désagrégation morale que celui-là, qui impose à une fille pauvre et belle les signes extérieurs de la richesse. (Ibid.)

Colette's observations of this ambiguous profession include her concern with the reduction of the physical body to pure image: 'elle est la conquête des regards [. . .] la passive réalisation d'une idée'. If the task of the mannequin is to address the artwork to the men and the mirage of the perfect, and purchasable, body to the women, it is clear that Colette's interest in them is not assimilable to either of these positions. She is interested in these women as working women, and in the instrumentalizing of their femininity – indeed, their sexuality – in the economics of desire.

So I return to the place of fabric in this economy. Fashion is a luxury industry, and Colette points out that the simpler and skimpier the style of dress, the more extravagant the textiles: 'ces défilés de robes, de jolies filles, de tissus que leur métrage, de plus en plus réduit, contraint à une magnificence sans cesse croissante' (ibid., p. 1116). Contrast this magnificence with the following:

> Celui qui tisse la lune, le soleil et les rayons bleus de la pluie sait qu'on ne touche pas par le prodige, ni par la splendeur, le fond de l'avidité féminine. Aussi recourt-il à certaines perversités.
>
> Cette année, il s'enferme avec un lot choisi d'écheveaux sans prix, filés par les vers de Chine, murmure une incantation, ondoie la trame d'un élixir talismanique, et apporte au jour, parmi des cris émerveillés . . . la plus parfaite imitation d'un petit lainage pied-de-poule à douze quatre-vingt-quinze le mètre! ('Soieries', pp. 1177–8)

This fabric designer works on the assumption that his customers – like the dandy of the early nineteenth century – may well find it more tasteful, and more aristocratic, to avoid ostentation. This fabric is a fiction: the comfort, the look and the discreet patternings of woollen cloth, reproduced in the finest silk. Its simplicity mimics humble cloths, but it is the *haut de gamme*.

The choice of fabric was not confined to the alternative between beading and embroidery on the one hand and weaving on the other. Printed designs were all the rage, whether on cotton, on satin or on silk velvet. Take this example:

> Elle ne vient pas me voir, elle entre en passant . . . Petit chapeau blanc, robe blanche, noire et verte [. . .] c'est chic d' « entrer en passant » chez une amie, à quatre cents kilomètres de Paris, avec un petit air d'être venue à pied . . . Au bas du pré, la mer humecte, d'une langue courtoise, le feuillage de fer et la fleur de flamme des chardons bleus. Mais mon amie Valentine ne voit ni la mer, ni la plage, ni le cap dépouillé par l'été, jaune et brun comme un fauve: elle pense aux vendanges. Les vendanges se portent, depuis deux ou trois ans, aussi assidûment que le kasha. Entre mon amie Valentine et la douce mer laiteuse s'interpose, saugrenu, un tableau de vendanges, d'une grâce arbitraire, et je plains cette jeune femme réduite, de par la Mode, à une constante prospection de l'avenir. ('Vendangeuses', pp. 1129–30)

Here Colette's interest is in the multiple dimensions of fashion, not merely in the look of the thing. Fashion is a set of behaviours – 'c'est chic d'entrer en passant chez une amie, à quatre cents kilomètres de Paris, avec un petit air d'être venue à pied'. She is noting the new casualness of visits given and received. Fashion is also a relation with the seasons – 'les vendanges se portent' – but this relation is fictional, it is not dictated by the weather: here we have a 'tableau' representing the patterns of rural life. Fashion is an urban phenomenon, depending upon the practical separation of urban life from rural realities. This separation is both geographical and a matter of attention, the involvement of persons in place and time: Valentine simply does not see the landscape she is visiting, just as the hunting outfit in this next quotation is not made for hunting:

> Les journaux de mode prônent cent tenues de chasseresses, aussi bien l'image flanque le texte et prouve que la chasseresse de 1925 n'a rien gagné sur celle de 1924. Ni gorge, ni croupe, elle s'affirme héronnière, et cependant dotée d'un buste interminable. Si j'en crois d'habiles dessinatrices, la chasseresse chausse de mignons escarpins, ou des bottines hautes en peau de gant. Elle s'arme d'une carabine longue comme une gaffe, d'une houppe à poudre, d'une cigarette et d'un bracelet-montre, qui marque sans doute la dernière heure du tireur le plus proche. Elle est quadrillée de grands carreaux comme une salle de bains, ou chevronnée comme un vieux guerrier. Elle porte, sous sa cravate masculine, un « chemisier » de crêpe de Chine blanc, moyennant quoi le gibier la voit, Dieu merci, de très loin. ('Poil et plume', p. 1133)

I wonder, too, if Colette is not making a further point: like Valentine who has popped in to show off the grape-harvesting outfit, fashion is always just visiting, always a 'tableau', always 'arbitraire' in that it is divorced from the patterns it borrows. Its own context – and the absence of the context to which it alludes – is registered in its temporality: it is 'une constante prospection de l'avenir'.

Nevertheless, this 'constante prospection de l'avenir' is marked by the citation and recycling of the past. It is precisely in, and through, the temporality of fashion that modernity is always already postmodern. In one place Colette ponders the use of new machinery for embroidery; in another, she notes that un maître de couture has decided to adorn his creation with 'une fleur verte, en laine tricotée, d'où pend une grappe saugrenue de cerises bleues, en laine tricotée, sommée de trois feuilles noires, en laine tricotée.'[4]

Her judgement coincides with Chanel's, whom she quotes elsewhere: 'Non, pas de petits machins sur un tissu qui se défend tout seul' ('Chanel').[5] But, again, this is not just about the look; it is about citation:

> Très tranquille, le couturier entame, en mon honneur, un couplet sur les travaux d'aiguille chers à nos grand-mères, il chante le naïf crochet tunisien, le *macramé* désuet et touchant – il réclame, pour ses ornements simplets, une place d'honneur sur nos robes d'air tissé et d'eau courante. Il prononce les mots, prévus, d'innovation, de tentative *amusante*. ('Le Maître', pp. 927–8)

The incongruity of the mix of knitting with silk is similar to the decontextualized tableau of Valentine's little print; 'la constante prospection de l'avenir' uses the past as a repository of novelty. Notice, as we speak of temporality, the verbs 'attendent' and 'revient': 'Reposons-nous parmi des jardins qui, fleuris cet hiver, attendent le soleil et les femmes de l'été prochain. La rose y abonde, une rose qui revient à une tradition picturale que nos mères chérirent vers 1880' ('Soieries', p. 1177). Alongside citation from the past, we also find citation from distant traditions of the textile arts, Persian carpets, for example: 'D'autres roses jonchent d'autres soieries, d'un goût rustique et ruineux: c'est la rose empruntée à la Perse, la rose des tapis, plate, écrasée, nivelée pour le plaisir d'un pied nu' ('Soieries', p. 1177). It is in design, specifically in fabric design, that the high visual arts meet the consumer market, and here that the paradoxical temporality of fashion mediates taste and hence desires both fleeting and intense. The title of the fashion magazine *Art-Goût-Beauté* seems to aspire to a traditional synthesis, while the juxtaposition on its cover of nostalgic nosegays and a bold geometric design is audacious.

Cultural memory does not provide the ground for continuity so much as a collection of motifs that can be quoted. Design brings together the imperatives of novelty and the familiar reassurance of memory, of memories: they are *souvenirs* from another place and time. Both these dimensions – novelty and nostalgia – are to be found not only in the visual design, but also in the technical conditions of textile production. Thus, when the *maître de couture* deposits a knitted ornament on a silk dress, he is citing a manner of making. Its opposite can be found in the strangest of textile innovations. Colette's satire is at its most hilarious in this sort of case:

Le roi des tisseurs ne se borne pas à inventer des tissus, il invente aussi leurs noms. Néologismes hardis, sons aussi riches que l'arabesque, aussi doux que la laine thibétaine, vous caressez l'oreille d'une harmonie qui participe de la sauvage mélopée et de la fumisterie . . .

The juxtaposition of 'mélopée' with 'fumisterie' – of the highbrow allusion to antiquity with the radical absence of serious content – pointedly reflects, as it reflects on, the pretentious innovations of fashion. 'Les oreilles caressées' to the point of 'une griserie phonétique', Colette is not merely engaged in mockery: she is making fun,

quand je lis le lot de la crépellaine, du bigarella, du poplaclan, du djirsirisa et de la gousellaine – j'en oublie! – une griserie phonétique me saisit, et je me mets à penser en pur dialecte poplacote. Souffrez qu'en vous quittant, lectrice, j'empoigne mon filavella, je chausse mes rubespadrillavellaines et je coiffe mon djissaturbanécla; la marée baisse, voici l'heure d'aller pêcher, dans les anfractuosités du rockaskaïa, le congrépellina et la dorade zibelinée. ('Nouveautés', pp. 1160–1)

It is no mere coincidence that textile invention is accompanied by textual innovation: this is the era of the rise of advertising and the fashion magazine. It is also the era in which handwork was industrialized, and in which looking was subject to new technical conditions as a result of electric lighting. As ever, Colette's attention to fabrics is firmly set in the material conditions of their display. She gives us to understand not only that fashion was the object of representation in advertising, not only that textiles themselves represented the world in which they were displayed, but also that they were, to borrow a term from Roman Jakobson, 'autotelic': they were designed to contribute technically to their own spectacularization. Ever a creature of the theatre, Colette intimates that the vogue for lamé was a response to artificial light: 'Que d'or, et d'argent, et de cuivre rouge, mêlés à la soie!' ('Soieries', p. 1176), she exclaims, again noting the incongruity of silk overlaid by metal: these precious stuffs were 'destinée[s] aux lumières artificielles' (ibid.) which they reflected back. The wearers of these garments became themselves the source of light, the stars in the firmament, their very brilliance rendering them insubstantial. However, these artificial conditions have a most unfortunate effect:

Lamés d'or, lamés d'argent, de cuivre, d'acier – ils se ressemblent par l'éclat sec, toujours un peu papier de chocolat, par la froideur râpeuse, et par l'odeur. La mode persistante du lamé démontre la grossièreté des sens féminins, particulièrement de l'odorat. Car le fumet d'une robe de lamé, humectée au cours d'une soirée chaude, oxydée pendant la danse, passe en âpreté le fier arôme du déménageur en plein rendement. Elle fleure l'argenterie mal tenue, le vieux billon, le torchon pour les cuivres; sa trame de soie ni les parfums qui l'imprègnent n'atténuent rien, au contraire. ('Arrière-saison', pp. 1163–4)

Is it really 'les sens féminins' as such that are unrefined? The careless misogyny of this comment is not uncharacteristic of Colette. Yet what we may nevertheless learn from it about women in this period is that their very attention to their own bodies is so controlled by the fashion industry that they become effectively oblivious to any sense other than that of sight. Colette suggests that the use of lamé is determined by the conditions of its display under artificial light. With its insensitivity to smell, and indeed to tactility, with its tableaux and its placement in tableaux, fashion is represented by Colette as an art of pure visuality, and the sensuality of women is reduced accordingly.

'Le luxe féminin' is 'exhibé' ('Mannequins', p.1117), she writes. Fashion parades are the obvious way in which this pure visuality is theatricalized:

[les hommes] viennent à cette solennité de la couture plus empressés qu'à une générale du boulevard. Ils font profession d'«adorer» ces défilés de robes, de jolies filles, de tissus [. . .] Ils confessent bien haut leur goût pour ces solennités vestimentaires que tout couturier coté organise avec un faste théâtral et religieux. ('Mannequins', pp. 1116–17)

Yet the designers refuse the status of true 'artistes' to their mannequins.

If the salons were theatrical spaces, the very bodies of the models were gallery walls, showing their rustic scenes and anything else that could be turned to the purposes of pure decoration:

Ah! ce dos! Quatre-vingts centimètres de dos, sans pinces ni pli. Monsieur le Brodeur, souriez: voici de quoi vous ébattre. Brodez, sur ce dos vertigineux, des pagodes, des fruits, des chiffres arabes, des scènes champêtres, des frises pompéiennes et des automobiles. ('Trop court', p. 1139)

Even the *maître de couture* does not touch his design – let alone his client – during a fitting:

> Le « maître » montre, d'ailleurs, une discrétion presque exagérée, j'allais écrire: dégoûtée. C'est d'un index lointain, comme aimanté, qu'il commande aux évolutions de sa cliente. Elle tourne, avance d'un pas, s'arrête, magnétiquement – il ne frôle même pas l'étoffe de la robe. ('Le Maître', p. 926)

We could contrast this depiction with the splendid portrait devoted to Chanel:

> La voici piétée sur des matériaux bruts, entre des pilastres de jersey, des poutrelles de foulard imprimé couchées. De longs drains de satin roulé chatoient ... Les parois mêmes de la pièce sont enflées de sourds molletons, de duveteux lainages, ici tout est silence. ('Chanel', p. 743)

Chanel's salon is a workroom, and Chanel, her mouth full of pins, 'sculpts' her customer: 'Chanel travaille des dix doigts, de l'ongle, du tranchant de la main, de la paume, de l'épingle et des ciseaux, à même le vêtement, qui est une vapeur blanche à longs plis, éclaboussé de cristal taillé. (ibid., p. 744) On her knees, using her arms, Chanel is a craftswoman engaged in physical work like that of 'une lavandière' (ibid.) whose task is to care for fabric. She designs the intimate relation of the body with that fabric, with its fall and its feel. She is the very opposite of the pretentious *maître* whose only concern is with novelty and look.

Nevertheless, the look and looking are our business, and Colette's concern with them is not so much to condemn them but to make us understand their centrality in fashion. The place of fashion as 'un art du spectacle' is 'acquis', and it fulfils its role there primarily through the fabrics themselves. In one of the finest pieces of ekphrastic writing she has given us, Colette describes what she saw at a showing of fabrics. We are not dealing here with the mannequins and their audience, but with the exhibition of the raw materials themselves. Long before they arrive at Chanel's workshop, they are art in their own right.

In the following, I dwell at some length on a single piece, entitled 'Soieries':

D'une obscurité profonde, où parfois glisse le reflet lent qui éclaircit les sources aux eaux abondantes et paresseuses, monte une ombelle énorme, une sorte d'astre. Son dôme, qui affleure la surface de l'eau, porte les couleurs du bégonia ardent, de la rose sanguine, ses bords noyés redescendent au rouge du métal chauffé, au grenat que l'ombre violace. Derrière la flottante créature empourprée, une ramille traînante, digitée, d'un vert d'algue se balance . . .

Il ne s'agit pourtant que d'un velours, et d'une fleur imprimée. L'auteur du dessin assure : «C'est un pavot . . .», et il le croit. Mais moi je sais bien que ventrue, ombiliquée, segmentée délicatement, frangée, et remorquant une traîne filamenteuse, sa fleur est une méduse. Si je dis au dessinateur que c'est une méduse, il protestera, sur un ton digne d'artiste incompris. La mer originelle est loin de nous. Le monstre ou la fleur qu'elle enfante en notre esprit émergent, comme fait le fruit de la châtaigne d'eau, au bout d'une tige si longue que nous ne pensons plus à sa racine submergée. Mais la beauté de la matière ouvrée révèle le secret d'une inspiration: au sein d'un velours riches en moires, touché du reflet aquatique qui court sur une surface buveuse de lumière, le pavot est devenu méduse. ('Soieries', p. 1175)

Colette describes the image as if she were describing the real thing: we have a modern version of the story of Zeuxis' grapes. But, 'l'effet du réel' denounces itself as the art of illusion: 'il ne s'agit que d'un velours, d'une fleur imprimée'. Furthermore, as Andrew Sprague Becker notes in his fine book on the Greek art of ekphrasis, 'ekphrasis describes an experience of representations, not just their appearance'.[6] This experience was physical – Colette tells us that she found it just too much at times – and it was an experience of interpretation. Thus Colette's reading of the image differs from the artist's intentions: 'si je dis au dessinateur que c'est une méduse, il protestera, sur un ton d'artiste incompris'. As in the tableau of the grape harvest, 'la mer originelle est loin de nous'. This is a 'matière ouvrée' whose art is such that it produces not just a realist illusion but a metaphor: 'le pavot est devenu méduse' – with which the metaphor deconstructs itself as a simile. Similes draw attention to them-selves as a verbal art, and as Colette shifts between the double illusion – the realism of the first image, its metaphorical transformation as the *fleur-méduse* – she requires us to read her own art. We are required thereby to note that this is a verbal text. Ekphrasis draws attention to itself, to the fact that it is different from the experience of viewing. It is made of words while the image is made of 'un velours riche en moires, touché du reflet aquatique qui court sur une surface buveuse de lumière'.

One of the ways in which ekphrasis draws attention to itself is by drawing attention, as Becker puts it, not only to the referent of the image, but also to the relation of that referent to the artisan and the artistry: in the case of Achilles' shield, this is achieved through the medium of worked metal.[7] In the case of Colette's fabrics, it may be the weaver's art, or it may be the new-fangled machines that have come to replace handwork:

> Les roses que je froisse baignent dans une brume légère, dans un air tremblant de chaleur, et je songe aux miraculeuses machines dont le doigt d'acier, posant ici un reflet de nacre, ici une goutte de lumière, ici le vert miroir d'une feuille mouillée, ne se trompe jamais. ('Soieries', p. 1177)

Another example makes these two aspects of ekphrasis very clear: Colette describes both the material art of the material and her own experience of viewing it: she has to touch it to understand how the illusion is produced, she has to show us both the image and how she deciphered it. As she is 'separated' from the roses by a 'brume illusoire', so we are separated from the experience of seeing; as she is drawn in, so are we. And as she multiplies her similes and her metaphors, so are we left with a double art of words, one that interposes itself like 'une toile d'araignée en argent fin' between us and the fabric, and yet reveals it to us:

> Quand le modéliste s'endort, le tisseur s'éveille, et fait des miracles. D'une torsion plus ou moins sévère, il refrène ou exaspère l'éclat du fil de métal, échauffe un fond, interpose une brume illusoire entre le dessin et le spectateur. Un trompe-l'œil me retient longtemps, et c'est du doigt que je cherche machinalement à quelle distance exacte peut flotter la toile d'araignée en argent fin, concave ici, convexe là, qui me sépare d'un rideau de roses indistinctes, jaunes, rouges, roses, sur un lointain ciel noir. ('Soieries', p. 1176)

We have visual metaphors here, but we also have metaphors of the visual:

> Je vois qu'on aime ici une certaine sorte de fantasmagorie, de duperie optique qui est bien près de l'humour. Des avenues de pastilles multicolores, énormes, vous

giflent l'œil, puis s'en vont selon la décroissance vertigineuse des réverbères nocturnes. Un jeu de lignes creuse, sur un crêpe candide, de trompeuses perspectives, et sur un autre crêpe l'œil embrasse à vol d'oiseau, comme du haut d'un avion, des cimes et des cimes d'arbres, des frondaisons crépues que souligne un petit trait, un bleu vif d'éclair. ('Soieries', p. 1176)

Yet the textile arts are different from the textual arts, seeing is different from reading. In my final example, Colette draws our attention to those differences by drawing a parallel between them as arts:

Il n'est point de plaisir sans fatigue, et celui des yeux, si on le prolonge, délabre particulièrement l'esprit. Tant d'or, rebrodé d'or sur fond d'or, tant de feux et de lignes, tant de lampas damasquinés, on gagne ici, à la fin, la lassitude qu'engendrent les musées trop riches. Encore notre satiété est-elle différée par une astuce d'artiste qu'on n'aperçoit pas tout de suite, et qui consiste à employer un gris, si j'ose écrire, invisible, distribué au revers d'une feuille, d'un pétale ardent, insinué entre deux feux de rouge, entre deux tranchants de vert. Un gris qui tamponne, qui calfate des fissures par où fuient les couleurs en fusion; un gris concentrique, pareil à la zone des reflets faibles qui cerne la rupture d'une eau tranquille. ('Soieries', pp. 1176-7)

Discovering the 'astuce d'artistes', Colette reveals her own by mentioning the very business of lexical choice as she writes: 'si j'ose écrire'. She does not merely create the metaphors and similes for how this invisible grey affects the experience of seeing the profusion of colours: 'calfater', 'tamponner', 'pareil à la zone des reflets faibles qui cerne la rupture d'une eau tranquille'; she also asks us to note them in their quality of stylistic tropes. In our experience of reading, what is this 'invisible grey', if not the line of writing and its unnoticed powers? The accumulation of riches is matched by the lists and the repetitions – 'tant d'or, rebrodé d'or sur fond d'or' – which make fun of themselves as they distance the reader from the experience of glut, keeping her attention as the writer's art defers the moment when we must look away.

Colette was a professional critic, and it is in this capacity that she attends the exhibitions and visits the showrooms. I have sought to convey an inkling of the writing work that she took this to involve. It is an art of words that describes what she sees, and makes us see it; it mediates the image through its own art; and it is an art of satire that takes us into the social and the cultural issues that are raised by 'la plus luxueuse industrie'. This satire is both deeply serious and very funny, and the people who invited her into their salons were quite aware of the risks they were taking. To recall the long-suffering *maître de couture*:

> J'accompagne ici, pour la première fois, mon amie Valentine, qui s'habille, bien entendu, chez un «maître de la couture». J'étudie le «maître», qui me le rend bien. C'est de Valentine qu'il s'occupe, mais c'est moi qu'il veut épater. Il s'attarde, il néglige d'autres sujettes impatientes – il pose, ne sachant au juste si je fais le portrait flatté ou la caricature. ('Le Maître', p. 927)

Colette's attention, however, is not merely drawn to individuals with dubious taste. Her critique reaches farther into the whole textile industry. Industrial modernity and the drive to innovation do have the strangest effects. From her matchless hands comes, *in fine*, a biting critique of fashion as industry and as fetish:

> Vous prenez un marabout, vous le rasez. Et pour que la mesure de son ignominie soit comble, vous le dégradez, avant de l'exposer à tous les regards [. . .]
>
> Heureusement, il ne s'agit que d'une garniture en vogue. Pour ce qui est de dégrader le marabout, passe encore. Du rose au rouge, du violet au bleu, il n'en sera pas plus laid. Mais le raser . . . Pourquoi pas tondre un poussin, ou épiler un angora? [. . .]
>
> Étrange industrie que celle qui s'empare d'une parure animale duveteuse, légère, chaude, suave au toucher, pour la détruire par la chimie ou l'électricité, et proclamer ensuite : «Voyez cette peau méconnaissable, dont nous avons fauché l'herbe vivante et laissé le chaume! Voyez ce balai quasi chauve.» ('Nouveautés', p. 1158)

We have read Colette describing fabrics; they are sometimes absurd, sometimes sublime, always the object of the writer's most exquisite verbal attention. If fabrics are also tactile, an experience of the skin, Colette's eye for textiles is an eye for how the visual has overridden all the other senses – not merely that it has done so, but *how*.

Notes

1   Colette, *Le Voyage égoïste*, in *Œuvres*, vol. II (Paris: Gallimard, Bibliothèque de la
    Pléiade, 1986), pp. 1091–81 (p. 1175). References will be from this text in this edition
    and will be included in the text with the subtitle noted. Different sections or volumes
    will first be introduced in the footnotes before again being included in the text.

2   For this point, concerning the restrictions on women's bodies required for the
    wearing of flapper fashion, see Anne Freadman, 'Breasts are back!: Colette's critique
    of flapper fashion', *French Studies*, 60/3 (July 2006), 335–46.

3   See, for example, the catalogue to the exhibition on fashion of the 1919–29 period
    held at the Musée Gallieri edited by Sophie Grossiord and M. Asakura, *Les Années
    folles* (Paris: Paris Musées, 2007). Alain-René Hardy, *Art Deco Textiles: The French
    Designers* (London: Thames & Hudson, 2003); Doretta Davanzo Poli, *Tissus du XXe
    siècle. Designers et manufactures d'Europe et d'Amerique* (Paris: Éditions Skira, 2007);
    and Sonia Rykiel, *Colette et la mode* (Paris: Éditions Plume, 1991).

4   Colette, 'Le Maître', in *Œuvres*, vol. II, pp. 926–30 (p. 927).

5   Colette, 'Prisons et paradis', in *Œuvres*, vol. III (Paris: Gallimard, Bibliothèque de la
    Pléiade, 1991), pp. 655–805 (pp. 743–4).

6   Andrew Sprague Becker, *Rhetoric and Poetics of Early Greek Ekphrasis: Theory,
    Philology and the Shield of Achilles* (London: Rowman & Littlefield, 1995), p. 11.

7   Becker, *Rhetoric and Poetics of Early Greek Ekphrasis*, p. 41.

Stars as Sculpture in the 1920s Fan-Magazine Interview

Michael Williams

The first two decades of the twentieth century witnessed the consolidation of the star system and the refinement of the discourse through which film stars were produced and consumed. As part of the project culturally to elevate both stars and the cinema itself, this discourse was frequently informed by the aesthetics of fine art, and particularly classicism, as a means of valorizing screen idols as quasi-mythical figures and to provide fans with the frameworks to appreciate them thus. What interests me about classicism is its ambiguous and context-specific nature. I use it as a complex term that references, in particular, the visual art of ancient Greece or Rome, and one that perhaps speaks as much of the context in which it is evoked as of the past itself. Thus successive classical revivals have reinterpreted the classical to endow the modern subject with an increasingly acculturated idea of idealized beauty and cultural value, ranging from the era of the Grand Tour to the physical culture of the 1920s, with stars as its most conspicuous exponents. Exploring implicit and explicit references to antiquity's most prized artefacts, I examine in this chapter the role of sculpture in British and American fan-magazines and use analysis of individual articles to connect this long history of the reception of classical beauty to the fan-magazines of the silent era. In a spirit of exploration I also draw from writing on ekphrasis to suggest that the sculptural form enabled magazines to negotiate the problems of stardom's intangibility and absent centredness – the way stars seem present and complete when beheld in the cinema, but seem to disintegrate into isolated fragments outside that experience – bringing together the performer and valorized art object in an imagined gallery space of exhibition and encounter.

Framing idols: the star as a work of art

In 1934, the American film fan-magazine *Photoplay* suggested a link for its readers between the privileged space of the museum or art gallery and that of the cinema and its stars. The article 'Hollywood, the world's sculptor', fashions this metaphor to equate Hollywood's transformation of actors into stars with the work of 'a gigantic sculptor, leaning over an immense bench, and the clay that responds to its long, sensitive fingers is the dramatic genius of the world'.[1] While the mere actor is but 'clay', the playful metaphor flatters the sculptor, cloaking the industrial scale, not to say imperial pretentions, of Hollywood's endeavour, in artisanal vestments. This artistic process is conceptualized with an unattributed quotation, from Alexander Pope's *Satires*: 'and marble, soften'd into life, grew warm'.[2] There is the intertext here of the Pygmalion myth, of desire and art creating life, or the illusion of something better than life, as well as a secularizing of both classical and Christian creation myths.

The *Photoplay* article is merely a more overt example of a classicized discourse that emerged in the mid-1910s and particularly in the 1920s, that equated stars with works of art, and particularly sculptures: as Edgar Morin observed in his book *The Stars*, a star's beauty is 'as eloquent as the beauty of statues'.[3] Morin's phrase alludes not only to the ideals of 'classical beauty' by which stars are valued, but implies that stars themselves are works of art (at least in the silent era before sound arguably lent these idols a more commonplace aura), displayed both within the frames of the cinema screen and in the pages of film fan-magazines. Sculpture might be particularly effective or conducive to appropriation in negotiating such encounters between stars, studio publicity and audiences, because among art forms, sculptures, as David Getsy puts it, 'are more self-evidently actual and obdurate things occupying space with their mass'. This materiality, he argues, is fundamental to 'the constitution of the sculptural object by and as actual matter – stone, metal, wax, ivory, and so on'.[4] Ideas and phenomena that are elemental or are intangible can thus be endowed with a patently physical form that shares space with the viewer. The significance of this for stars becomes apparent when one recalls here the characteristics of stardom as defined by John Ellis, following Richard Dyer:

> Stars are incomplete images outside the cinema: the performance of the film is the moment of completion of images in subsidiary circulation, in newspapers, fanzines, etc. Further, a paradox is present in these subsidiary forms. The star is at once ordinary and extraordinary, available for desire and unattainable. This paradox is repeated and intensified in cinema by the regime of presence-yet-absence that is the filmic image.[5]

The sculptural metaphor is thus one way of endowing the star with imaginative shape, and above all, *presence*. The metaphor invites the viewer, in order to move around stars, to take in the different angles and gestures of their pose, to notice details as if in close-up, sharing their environment, framing their bodies from different perspectives and negotiating the play between image and object. As we shall see, to evoke sculpture in writing on cinema and its stars is to foreground the tension between past and present, and particularly action and stasis, as the calm grandeur associated with the canon of Hellenistic art is juxtaposed with these most dynamic exponents of modernity. The classical art object projects substance, cultural prestige and historical durability onto the star, and dramatizes the very idea of encounter between star and audience in a mutual space beyond the cinema. It also, perhaps, brings with it the aura of an art object that enhances the sense of elevated otherness, even other-worldliness, often attributed to stars. Yet, as we shall see, even in what can be a throw-away reference to stars as sculpture that hints at a gallery where one might view, or even meet, a star, this dynamic exchange of warm flesh for cold marble bodies can only delay our perception of the kind of poignant unattainability suggested above. Though the divinizing adjectives of classicism channelled through the visual arts point to an apparently prefabricated discourse designed to flatter both star and studio, there is more at stake here.

The implicitly eulogistic aspect to stardom that Ellis evokes had added resonance in the Great War period, where fan-magazines were poems and letters full of longing to intangible, fading film stars. Perhaps a product of the reality of love and separation in this historical context, such lines anticipate the familiar rendering of stars through a vernacular of shining light, idealized youth and sometimes uneasy vitality, fuelled partly through the influence of the war's poetry and memorial architecture on the post-war cultural memory.[6] We might term this trope 'shadow love' in sympathy with the fleeting shadows and devotional poems written to stars in the period, typified by the final lines of a 1916 issue: 'The girl for me beyond a doubt –| And then the film just faded out'.[7] Such evocations attest to what is presented in this period as an almost desperate search for appropriate language to construct film stardom, often with recourse to language that may appear florid to us today. One example from 1920, a self-titled 'futurist impression' from a Corrine Griffith fan, is at the abstract end of the scale, describing the idol as 'Tropic moonlight; the Mediterranean at azure night; perfumes of India; a silken gemmed butterfly in a garden of orchids'.[8] In attempting to describe what a star means for them, and what it is that stars *do*, audiences perhaps share a desire to overcome what Stephen Bann notes to be 'the modern conviction (deeply rooted at least since the time of Baudelaire) that a good proportion of what is experienced in looking at a work of art simply cannot be expressed in visual terms'.[9] Hence perhaps the reasons such references typically grasp at a more tangible form of evocation, while maintaining the sensuality of metaphor and vividness of imagery evoked above.

In parallel with the development of film actors from their earlier incarnations as initially anonymous players in the early 1900s, to picture personalities, thence to stars, so the fan-magazines that emerged in the mid-1910s sought to refine increasingly valorized frameworks in order to display stars to their readers outside the architectural environment of cinema itself, or rather extend its apparatus of display.[10] These frames were often literally conceived, as in *Picturegoer*'s 'portrait gallery of screen stars', a regular feature beginning in August 1915.[11] Like the sculptural references that would proliferate after the war, they served to familiarize readers with the names and faces of stars, but they also stand in for the visual presence for the star. At the same time, such galleries, whether overt or more implicit, contributed to the elevation of cinema itself as an increasingly dominant art form; they flattered the interest and assumed the discernment of the audience in appreciating the stars so carefully constructed for them, while also providing an imaginative means of interacting with stars and other followers. As a means of documenting the mythic-real lives of the stars, such strategies belong to a long tradition of art-historical appropriation. Notable among these is the 'Historical Style' of Joshua Reynolds in the mid-eighteenth century, which deployed classical settings and contrapposto poses to elevate both art's subjects and the artist himself for a nascent celebrity culture.[12] In the post-war 1920s, such strategies provided an ideal imaginative template, with reassuringly historical patinas, for transposing the art that has faithfully preserved and reinterpreted the ancient idols, and their Grand Tour pretenders, into the new pantheons of the picture-palace.

Stars and iconotexts

Sculpture was referenced in star discourse in a number of ways in 1920s fan-magazines while also functioning as an explanatory metaphor for the tensions inherent in stardom itself. First, and perhaps most familiar, is the long-established use of classical metaphors to construct the physical beauty, artistic and heroic qualities of stars. *Picture Show*'s 1923 article 'A ready-made enchantress' provides an interesting example.[13] Part of its 'Expressions' series, the article examines the image and personality of Pola Negri, focusing in particular on an American interviewer's attempt to produce what it terms 'An arresting pen picture'.[14] Taking as its starting point that writer's failing to find suitable adjectives, the magazine draws a typically complex picture of the Hollywood star for its British readers, perhaps undermining its title statement of how 'ready-made' she actually was for the screen. But perhaps that was precisely the point.

From establishing the inadequacy of language through which to describe the star, the article pursues a motif of remoteness, recalling the absence noted by Ellis. The reader, we are told, cannot imagine 'Pola Negri' without having seen her both on and off the screen; her film image leaves a perceived vacuum which requires compensation, while her on-off relationship with Charlie Chaplin and her Polish origins portray her as romantically remote (but possibly available) as well as embodying the Old World as viewed from Europe (her arrival in America even equated with Cortés' conquest of Mexico). Into this carefully constructed remoteness, a metaphorical empty frame, is then set an array of cultural references:

> For Pola Negri, as I have seen her on the screen, is the very essence of all the famous women in history who ever tempted men. I write 'the essence' for Pola is not a copy of Cleopatra, Helen of Troy, Du Barry, Nell Gwynne, Circe, Carmen, or any of the 'Vamps' of history, mythology or fiction. If some magician wished to produce in the form of modern woman an enchantress having something of all these women, he would find her ready made in Pola Negri.

Negri is like all of these eclectic comparators and like none of them: she is a blend of history, mythology and fiction. The combination of mythic-historical reference points is necessary to realize her 'essence' or charisma, which is then internalized, embodied in a modern incarnation. This primes the reader for the hermeneutic leap in the final paragraph, the 'pen picture' itself, which ties together the preceding prose and visual imagery.

The magazine then informs us, with a touch of anthropomorphism, that Negri 'has a beautiful but rather mystic face which seems like a living cameo'. From the incorporeal figure thus far evoked, the star is now likened to a tangible object with features in relief, the photograph juxtaposed against this text even presenting the star in profile as if realized by the preceding description in the form of a cameo. However, the article again concedes to an elusiveness of form, the pen portraitist admitting 'even her build eludes me as I write', as if she were once again disappearing from view. Shifting from an effective close-up of the face, the eye is likely to be drawn back before turning the page to a three-quarter-length photograph of Negri, which immediately recalls the figure of Venus, particularly the most famous canonical sculpture of the Venus de Milo. Negri as Venus is the most fully realized version of a whole series of intermedial plays around image and text in the article. The art deco-esque circle behind Negri draws the eye and suggests sculptural relief on the page, while the fur she wears mimics the folds of classical drapery to connote modern opulence rather than classical simplicity. Her nude body is suggested underneath, evoking contrasting traditional representations of the clothed and unclothed Venus, and her dual mythology of both serene innocence and earthly sensuality. Venus is mentioned nowhere in the text, but visualizes its mythic themes, and could thus be described as an iconotext, which Peter Wagner defines as 'the use of (by way of reference or allusion, in an explicit or implicit way) an image in a text or vice versa'.[15] Interpreting such images (in stills or film) as iconotexts within allows us to achieve a degree of critical traction on the relationship between these heavily acculturated images, the personae and the multiple cultural associations of the stars themselves for different audiences.

A particularly bold sculptural iconotext can be found in a 1922 *Picture-Play* image of American star Gloria Swanson, a promotional still taken on the set of *Her Husband's Trademark* (Sam Wood, 1922), in which the star is directly compared to a statuette of the Venus de Milo.[16] Like the Negri image, Swanson replicates the pose of the statue; her flowing silk sleeves mask her forearms to mirror a resemblance to the copy of the statue that stands beside her. Each icon reflects upon the other. Unsurprisingly, given her attributes as the goddess of love in mythology, Venus was the favoured figure from antiquity appropriated by magazine columnists to divinize the female star, and the goddess' iconography continues to influence star iconography. The broken arms of the statue that testifies to its long and evidently damaging passage through history renders Negri and Swanson more complete, and present, in contrast. Moreover, these stars have been fashioned to the aesthetic tastes of 1920s modernity in their styling and slim body shapes and here, as the subtle frame of Negri's portrait acknowledges, the influence of a trend that would become known as art deco or 'Art Moderne' following the Paris Exposition Internationale des Arts Décoratifs et Industriels Modernes in 1925, is pronounced. As Lucy Fischer has shown, later stars such as Greta Garbo drew strongly from the visual culture of art deco and the women it constructed.[17] However, this earlier use of classicism and the far-reaching significance of its use in constructing film stardom itself have been neglected. Unlike the Negri image, Swanson is placed within the same space as the Venus as if to challenge the viewer to compare these carefully constructed images of female beauty, taste and cultural authority. The star draws icono-graphic power from the Venus, even as, once more, the broken limbs of her ancient counterpart cruelly foreshadow the fate of all idols, whether cast in stone or, less still, the fragile emulsions of celluloid.

While Swanson's ostentation fitted her extravagant persona, most stars would avoid at all costs possible accusations of appearing to pose. Thus, while one's grace could be compared to that of a statue, it would not do to appear mannered. Hence the significance of framing discourses outside the body of the star, sometimes vicariously, through the adoration of sculpture. The point is implicit in *Picture Show*'s description of actress Constance Collier: 'Though grace and dignity were in every line of that splendid body, there was an entire absence of *pose*'.[18] Thus, while the production of films invariably involved posing, in the fan-magazine an emphasis on animation needed to compensate for the static nature of the images. The prose of such features also provided an opportunity for stars to reassert their authorship in order to address the tension between sculptor and clay with which I started. In constructing a means for the star to move and speak and 'come to life' through another medium, the star is seen to implement a certain iconic agency to compensate for both the image of the posed art object, and the conception of the actor as puppet of the director and studio. Galatea can thus assert her independence. The proverbial clay still clings, however. Mary Thurman is clearly presented as such in *Picture Show*'s 1920 'Measuring a film face' article, where producer Allan Dwan sets about the actress with a T-square, two triangles and tape measure.[19] 'Not only are the proportions perfect', we are told 'but planes and contours are so chiselled as to lend themselves most advantageously to artistic lightings'. Here, the face is conducive to art, but the term 'chiselled' implies that she is already sculptural. This oscillation between metaphor and simile seems somehow guided by the ambiguous status of the star as both an artist and a model in these promotional pictures. Indeed, stars often also worked as models in other media, and this was seen to have the artistic advantage of their being recognized as either beautiful or culturally significant, aside from being further 'immortalized'. Under the title 'A "model" man', *Picture Show* detailed the modelling work of Monroe Salisbury for a sculptor who, it tells us, made his selection because of his remarkable physique:

'I had nothing to do with my physique,' said the modest Salisbury, 'except to keep in shape.' 'Still,' said a member of the company, 'you've done the hardest thing a man could do. Many of us have broken into print, but you're the only one who has broken into stone.'[20]

Sidestepping allegations of narcissism and all that signifies, Salisbury here denies awareness of his physical appeal, and responsibility for shaping it, and substitutes kinetic metaphors for static posing. Just as Swanson seemed to have broken *out* of sculpture in her portrait, such accounts construct stars not only as latent art, but the figure of the absent model, the 'real' person who exists outside the still image, the text, or indeed, the statue.

Stars and ekphrasis

The problem of stardom's absences, to which Ellis referred, is a pronounced symptom of the challenge to traditional cultural values, of which film is the exemplar, witnessed in the age of mechanical reproduction described by Walter Benjamin. Here, as Benjamin asserts, 'even the most perfect reproduction of a work of art is lacking in one element: its presence in time and space', which would also attest to its authenticity. Even if the photographic reproduction does enable 'the original to meet the beholder halfway', in such situations 'the quality of its presence is always depreciated'.[21] The fan-magazines perhaps attempt to restore this 'aura', which Benjamin deems lost, replacing it with what he refers to as 'an artificial build-up of the "personality" outside the studio'.[22] In artfully framing stars as artefacts and presenting ekphrastic frameworks within which to interpret them, fan-magazines imply something of the gallery or museum setting, a privileged space for imparting traditional values upon these very modern figures.

Looking through these interviews and features one finds the interviewers work hard to paint pictures, to present the movements and subtle idiosyncrasies of the star that one could only detect in their physical presence; the interviewers discursively moving back and forth from the literal to the fantastic as if animated by the very doubt that stars *have* a physical body. Getsy's work on the new corporeality of sculpture in Britain at the end of the nineteenth century explores the relationship between the sculptural form and the 'real' bodies for which it stands in.[23] Getsy likens the sculpture to the double who replaces a film actor for lighting tests or publicity stills, which in composite provide a 'substitute physicality and its visual idealization'.[24] Thus various framings and poses form the ideal body in composite, with the actor, like the sculpture, the product of those fragmented and absent elements. The Negri feature could be seen as a counterpart to this process, re-forming the absent parts through the substitute physicality of the statue. The gap thus implied might also extend to the uncanny nature of beauty in cold marble that suggests something of death, a recurring theme in responses to sculpture as Getsy notes, where frustration might result from the way the more a sculpture emulated the human form, the more it dramatized 'the gap between the immotile marble or bronze statue and living, moving bodies [...] however convincingly a sculpture might conjure up a warm living body, it remains a cold, inert object'.[25] It is perhaps to counteract this perception that fan-magazines often seek to conjugate ancient art with emotion, health, and above all modernity, as in the insistence on warm sun in this 1920 description of British star Ivy Close:

> You must all know her. Know that seductive face that stands for English beauty unadorned. I mean Ivy Close. No need to rhapsodise over her beauty, but I can't help myself. Her hair is just a crown of straying sunbeams, her face, a perfect cameo, flushed delicately with life. And her eyes, her lips, her slim exquisitely modelled figure, are all in keeping. To few of us does Nature grant such all-round grace, and perfume it with such unaffected charm.[26]

Like many of the fan-magazine descriptions I have quoted in this essay, *Picture Show*'s words are gushingly effusive and yet fascinating in the way they have been crafted for the purpose of presenting the star as art object for the reader/viewer. Most strikingly, the description identifies itself as an act of ekphrasis in the first person; it rhapsodizes over Close as a 'modelled figure' and a cameo (like Negri), crowned by the classical sunbeams of an Apollo, or here perhaps, Aurora that designate divinity as well as the halo of a great work of art. Yet she is also rendered human, and alive, by the 'flush' of life that animates her as in the myth of Pygmalion's sculpture of Galatea brought to life. It seems that only artistic reference points can fully articulate the attributes of 'Nature' bestowed upon this sensual cameo, and there is certainly a tension between action and stasis, and particularly the 'unadorned' and 'unaffected' versus the constructed and posed here.

The sensations evoked by these articles also speak to the fan's desire to touch the star's body (to test that it is 'real' and make concrete his or her interaction with that body), a sensuality shared with the medium of sculpture and an incredulous reaching out which became exemplified by the 'phrenological' studies of stars run in magazines in the 1920s.[27] A 1919 interview with Phyllis Monkman, for example, presented this sense of increasing intimacy in these lines, printed next to a close-up of the actress leaning forward and smiling into the camera: 'Miss Monkman tilted her chin upward with a gay smile, and as I looked at her, with all her brightness and vivacity, I suddenly felt very, very old. Here was *youth* – youth of soul and body. Youth there bubbled over and spilt itself recklessly.'[28] The eloquence of these star portraits of image and text not only connotes an *immediate* emotion and an *immediate* context, but also speaks to a wider cultural history. Monkman's description begins with the specific tilt of her chin, moves through the apperception of physical age and then, italicized, that of universal youth. As in the feature on Negri, the article finally returns to abstraction as youth metaphorically spills over, evoking the effervescence of champagne as a symbol of modernity and certainly a degree of sexual innuendo. Within those two sentences the restless shifts from eternal truths to physical specificity, from bright modernity to the aged and ancient, from form to dissolution, and from high-art references to kitsch, are dizzying: they are typical of the fan-magazine writing in this period. Could the film fan-magazine, in effectively bringing to sight the persona of a work of art, and offering a sense of proximity to the stars, be understood as offering a form of ekphrasis?

Ekphrasis is the rhetorical art of description, typically in which a visual form is described in literature. Its root meaning is of 'speaking out' or a 'telling in full', James Heffernan reminds us; it is a process of speaking both of and for a work of art in a way that animates it.[29] In thus evoking the 'power of the silent image', one can view this mode of description as having strong resonances with the presentation of stars in the pre-sound era, constructing imaginative images whether or not juxtaposed with photographic ones, and ensuring that even without speech such stars were never silent. For Heffernan, rather than merely nebulous juxtapositions and impressionistic affinities, ekphrasis establishes instead 'tangible and manifest' relationships between the arts. However, Heffernan also explores the sense of a 'duel' in ekphrasis that can be read as gendered where a male narrative attempts to 'overcome the fixating impact of beauty poised in space, namely a feminine image that is both alluring and threatening'.[30] This is the concept of 'ekphrastic fear' that Heffernan borrows from W. J. T. Mitchell, the 'medusa model' of 'conflict between male authority and the female power to enchant, subvert, or threaten it'.[31] One might here recall the way the Negri article struggled fully to convey an impression of the star, listing a series of historical 'vamps', including Circe (it may have been a step too far to include Medusa), the sorceress who attempted to enchant Odysseus' men, before the prose dissolved into formlessness. However, as Heffernan notes, this polarized view of gender is as misleading as it is dubious, for the viewer-reader is as likely to be female as male, which is very likely to be the case for the readership of film fan-magazines, who were primarily female. Mitchell's *Picture Theory* points to two additional perceptions of ekphrasis, 'ekphrastic hope', where imagination and metaphor can overcome the underlying 'impossibility' of ekphrasis and allow us to 'see' an object, and also 'ekphrastic indifference'. The latter is founded on a claim that an object can be verbally referred to, but never brought to visual presence in the way that pictures can. From this perspective, 'words can "cite" but never "sight" their objects'.[32] As Mitchell relates, these conceptions of the possibilities offered by ekphrasis are ambivalent by nature, denoted by an ever-shifting play of action and passivity between the object being represented, the individuals representing it, and the imagination of the self. Most significant in terms of this chapter is the way that the very promise of ekphrasis to bring the object to sight is dependent on the object being absent in the first place. While a photograph might usually render an object literally visible, for the cinematographic star, this only attests to the curiously evanescent quality that makes them so elusively desirable to the audience, as if a lost work of art. Such tensions perhaps explain the impossibility of rendering Negri, and indeed all stars. Any attempts to unify their fragments outside the cinema screen only amplify the ethereal nature of stars.

Barbara Fischer explores this more meditative form of gaze in her study of how the gallery or museum encounter precipitates ekphrastic language that evokes love and faith when addressing art. One example that Fischer highlights is Robert Hayden's poem 'Water Lilies', written during the Vietnam War in 1966 as a response to Monet's 1906 painting. Hayden responds to the 'illusive flesh of light' and describes, in the final lines, his perception that: 'Here is the aura of that world / each of us has lost. / Here is the shadow of its joy'. As Fischer remarks:

> [the museum experience] allows an 'aura' of that lost world to be regained. Based in feelings of love and faith, the speaker's response to the painting exemplifies what Bourdieu has called the 'charismatic ideology,' the belief that aesthetic experience is a spontaneous 'descent of grace (*charisma*) [. . .] a visitation, as the theological term suggests, of a divinely conferred gift or power [. . .] we do not find serenity in a museum without being reminded why we need to search for it.[33]

This Janus-like view of the elusive art object and the return view of ourselves in pseudo-religious awe recall the 'shadow-love' of the 1910s. Indeed, both draw upon poetic traditions to express loss and desire. The imagined museum setting, for the ekphrastic poets whom Fischer discusses, is one that is condemned for enshrouding art in a 'sacralizing aura that obfuscates the conditions of a work's making', and for being elitist and removed from every-day life. But it is also a space of sensory intensity in the 'figures for desire' it produces.[34] There are parallels with film stardom where semi-sculptural idols constructed for audience desire are framed somewhere between art and commerce. Here, the discernment of grace, an attribute of divinity in both classical and Christian discourse, usefully connects to Richard Dyer's reading of 'charisma' as a social function; the appeal which a particular star holds for the historical needs of particular audiences in a given context, here revealing the culturally heightened aspects of love and loss.[35] For Fischer, ekphrasis constructs a place of 'anxiety and suspect pleasure', which is perhaps fitting for the way serene visions seem blown away from vision at this time of war.[36]

A fan writing to *Picture-Play* in 1923, and perhaps an example of what Mitchell terms 'ekphrastic hope', praised one star interview for not breaking 'the silvery halo encircling the head of all motion-picture artistes [. . .] which *nothing* seems able to displace'. Here the fan's words evoke a sense of the cultural (and mythological, fitting the subject) aura surrounding great art, and also alludes to the kind of transcendent glow used to designate beauty, purity and, often, white femininity in film and in wider Western art.[37] Against this ethereal, if elevated, image, the fan also perceives something more substantive: 'One of your interviewers, *who really can write*, gives a wonderfully convincing and very frank picture of Lila Lee . . . I can just visualize little Miss Lee'.[38] The mythic aspect seemingly coheres to enable an imaginative, if not physical, encounter, bringing the star to sight through description. In this instance the fan seems to experience 'ekphrastic hope', the moment, as Mitchell puts it: 'when the impossibility of ekphrasis is overcome in imagination or metaphor, when we discover a "sense" in which language can do what so many writers have wanted it to do: "to make us see"'.[39] We might also here remember Giuliana Bruno's urge in her *Atlas of Emotion* for us to move away from the primacy of the gaze and consider the 'haptic' experience of cinema as a lived engagement with art. Bruno argues that cinema makes a psycho-geographic appeal to tactility and other senses through an array of sensual encounters, which also reference architecture and travel. We might link this approach with the Negri article (and what is the 'pen picture' if not ekphrastic?), with its evocation of the physical and emotional journey, and particularly the star as an almost three-dimensional, sculptural artefact moving, to appropriate Bruno's terms, 'within and through historical trajectories'.[40] The star's body becomes a site where we may glimpse the ancient if the pose or prose permits.

A delightful illustration can be found in columnist Herbert Howe's imagining of another historical exchange upon Ramon Novarro's departure from America to begin filming *Ben-Hur* (Fred Niblo, 1925) in Italy. Howe (who, coincidentally, or not, was also Novarro's lover) constructs his subject as one of the most eulogized objects in Western art:

> Novarro's chief handicap has been his youth and good looks. If he ever visits the Vatican the Apollo Belvedere is going to get down and apologize for having taken up so much time. Both for classic countenance and physique Ramon could easily pass as an authentic Phidian athletic.[41]

The cold, ancient marble is thus substituted for a youthful, living star and the desires that may be projected upon them, whether homo- or hetero-erotic. Apollo willingly displaces himself for the new idol, an effortless hermeneutic leap that can only be achieved through audience complicity in a tradition that valorizes the classical past and routinely projects its views upon the present. Novarro here literally steps into the space vacated not only by the represented god, but that of the model(s) before them. Homoerotic vitality is uppermost in this instance but, as this chapter has argued, death and absence also inform the reception of stars and statuary alike. Such works solicited a sense of intimacy: they evoked sensuality while preserving the prohibition on actually touching art, by inviting one to look around them, to move around to appreciate all angles, and to search for completeness in the face of the fragments and absences of stardom. Thus, they echoed the imaginative strategies we deploy when we contemplate the ruins and evocative fragments of the art and culture of antiquity.

Fan-magazines in the late 1910s and 1920s offered their readers a fascinating blend of the visual and textual, driven by the dynamic cultural forms emerging during and after the Great War, and by a search for appropriate language. Like Richard Dyer's notion of star charisma, where particular star qualities are seen to be most effective 'when the social order is uncertain, unstable and ambiguous', and where the star can either resolve or expose those social tensions, so the particular aspects of stardom are perfectly, or perhaps imperfectly designed for their social context.[42] Here, the forms of modernity, both beautiful and terrible, were negotiated with a sense of history for what was created, and lost, in the past. Sculptural metaphors, among others, presented a way of re-evaluating the past against the modern, and a means of scrutinizing tensions between stasis and action, the mythic, real and ideal, the quotidian and the universal, the original and the copy, and the present and the absent. It furnished a material need to embody the remote or lost, and provided an imaginative means of suggesting a way for stars seemingly to embody space and remain apart from us. As I hope to have indicated, these ever-shifting physical and temporal qualities fragmented across a variety of textual forms, are fundamental to their enduring appeal.

Notes

1. Winifred Aydelotte, 'Hollywood, the World's Sculptor', *Photoplay*, March 1934, 79.
2. Ibid., 80. The quotation derives from Alexander Pope, *Satires, Epistles, and Odes of Horace*, epistle I, book ii, line 147.
3. Edgar Morin, *The Stars* (Minneapolis: University of Minnesota, 2005 [1957]), p. 131.
4. David J. Getsy, *Body Doubles: Sculpture in Britain, 1877–1905* (London: Yale University Press, 2004), p. 10.
5. John Ellis, 'Stars as a cinematic phenomenon', in *Visible Fictions* (London: Routledge, 1992), p. 91.
6. See Paul Fussell, *The Great War and Modern Memory* (London: Oxford University Press, 1975). Stars, of course, held specific significance for their context, as I have explored in a case study of British star Ivor Novello, heralded as 'England's Apollo' in the wake of the Great War. See Michael Williams, *Ivor Novello: Screen Idol* (London: BFI, 2003).
7. Robert Foster, 'In the spring of a young man's fancy', *Picture-Play*, April 1916, 63.
8. 'Vitagraph Star', *Picture Show*, 14 February 1920, 8.
9. Stephen Bann, *The True Vine: On Visual Representation and the Western Tradition* (Cambridge: Cambridge University Press, 1989), p. 28, quoted in Peter Wagner, *Icons–Texts–Iconotexts: Essays on Ekphrasis and Intermediality* (Berlin and New York: Walter de Gruyter, 1996), p. 7.
10. See Richard de Cordova, *Picture Personalities: The Emergence of the Star System in America* (Urbana: University of Illinois Press, 1990).
11. 'Our Portrait Gallery of Screen Stars', *Picturegoer*, 21 August 1915, 191.
12. See Malcolm Bull, *The Mirror of the Gods: Classical Mythology in Renaissance Art* (London: Allen Lane, 2005), and Martin Postle (ed.), *Joshua Reynolds: The Creation of Celebrity* (London: Tate Publishing, 2005).
13. 'The expressions of Pola Negri: a ready-made enchantress', *Picture Show*, 3 November 1923, 19.
14. Ibid.
15. Wagner, *Icons–Texts–Iconotexts*, p. 15.
16. *Picture-Play*, September 1922, 82.
17. See Lucy Fischer, *Designing Women: Cinema, Art Deco and the Female Form* (New York: Columbia University Press, 2003).
18. 'Constance Collier talks', *Picture Show*, 26 July 1919, 10.
19. 'Measuring a film face', *Picture Show*, 11 December 1920, 9.
20. 'A "model" man', *Picture Show*, 3 July 1920, 3.

[21] Walter Benjamin, 'The work of art in the age of mechanical reproduction', in *Illuminations* (London: Pimlico, 1999 [1936]), pp. 214, 215.

[22] Ibid., p. 224.

[23] Getsy, *Body Doubles: Sculpture in Britain, 1877–1905*, p. 5.

[24] Ibid., p. 1.

[25] Ibid., pp. 1, 12. Getsy quotes Alex Potts, *The Sculptural Imagination: Figurative, Modernist, Minimalist* (London: Yale University Press, 2000), p. 50.

[26] 'Ivy Close: a famous British film actress', *Picture Show*, 3 January 1920, 11.

[27] See, for example H. H. Faulkner, 'A phrenological study of some famous stars', *Photoplay*, March 1922, 30–1.

[28] '"My screen début" Phyllis Monkman tells why she loves film work', *Picture Show*, 17 May 1919, 13.

[29] James A. W. Heffernan, *Museum of Words: The Poetics of Ekphrasis from Homer to Ashbery* (Chicago and London: University of Chicago Press, 1993), p. 6.

[30] Heffernan, *Museum of Words*, p. 1.

[31] Ibid., p. 108; Heffernan draws from W. J. T. Mitchell, 'Ekphrasis and the Other', *South Atlantic Quarterly* 91 (1992), 695–719.

[32] W. J. T. Mitchell, *Picture Theory* (London and Chicago: University of Chicago Press, 1995), p. 152.

[33] The discussion of the book *Transforming Vision* (1994) by Robert Hayden, containing the 1966 poem, features in Barbara K. Fischer, *Museum Meditations: Reframing Ekphrasis in Contemporary American Poetry* (New York and London: Routledge, 2006), p. 16. The quotation from Bourdieu is taken from his *Love of Art*, p. 54.

[34] Fischer, *Museum Meditations*, p. 5.

[35] See Richard Dyer, 'Charisma', in Christine Gledhill (ed.), *Stardom: Industry of Desire* (London: Routledge, 1991), pp. 57–9.

[36] Fischer, *Museum Meditations*, p. 5

[37] See Richard Dyer's *White* (London: Routledge, 1997).

[38] 'Fans will be fans', Miss Fannie Cisch, Brooklyn NY, *Picture-Play*, October 1923, 108.

[39] Mitchell, *Picture Theory*, p. 152.

[40] Giuliana Bruno, *Atlas of Emotion: Journeys in Art, Architecture, and Film* (London: Verso, 2002), p. 6.

[41] Herbert Howe, 'A prediction', *Photoplay*, May 1924, 131.

[42] Richard Dyer, 'Charisma', p. 58.

III

Visual negotiations and adaptations

Victor Hugo and Painting: The Exceptional Case of the *Orientales*

Karen Quandt

On doit comprendre qu'il est un moyen de laisser voir la pensée, sans s'épuiser à la peindre.

Sainte-Beuve (*Le Globe*, 9 January 1827)[1]

Victor Hugo did not have much to say on the subject of painting, but his *Orientales* (1829), in their attention to the visual and the image, afford us ample reason to stop and wonder about this omission. At a time when Hugo was actively collaborating and corresponding with painters and sculptors, the state of the visual arts was of distinct concern in literary circles.[2] For Emile Deschamps, an enthusiastic member of and fervent spokesperson for Hugo's 'Cénacle', both painting and music were essential for a modern poetic sensibility that heightened the workings of the imagination:

> Or, la poésie n'est pas seulement un genre de littérature, elle est aussi un art, par son harmonie, ses couleurs et ses images, et comme telle c'est sur les sens et l'imagination qu'elle doit d'abord agir, c'est par cette double route qu'elle doit arriver au cœur et à l'entendement.[3]

Hugo's general silence on painting – whether in his poems, essays, prefaces, or even correspondence – is thus curious, above all when it comes to the

Orientales, a book that makes major concessions to the image. 'Sara la baign-euse', to take one notable example, is not only painterly with its touches of colour, detail and attention to foreground and background, it is also sculptural in the way that the young girl poses:

> Elle est là, sous la feuillée,
> Eveillée
> Au moindre bruit de malheur;
> Et rouge, pour une mouche
> Qui la touche,
> Comme une grenade en fleur. (ll. 37–42)[4]

Hugo's silence regarding the visual arts is not only curious, but suspicious. In the case of the *Orientales*, Hugo's neglect to make an explicit nod to the influence of painting is consistent with a tradition of hierarchy in the arts, where poetry sits at a categorical pinnacle. Hugo, mindful in his organicist model of art that the new has its roots in the old, let the ruins of the past breathe.[5] The foundation of tradition remains solid underneath the turbulent and varying contingencies of the contemporary. As experimental as they may be, the *Orientales* reveal a poet who remains unconvinced by the effects of the image; their seductive – but momentary – imprint leads in the final poem to a dull and gray winter: 'C'est Paris, c'est l'hiver. – A ta chanson confuse / Odalisques, émirs, pachas, tout se refuse' ('Novembre', ll. 25–6). It is the dark and intimate interior of the poet that is the source of the sublime in art.[6] To borrow Edmund Burke's language, this is 'because the imagination is entertained with the promise of something more, and does not acquiesce in the present object of the sense' (II.11).[7] Hugo's Muse, though she laments the disappearance of the exotic ('Pleurant ton Orient, alors, muse ingénue', l. 31) is quickly revived through the notes of the lyric song, and is now safe from the scrutinizing gaze of others: 'Et nous nous asseyons, et, loin des yeux profanes, / Entre mes souvenirs je t'offre les plus doux' (ll. 38–9).

The effects of painting in Hugo's *Orientales* are potent, but they are not meant to be subservient to the art of poetry. We can support this claim by gleaning a few key concepts in Hugo's theories of art from around the same period. Specifically, my reading will situate Hugo's major emphasis on the role of the eye in the work of art, as well as his particular application of the term 'picturesque' to poetry; both reveal how eye and image in the *Orientales* paradoxically make the case for the lyric.[8] As a conclusion, I will propose what might be called a collusion of Hugo's *Orientales* with Delacroix's *La Mort de Sardanapale*. The poem 'Mazeppa' in particular reveals the degree to which Hugo – in all of his attention to the painterly – sought to preserve the imperial status of the poet.

Before attempts are made to convince the reader of Hugo's sceptical stance regarding painting, it is necessary to give a brief historical context concerning the question of 'ut pictura poesis', and how it was addressed (albeit indirectly) by the generation of French writers that preceded Hugo's own. La Harpe, the champion of the neoclassical aesthetic at the dawn of the French Empire, did not mince his words: 'Le premier de tous les talents est d'être éloquent en vers.'[9] Chateaubriand's *Génie du christianisme ou Beauté de la Religion Chrétienne* (1802), the undisputed point of reference for Hugo and his literary contemporaries, is a vast manual on poetry in which the other arts seem merely an afterthought: poetry makes up five books, while music, painting, sculpture and architecture combined make up just one.[10] All arts do as poetry does; this is not to say that they are on equal footing, but that the painter or sculptor is resigned to choose from what the epic poem or ancient tragedy has already furnished. The Word is first, and painting serves as an imitative second, or as Chateaubriand phrases it: 'Le Nouveau Testament change le génie de la peinture' (III.I.4).

This hierarchy stems from an ingrained tradition in the history of aesthetics, one that had only recently been called into question in France with the advent of art criticism as a genre.[11] It is no coincidence that descriptive poetry, with its concern for pleasing the eye of the reader, flourished in the eighteenth century, as painting became a philosophical and psychological (as opposed to merely aesthetic) object of inquiry. The capacity for painting to emulate the movement of the epic and the temporality of the theatre seemed a distinct possibility.[12] But ever ready to seize the chance to refute the 'philosophes' and their insistence on the empirical and the sensual, Hugo maintained a neoclassical sense of the hierarchy of arts as it was perpetuated at the dawn of the French Empire.[13] Theatre, the seventeenth-century genre par excellence, thus rules supreme, and the 'Preface to *Cromwell*' (1827) reiterates as much.

Hugo's iconoclasm in this manifesto is directed against descriptive poetry and bourgeois theatre (eighteenth-century genres), and *not* against the classical taste for form and scenes worthy of the epic. The difference was, in a post-Revolution and post-Empire society, the everyday (the people, the masses) *was* the epic; the dramatist could not only choose one moment, but had to keep up with all of them.[14] The result is multiple points of views and an anticlimactic sense of ambiguity; nothing is resolved at the end of *Cromwell*, and the play ends with the question that put it into action: 'Quand donc serai-je roi?' (V: 6413).[15] But the element of the grotesque, which appears in the form of the despot's court jesters, will serve as an antidote to this uncertainty; although figures on the margin, they are the ones who 'see' through the uncertain. The 'fou' Gramadoch expresses this profound and privileged point of view: 'Le Cromwell, qui croit tout soumettre à son contrôle, / Ferait bien d'emprunter l'œil de ses quatre fous' (III.2377–8).

The modern poet, through the prism of his own unique perspective, or idea, was expected to capture the realities and accidents of a nineteenth-century moving history.[16] If Hugo valorizes Molière above all ('Molière occupe la sommité de notre drame', Preface to *Cromwell*, p. 94), it is because the form of his verse, his idea, does not stray from the drama and accidents of the human condition. What at first appears ordinary or mundane becomes art through the device of the eye; it is not an eye that merely sees, but an eye that initiates a process. Capturing nature, or what is true, is no longer imitative, but creative:

> Chez lui [Molière] le vers embrasse l'idée, s'y incorpore étroitement, la serre et la développe tout à la fois, lui prête une figure plus svelte, plus stricte, et nous la donne en quelque sorte en élixir. Le vers est la forme optique de la pensée. Voilà pourquoi il convient surtout à la perspective scénique. Fait d'une certaine façon, il communique son relief à des choses qui, sans lui, passeraient insignifiantes et vulgaires. (Preface to Cromwell, pp. 94–5)

Hugo's construct of the 'forme optique de la pensée', which could be described as the unique prism of the poet, guides us through a reading of the *Orientales*. As his discussion of Molière reveals, Hugo's theory of art calls for a careful combination of the real and the ideal; what the eye initially takes in subsequently takes form as idea. This is a theory that took root in his very first published volume of poetry, *Odes et poésies diverses* (1822), whose preface states: 'Sous le monde réel, il existe un monde idéal, qui se montre resplendissant à l'œil de ceux que des méditations graves ont accoutumés à voir dans les choses plus que les choses'.[17]

In the case of the *Orientales*, this 'idea' is that of the poet himself. Despite their apparent pretence to escapism and to the exotic, the *Orientales* – all forty-one of them – are grounded in Hugo's actual viewing of a sunset: 'à quoi bon ces *Orientales*? [. . .] Il [l'auteur] répondra qu'il n'en sait rien, que c'est une idée qui lui a pris; et qui lui a pris d'une façon ridicule, l'été passé, en allant voir coucher le soleil' (Preface, p. 578). If we think of this sunset as what it actually is, that is to say, not as a 'Romantic' trope that signifies mortality or the yearning for something beyond the horizon, but as a descending agent that produces constantly changing effects on the earth's atmosphere, we need to find the poet's steady point of view within these changes.[18] All points of the book, no matter how far removed from the here and now, refer back to the poet's controlled and controlling eye. The first preface shows us in decidedly visual terms how this works; after claiming matter-of-factly that the inspiration of the book was the 'ridiculous' act of viewing a sunset, what immediately follows is a lush, long and dizzying description – in a single sentence that takes the space of a page and a half – of his imaginary view of the East. Out of the source of the eye grows the poem; the creative possibilities associated with sunrise (light, colour, warmth) come out of the darkening sky of the West. The *Orientales* put into action what Hugo had observed in the 'Preface to *Cromwell*': 'le coucher du soleil a quelques traits de son lever' (p. 77). Thus it makes sense that the book would end in a dark 'Novembre'.

A recurring crescendo–diminuendo effect underscores this dynamics of control amid movement, and appears most visibly and dramatically in 'Les Djinns'.[19] Hugo's overall attention to decoration and landscape is not there for our viewing pleasure, but to display how the poet's eye strives to interpret surface detail and reconcile it with his subjective vision. Thus, creation some-how emerges from destruction: in 'Le Feu du ciel', the opening poem of the book, the poet's vision of Sodom and Gomorra somehow resists the destruct-ive act of the sulphurous cloud. In the poem's eighth section, the city is described at the same time as it is incinerated. In the end, every detail of the long poem seems to coalesce in the final image of the frozen lake, described as a hardened 'miroir du passé'; but it is nonetheless (and paradoxically) a smouldering lake, one whose fumes escape from its hardened surface: 'Qui fume comme une fournaise!' (p. 336). The cloud's punishing flames, in that they do not entirely destroy, are actually a testimony to a creative imagination that is in the process of rehabilitating art. And so the movement of drama, with surface details (from architecture to insects) serving as a cast of characters, emerges as the 'idée' of the book.

Because Hugo underscores the device of narrative in the *Orientales* in order to capture what will turn out to be constant change and movement, it is, paradoxically, the poet's eye that sees best. Hugo's grandiose plea 'que le poète donc aille où il veut' (Preface, p. 577) cannot apply to the painter; 'Le Feu du ciel', for example, opens with an invitation to see movement: 'La voyez-vous passer, la nuée au flanc noir?' (l. 1). Hugo insists on the advantages of his access to simultaneity: 'On croit voir à la fois' (l. 4). Despite apparent indications to the contrary (his use of colour in both *Cromwell* and the *Orientales*, as well as a painterly vocabulary), Hugo states the claim of the poet who – above and beyond the painter, sculptor, musician and architect – can best encompass the 'tout': history's movement and turbulence, the underlying source of the poet's subjectivity, as well as the exterior of the surface. At a critical impasse between the universal and ideal models of art that persisted in the first few decades of the nineteenth century, and the subsequent turn to the contingent and the real that would flourish during the July Monarchy, only the poet-dramatist, as Hugo saw it, could effectively achieve a union of the aesthetic potential of each:[20] 'Le drame, unissant les qualités les plus opposées, peut être tout à la fois plein de profondeur et plein de relief, philosophique et pittoresque' (p. 76).

The *Orientales*, then, do not give us a gallery of framed images, but reinforce the traditional distinction of narrative (poetry, writing) and the pregnant moment (painting). No doubt aware of the limits of poetry and painting that Lessing had posited in his *Laocoön* (1766), Hugo reverts to a model of art where poetry simply encompasses all.[21] Poetry knows no limits, and Hugo (with a posture of naivety) makes use of the word, even italicizing it: 'L'auteur ne savait pas en quoi étaient faites *les limites de l'art*' (*Les Orientales*,

Preface, p. 578). Even more revealing is a specific reference to the poet's ability to achieve the simultaneous, or the 'tout': 'L'espace et le temps sont au poète' (p. 577). Not subject to a frame or to a moment, the *Orientales* take the form of a narrative that opens up to further possibilities.[22] The book is not an assemblage of various landscapes, but a unified, moving tableau that keeps emanating from that controlled and controlling eye. The 'telos' is free and responds to the central declaration of the book: 'Que le poète donc aille où il veut, en faisant ce lui qui plaît; c'est la loi' (ibid.). A law of freedom is a paradox, but here Hugo guards us from the metaphysical impasse of the infinite; wary of accusations that the 'Romantic' was nebulous or vague, Hugo is sure to formulate a site from which the work of art will take strong root:[23] 'Le poète est libre. Mettons-nous à son point de vue, et voyons' (ibid.). Appropriating the tool of the painter – the eye – Hugo absconds with it and uses it to the poet's advantage.

Hugo's reticence toward painting was not only an attempt to exhibit the superior vantage point of the poet; it was also symptomatic of a more general concern that the nineteenth century was no longer poetic, but 'realist' or mundane. There are several significant relays between Hugo's 'Preface to Cromwell' and Stendhal's *Racine et Shakespeare* (1823, 1825) – the artist needs to have a more attentive eye, and be in tune with contemporary society.[24] However, their essential difference lies in Stendhal's aversion to the form of the verse: 'Le vers alexandrin n'est souvent qu'un cache-sottise' (Lettre I). As the pre-eminent Salon writer of the period, and a convinced inheritor of Diderot and his emphasis on the sensual in the work of art, Stendhal high-lighted the rapid and the fleeting as opposed to slow growth and the labours of the poem; in the first version of *Racine et Shakespeare*, he notes the speed with which his brochure came about, 'écrits en quelques heures et avec plus de zèle que de talent' (Preface). Hugo, when it was his turn, would refer to prose as 'timide' in the 'Preface to *Cromwell*'.

The increasing popular genre of landscape painting also reveals the extent to which 'the real' was gaining ground in artistic circles.[25] Although the Barbizon school would not fully come into its own until after the July Monarchy, landscape painting was already gaining considerable ground during the Restoration. The line between nature and art, as the neoclassical veneer disappeared from landscapes, became a fine one; paintings executed in 'plein air' in the Fontainebleau forest, for example, could be considered prototypes of the photograph.[26] Notably, Camille Corot, in the important lineage of Pierre-Henri de Valenciennes and his emphasis on the direct study of nature in Eléments de perspective pratique (1800), was producing highly finished studies of tree trunks at Fontainebleau as early as 1822.[27] What and how the eye saw became the actual subject of art and, as such, it increasingly appeared as if the liberties of the creative imagination were being challenged by the copy.

However, Hugo was careful to distinguish himself from this model of an imagination based primarily on the empirical; once again, in a text that heralds the liberty of the artist, Hugo imposes the 'limite infranchissable qui sépare la réalité selon l'art de la réalité selon la nature [. . .] L'art ne peut donner la chose même' (p. 89). Eye and idea must always coincide in Hugo's scheme of things: 'le but multiple de l'art [est] d'ouvrir au spectateur un double horizon, d'illuminer à la fois l'intérieur et l'extérieur des choses' (p. 91). In contradistinction to Stendhal's 'miroir de la route' in Le Rouge et le noir (1830), one that merely reflects either the azure of the sky or the mud below, Hugo's 'miroir de concentration' is a process as opposed to a gesture.[28] A traditional (mimetic) mirror provides a pale copy of the object, while the poet-dramatist's mirror concentrates the object's effects: 'Il faut donc que le drame soit un miroir de concentration qui, loin de les affaiblir [des objets], ramasse et condense les rayons colorants, qui fasse d'une lueur une lumière, d'une lumière une flamme' (p. 90). As Jean-Pierre Reynaud has noted, a dialectic in Hugo's oeuvre between the infinite and the concrete results: 'l'infini ne se laisse jamais complètement ou durablement maîtriser. Conquise sur lui, l'image est constamment remise en question par lui' ('Le Contour et l'infini').[29] Art is not the fast and easy mark of pleasure, then, but the arduous path that requires the maintenance of this balance. The telling of Cromwell's story through the dull reflection of prose, or the reduction and deformation of his grandeur onto a two-dimensional canvas, would be to sell it short. Cromwell needed the alexandrine, and so Hugo worked to maintain a distinctly poetic eye.

Apart from the question of realism in the Orientales, there is also that of 'l'art pour l'art'. Is Hugo a proto-Gautier, one who glosses over and, in the manner of Ingres, twists and exaggerates limbs in order to achieve a sculptural effect? From what we have already seen concerning Hugo's inclusion of the 'laid' in his theory of poetry, clearly not. Yet critics, both contemporary to Hugo and present day, have been quick to claim that the *Orientales* are an aberration within Hugo's oeuvre, a passing fancy of experimentation where form has the last say. The emphasis on plasticity in 'Sara la baigneuse' is certainly striking:

> Et la frêle escarpolette
> Se reflète
> Dans le transparent miroir,
> Avec la baigneuse blanche
> Qui se penche,
> Qui se penche pour se voir. (ll. 7–12)

But, once more, narrative will 'disturb' the stillness of this image. Hugo finds small but effectively powerful ways to break the young girl out of her form:

> Elle bat d'un pied timide
> L'onde humide
> *Où tremble un mouvant tableau,*
> Fait rougir son pied d'albâtre,
> Et, folâtre,
> Rit de la fraîcheur de l'eau. (ll. 19–24, my emphasis)

All of the arts are combined in the poem (music, painting, sculpture, even the imagined architecture of a palace), but the story behind Sara is what motivates the reader through each stanza. This short poem even takes the form of a drama, complete with a monologue and a surprise ending; our pleasure stems not exclusively from the presentation of Sara's beauty, but more from the intrusion of her reality: this is not a Bathsheba of Babylon, but a peasant girl who can only dream of taking baths in amber.

So why has there been a general tendency to reduce the *Orientales* to a smug enterprise, as if Hugo were saying, 'Look, I can paint!'? This glossing over seems to be centred on the word 'picturesque', a term that, due to its original meaning ('pittoresco': 'in the manner of painting'), came to connote the surface of things.[30] The word eventually became synonymous with the genre of descriptive poetry as considerations on the 'true' representation of nature formed *the* major discourse in eighteenth-century aesthetics. It comes as no surprise, then, that the term 'picturesque' became derogatory in Romantic circles as the faculty of the imagination resisted the process of imitation. But the French Romantics, especially Hugo, Deschamps and Sainte-Beuve, and even earlier, Prosper de Barante in the preface to his *Histoire des ducs de Bourgogne* (1824), re-motivated the term; that is to say, they appropriated a used and abused word in order to discuss a newly modernized concept. Barante places the faithful representation of surface detail in a harmonious relationship with the creative imagination, and he sums up the writing of history thus: 'manifester tous les dons de l'imagination dans la peinture exacte de la vérité'.[31] This imagination is mobile, not reliant on the retrieval of impressions: 'Cette mobilité de l'imagination, si précieuse pour tout peindre'. This is what Hugo meant by 'L'autre poésie était descriptive, celle-ci serait pittoresque' ('Preface to *Cromwell*', p. 96); the terms were once conflated, but Hugo latched onto the latter in order to stress the image itself (what the poet does with an object) as opposed to a mere accumulation of things. Indeed, Hugo conflates 'picturesque' with the imagination; the gro-tesque fertilizes poetry with 'mille imaginations pittoresques' (ibid., p. 71).[32] The picturesque did not have to do with the description of gardens or land-scapes (Delille), or with travel narratives that seek to 'show' the reader a specific locale; rather, it described the working (the process) of the poet-historian-dramatist's eye, and how the artist keeps to the idea without straying from a sense of precision.[33] The use of the term was fair game, then, as long as it was conceived as part of the whole, as opposed to an end in itself: 'Le drame, unissant les qualités les plus opposées, peut être tout à la fois plein de profondeur et plein de relief, philosophique et pittoresque' ('Preface to *Cromwell*', p. 76).

In the *Orientales*, Hugo uses the pictorial against itself. In what could be described as a challenge to the genre of painting, every image in the *Orientales* is subservient to the whole of an even more exotic landscape: that is, Hugo's own emanating process of poetry, in which the panorama of images, spilling out of any sense of border, serve as a metaphor for the poet.

It is curious nonetheless that, despite his resistance to painting, Hugo makes no reference to Delacroix in a book of poems that revels in colour, enthusiasm, movement, Greece, veils, tigers, sultans and slaves. Delacroix had only very recently exhibited a number of Orientalist paintings at the 'Exposition de tableaux au profit des Grecs' (1826). It is curious especially because 1827 marks the transient moment when poet and painter were on friendly terms. From the minimal mention that Hugo made of Delacroix, we do know that the poet was particularly drawn to *La Mort de Sardanapale*, exhibited in the third instalment of the Salon of 1827. Though the target of unanimous criticism, Hugo (albeit in a private letter) eagerly defended it: 'Son *Sardanapale* est une chose magnifique, et si gigantesque qu'elle échappe aux petites vues.'[34] Given Hugo's central tenant in the 'Preface to *Cromwell*' that 'la muse moderne verra les choses d'un coup d'œil plus haut et plus large' (p. 69), this was no passing remark. Appearing only weeks after *Cromwell*, Delacroix's ambitious and expansive canvas meets Hugo's main criterion for the modern work of art: the widening and active eye. Delacroix 'sees' what the eye normally resists, leading him ever closer to the 'tout'; he combines in *Sardnapale* the lush material, the sensuous flesh, the attention to human form ('le beau') with a strange palette, a lack of perspective and arbitrary violence ('le grotesque').

With the appearance of the *Orientales*, written in the wake of the Salon of 1827, the chief exponent of Romantic poetry thus comes 'eye to eye' with the leading Romantic painter. But this 'meeting' produces a sense of friction, with Hugo's volume posing as a response meant to safeguard the poet's absolute place of privilege. Hugo, looking to beat the painter at his own game, tells his own story through the ocular. This rivalry is most apparent if Hugo's 'Mazeppa' is viewed, so to speak, alongside Delacroix's provocative painting. Both works are based on Byron; both highlight despotism; and both emphasize the figure of the protagonist's eye. And, if Hugo's 'Preface to *Cromwell*' was a manifesto, the stakes were equally high for Delacroix in 1827; later musing on *Sardanapale*, he would say: 'ce fut mon Waterloo.'[35] These essential similarities not only allow for comparison, but due to Hugo's wariness regarding painting, they should motivate us to find the contrasts.

Byron's 'Mazeppa' (1819) is a love story within a larger narrative of history.[36] The length of Hugo's version is miniature in comparison, but its power of suggestion is expansive as it puts into action the device of the 'miroir concentré'. At what for Byron was the midway point, Hugo begins at the split second before the horse begins his long and frenzied run ('Away! Away!'

serves as Hugo's epigraph). It becomes apparent, as Hugo's horse makes its way with the load of its victim, that Hugo further condenses Byron's narrative to Mazeppa's eye. The poem, in fact, begins with a reference to what Mazeppa sees: 'Ainsi, quand Mazeppa, qui rugit et qui pleure, / A vu ses bras, ses pieds, ses flancs qu'un sabre effleure' (ll. 1–2). As they fly across the landscape, the eye somehow still manages to take it all in; the details are surprisingly specific:

> Il voit courir les bois, courir les larges nues,
> Le vieux donjon détruit,
> Les monts d'un rayon baigne les intervalles;
> Il voit; [. . .] (ll. 36–41)

Mazeppa can even see in darkness; as night falls, he makes out the massive flocks of birds of prey that follow intently. This hero can discern black upon black:

> Entre le ciel et lui, comme un tourbillon sombre,
> Il les voit, puis les perd, et les entend dans l'ombre
> Voler confusément. (76–8)

But the climax of the poem occurs in the second part, when the figure of the suffering poet who struggles with his genius replaces Mazeppa and the horse, respectively. And so the drama comes not from Mazeppa's vindication, but when we learn that the *poet* sees all: 'Il voit tout' (l. 124). The poet has gone from the image of ropes that bind Mazeppa to the moons of Saturn, but with his eye at the centre (in control) at all points in time.

However, in addition to the poem's epigraph, there is also the dedication to Louis Boulanger, a painter and Hugo's close friend. The facts tell us that Boulanger submitted *Le Supplice de Mazeppa* to the Salon of 1827 (the same year as *Cromwell*, and the same year as *La Mort de Sardanapale*), but Hugo in no way concedes to ekphrasis (see fig. 9.1). While there is a sense of fluidity and action as Hugo's figure of the horse runs its course, the horse in Boulanger's representation is stuck in a mannerist, oddly assembled patchwork of figures. The painter's representation of the story in light of Hugo's is a stark point in contrast, not just due to the limits of painting, but mostly because of Boulanger's disorienting positioning of human figures. Boulanger emphasizes details as *limits* (the court, the court's henchmen, the imposing architecture,

Fig. 9.1. Louis Boulanger, *Le Supplice de Mazeppa*, Salon of 1827, Rouen,
Musée des Beaux-Arts. RMN-Grand Palais/Agence Bulloz

the ropes, the crowd), rendering it difficult for the viewer to gain access to the protagonist. Shapes preclude detail, suggesting that this painter's eye is not wide open. This is another way of saying that Boulanger is descriptive, as opposed to what the Romantics called 'picturesque'. The viewer's eye is drawn upward to the group that stands above and in the background, as opposed to Mazeppa himself, who is lost in a wash of white. The power of suggestion is feeble; it is not even certain that this horse will take off (how can it move out of this throng? will it run into the onlookers, or even better, the fortress?). Boulanger, in effect, chokes under the weight of Byron's poem, while Hugo delights in running with it, 'away, away' from the limits that we see here.

Where Boulanger is static, Delacroix evokes movement with every brush-stroke. Despite the crowded nature of Delacroix's *La Mort de Sardanapale* there is an unmistakable fluidity to its lines and placement of figures.[37] Delacroix's murky representation of Sardanapalus somehow calls out to our eye as it gleams from within the darkness. If it is hard to find a sense of perspective in the painting, due to the abundance of material, colour and serpentine lines, it is the king's eye that orders our own. The painter, despite a scene that seems to carry him away, reveals a sense of fixity. This is an original retelling, not a 'history painting'; Delacroix identifies not with the pathos of the scene, but with the figure that shows the utmost sense of restraint and order.[38] Independent of the word, Delacroix paints his own poem. The eye of Sardanapalus is to Delacroix what the sunset is to Hugo in the *Orientales*: the idea that orders everything else. The flesh, the jewels and the slaves, however gorgeous and lush they may be, are secondary to the source of this 'point optique'.

With this fixed eye, Delacroix offers a challenge to the poet; and Hugo, true to his nature, was quick to respond to it. Boulanger's version of Mazeppa merely upheld the traditional distinction between the fixed, pregnant moment in painting and the movement of narrative in the epic poem: Mazeppa's horse is just about to take off, and we see the gaping hole of the page's mouth as he resists this moment with all his might. This is the 'Laocoön' moment par excellence, the moment of the sigh, complete with ropes that might as well be snakes; Boulanger makes it too easy.[39] But Delacroix chooses a different kind of moment, the one that comes after heightened anticipation:

the fall into chaos. Yet this turbulent movement is countered by a strong sense of fixity, of calm and of order. Delacroix, in other words, was not obedient to the traditional distinction of word and image, but emulated Hugo's theory of poetry in the 'Preface to *Cromwell*'. The size of the canvas, the attention to colour, a *dramatic* history painting, the unique retelling of Byron's story: Delacroix expands, combines, concentrates and achieves 'le tout'. Through chiaroscuro light meets the mysterious and dense counterweight of black, of the artist at work behind the scenes. *La Mort de Sardanapale* shows a painter who has achieved the poetic. Michèle Hannoosh's commentary on the role of poetry in Delacroix's oeuvre could apply to Hugo: 'The pictorial must be reconsidered, reconceived in terms of the natural instability, the "literary" temporality, of the imagination.'[40] But not quite at ease with painting's 'intrusion' into the poet's privileged sphere of freedom, Hugo problematizes Delacroix's harmonizing of word and image with an implicit reminder of the painter's limitations.

The *Orientales* are not as arbitrarily fantastical as they may first appear; on the contrary, they require a reader who is in tune with the critical shift in the role of the imagination that emerged most notably from Hugo's own 'Preface to *Cromwell*'. The few critics who have approached the *Orientales* explain the book's emphasis on imagery, form and colour by dutifully reminding us of facts and incidentals. The volume is hermetic, a closed case, an unexpected hiccup within the broader scheme of Hugo's progression towards the cosmic grandeur of *Les Contemplations* or *La Légende des siècles*.[41] Because the *Orientales* are an exception to the rule, a prototype of art for art's sake, it is as if the reader is excused for glossing them over.

However, the import of this moment of time within Hugo's career, between the publication of *Cromwell* and *Hernani* (1830), cannot be overstated; an imagination that had been fermenting and in flux in the wake of Chateaubriand and Mme de Staël was now more sharply defined and in control. Sainte-Beuve even refers to the *Orientales* as the period's crowning achievement; Hugo's most unique and 'glorious' speciality, he writes, is 'l'ode pittoresque ou d'imagination, dont les *Orientales* lui assurent le sceptre parmi les contemporains.'[42]

Notes

[1] Review of Victor Hugo's *Odes et ballades* (4th edn, 1826).

[2] Just a glance at Léon Séché's volume 'Victor Hugo et les Artistes', which is part of a broader study of *Le Cénacle de Joseph Delorme (1827–1830)* (Paris: Mercure de France, 1912), shows that Hugo's association with sculptors and painters during the writing of the *Orientales* (mostly in 1828) was far from negligible: David d'Angers, the Devéria brothers, Louis Boulanger, Charles Robelin, Paul Huet, Eugène Delacroix, the Johannot brothers, Célestin Nanteuil and Charlet are all included. Jean-Bertrand Barrère's 'Victor Hugo et les arts plastiques' (*Revue de littérature comparée*, 30 (1956)) and Tony James's '*Pictura poesis* ou art rêveur ?' (in Hugo's *Œuvres complètes*, ed. J. Massin, XV/XVI, no. 1) offer critical examinations of the impact of painters and painting on Hugo's oeuvre in general.

[3] Émile Deschamps, *Études françaises et étrangères* (2nd edn, Paris: Urbain Canel, 1828), p. xviii.

[4] All references to the *Orientales* are from Pierre Albouy's edition of Hugo's *Œuvres poétiques*, vol. 1 (Paris: Gallimard, 1964). Though there are two prefaces, I refer to only one ('Préface de l'édition originale'), using the much simpler indication 'Preface'.

[5] In the words of Suzanne Nash, 'Hugo's germ will grow into the roots of a plant which will break down the walls of the fortress, opening the way for new forms to be born out of the now generative ruin'. 'Victor Hugo's *Odes et Ballades* and the romantic lyric', in William Paulson (ed.), *Les Genres de l'hénaurme siècle* (Ann Arbor: University of Michigan Press, 1989), 73–95 (75).

[6] Ton beau rêve d'Asie avorte, et tu ne vois
   Sous tes yeux que la rue au bruit accoutumée,
   Brouillard à ta fenêtre, et longs flots de fumée
   Qui baignent en fuyant l'angle noirci des toits. ('Novembre', ll. 9–12)

[7] Edmund Burke, *A Philosophical Enquiry into the Origin of our Ideas of the Sublime and the Beautiful*, ed. Adam Phillips (Oxford: Oxford University Press, 1998 [1757]), p. 70.

[8] David Scott specifically refers to both the 'Preface to *Cromwell*' and the *Orientales* in the context of the 'ut pictura poesis' debate, framing the texts as 'the writer's attempt to rival in literature the success of painting in expressing visual experience'. See David Scott, 'Poetry and painting: *Ut pictura poesis* reconsidered', in *Pictorialist Poetics* (Cambridge: Cambridge University Press, 1988), chapter 1, pp. 5–19.

[9] Quoted in Charles Bruneau's 'L'Epoque romantique', vol. 12 of Ferdinand Brunot's *Histoire de la langue française des origines à nos jours* (Paris: Armand Colin, 1968), p. 23. The quotation comes from vol. IX of La Harpe's *Lycée, ou Cours de littérature ancienne et moderne* (1798–1804).

[10] François-René de Chateaubriand, *Génie du christianisme* (Paris: Flammarion, 1966 [1802 by Migneret]), 2 vols.

[11] As Lockean theories took hold on English and French eighteenth-century theorists, sight became a primary target of investigation; the impact of the visual implicitly turned studies on psychology into treatises on painting. Consider Burke's musings on the colour black: 'Black will always have something melancholy in it, because the sensory will always find the change to it from other colours too violent' (*A Philosophical Enquiry* IV.XVIII).

[12] Consider Diderot's review of Greuze's *La jeune fille qui pleure son oiseau mort* (Salon of 1759), where he repeatedly refers to the painting as a poem; we will also note that, in this case, the poet (Gessner) works from the painter: 'La jolie élégie! le charmant poème! la belle idylle que Gessner en ferait!' (*Œuvres esthétiques*, ed. Paul Vernière (Paris: Garnier, 1959), p. 533.

[13] To Hugo, it was almost as if the eighteenth century had never happened. In his examination of Voltaire, he remarks: 'Le dix-huitième siècle paraîtra toujours dans l'histoire comme étouffé entre le siècle qui le précède et le siècle qui le suit' (*La Muse française*, December 1823, later published as 'Sur Voltaire' (1834); in Hugo, *Œuvres complètes* (Paris: Laffont, 1985), vol. 13, p. 141).

[14] This was one of the guiding themes of the *Odes et Ballades* (in *Œuvres poétiques*, vol. 1). 'Le Rétablissement de la statue de Henri IV' (1822) is one of Hugo's most vivid examples of the people's participation in history.

[15] The Garnier-Flammarion edition of *Cromwell* is used here (Paris, 1968).

[16] Napoleon was the current-day Cromwell.

[17] Hugo, *Œuvres poétiques*, vol. 1, p. 265.

[18] Lamartine provides several examples of this trope in his *Méditations poétiques*. As the sun sets, the poet arrives at his last breath: 'Aux regards d'un mourant le soleil est si beau!' ('L'Automne', l. 20). Alphonse de Lamartine, *Méditations poétiques et Nouvelles méditations poétiques*, ed. Aurélie Loiseleur (Paris: Livre de poche, 2006).

[19] The famous poem in which two beats per line steadily increase (per stanza) to ten. Hugo does not only depict the anticipated moment of 'just before' but the whole drama of the coming and going of the furies.

[20] They are, for Hugo, one and the same, since the modern-day dramatist is a natural result of the epic poet (the ancient) and the lyricist (the primitive).

[21] A French translation of the *Laocoön* appeared in 1802, and Mme de Staël makes frequent reference to Lessing in *De l'Allemagne*. Though we cannot be sure that Hugo read the *Laocoön*, he would have been familiar with its main line of inquiry.

[22] In general, the poems make a progressive move from East to West, and at the same time, an equally gradual descent from clouds ('Le Feu du ciel') to the poet's windowpane in Paris ('Novembre').

23 In the words of Mme de Staël, 'il faut, pour concevoir la vraie grandeur de la poésie lyrique, errer par la rêverie dans les régions éthérées, oublier le bruit de la terre en écoutant l'harmonie céleste, et considérer l'univers entier comme un symbole des émotions de l'âme' (in *De l'Allemagne*, 2 vols (Paris: Garnier-Flammarion, 1968), II.X, 'De la poésie').

24 In Stendhal, *Œuvres complètes*, ed. Pierre Martino, vol. 37 (Geneva and Paris: Slatkine Reprints, 1986).

25 As submissions of history paintings to the Salon of 1827 decreased, those of land-scapes increased by 25 per cent. For a brief history of the Salons in this period, see 'Le Salon à Paris de 1815 à 1850', in the exhibition catalogue, Jean Lacambre and Isabelle Julia (eds), *Les Années romantiques: La Peinture française de 1815 à 1850* (Paris: Réunion des Musées Nationaux, 1995).

26 A 2007 exhibition at the Musée d'Orsay in Paris blurred the distinction between canvas and lens. See the accompanying catalogue, Chantal Georgel (ed.), *La Forêt de Fontainebleau: Un atelier grandeur nature* (Paris: Réunion des Musées Nationaux, 2007).

27 Ibid. pp. 29–35.

28 Stendhal, *Le Rouge et le noir* (Paris: Flammarion, 1964), part II, ch. XIX ('L'Opéra bouffe').

29 In M. Blondel and P. Georgel (eds), *Victor Hugo et les images* (Dijon: Aux amateurs du livre, 1989), p. 218.

30 Although quite schematic, Wil Munster's *La Poétique du pittoresque en France de 1700 à 1830* (Paris: Droz, 1991) considers the history of the term 'picturesque', and highlights how the Romantics appropriated it.

31 Prosper Brugière de Barante, *Histoire des ducs de Bourgogne de la maison de Valois*, 13 vols (4th edn, Paris : Ladvocat, 1826), vol. 1, p. 3.

32 This is also Sainte-Beuve speaking. Referring to Hugo's ballads as picturesque odes, he equates them with the 'ode d'imagination et de fantaisie' (Charles Augustin Sainte-Beuve, 'Prospectus pour les œuvres de Victor Hugo', *Premiers lundis*, vol. 1, ed. Maxime Leroy (Paris: Gallimard, 1949), pp. 297–303 (p. 299)).

33 Hugo conflates them all in the 'Preface to *Cromwell*': 'Nous constatons un fait. Nous sommes historien, non critique' (p. 70). The debt that Hugo's preface owes to Barante's is not negligible.

34 Letter to Victor Pavie, 3 April 1829.

35 Quoted in Vincent Pomarède's, pamphlet published by the Réunion des musées nationaux (1998) to accompany *La Mort de Sardanapale*; see below, note 37.

36 The story is long and complicated. What follows is a truncated annotation from Byron's *The Major Works*, ed. J. J. McGann (Oxford: Oxford University Press, 2000).

Using Voltaire's *Histoire de Charles XII* (1772) as a reference, Byron recounts the trials and tribulations of Ivan Mazeppa (1632?–1709), a page at the court of John Casimir V of Poland. Mazeppa was punished because of his affair with the wife of a nobleman; but later he was made Hetman of the Ukraine by Peter the Great, and later still defected to Charles XII of Sweden (Byron's poem speaks through Mazeppa himself as he recounts his story to Charles).

[37] Ancient accounts tell us that Sardanapalus was king of the Assyrian empire; rather than see it fall to the Medes, he orders that it be destroyed. Essential to any study of *La Mort de Sardanapale* is Vincent Pomarède's accompanying pamphlet published by the Réunion des musées nationaux (1998). Also helpful for a very close analysis of the story of Sardanapalus (which goes well beyond Byron's version) is Beatrice Farwell's 'Sources for Delacroix's *Death of Sardanapalus*', *Art Bulletin*, 40/1 (1958), 66–71.

[38] In his commentary, Alain Daguerre de Hureaux prompts us to consider *Sardnapale* apart from Byron's influence, noting that Delacroix did not provide a source in the Salon pamphlet: 'Contrairement à la coutume, aucun nom d'auteur ne suit le texte du livret du Salon et un tel procédé peut justifier l'outrance de la représentation par une prétendue source littéraire que le peintre aurait simplement suivie à la lettre.' *Delacroix* (Paris: Hazan, 1993), p. 79.

[39] See Lessing's description of the *Laocoön* (1766), chapter 5.

[40] Michèle Hanoosh, *Painting and the Journal of Eugène Delacroix* (Princeton: Princeton University Press, 1995), chapter 1.

[41] Pierre Albouy, in his notice to *Orientales* in Hugo's *Œuvres poétiques*: 'un poème comme *le Feu du ciel* serait presque digne de figurer dans *La Légende des siècles*' (p. 1299).

[42] Sainte-Beuve, *Premiers lundis*, p. 300.

Visions and Re-visions: Zola, Cardinal and *L'Œuvre*

Kate Griffiths

Adaptations, whatever their medium, are frequently criticized for their revisions to an original author's work. Pierre Cardinal's 1967 television production of Emile Zola's 1886 novel *L'Œuvre* appears to open itself to such criticism since it offers a clearly cropped vision of Zola's panoramic novel surveying the art and society of late nineteenth-century France. However, Cardinal harmonizes with Zola's textual vision in three key respects. First, the intimacy of the television aesthetic in general, and that of Cardinal's adaptation in particular, bring the viewer closer to Zola's intention to provide, in an intimate close-up, a dissection of his characters. Secondly, whilst Zola's novel explores the power of the characters' vision to capture reality, Cardinal's programme questions self-reflexively the power of its own adaptive vision, its ability to show Zola's text in a different medium. Finally, Cardinal's offering, whilst it does revise Zola's novel, echoes and furthers the nineteenth-century author's conceptualization of authorship, not as a moment of originary purity, but as an essentially revisionary process. As Zola adapts the techniques of art to his fiction, evaluating and inhabiting the interstices between pen and paint, so Cardinal's work probes the boundary between painting and television, dramatizing the interaction of canvas and camera in an adaptation

Chapter 10

which, like the source text from which it stems, assesses the adaptive nature of artistic creation.

Television adaptations generally offer a very different vision of Zola's texts from that of the novelist's works. The traditional television aesthetic, reliant as it has been on short, boxy shots in dialogue-heavy interior productions, amputates Zola's panoramic visual aspirations in the novel in which his protagonist's artistic aim is 'tout voir, tout faire, tout conquérir'.[1] Cardinal's adaptation is no exception. Zola's *L'Œuvre*, in the novelistic equivalent of an establishing shot, systematically directs the viewer's gaze through the lines and details of the landscape, reaching as far as the eye can see:

C'était une trouée immense, les deux bouts de la rivière s'enfonçant à perte de vue [...] Les plus minces détails apparurent, on distingua les petites persiennes fermées du quai des Ormes, les deux fentes des rues de la Masure et du Paon-Blanc, coupant la ligne des façades; [...] tandis que, de l'autre côté, sous le pont Louis-Philippe, au Mail, les tours alignées sur quatre rangs avaient flambé. Et l'on vit [...] tout un monde emplissant l'énorme coulée, la fosse creusée d'un horizon à l'autre. (p. 437)

Cardinal's adaptation not only offers no such establishing shot, but, with the exception of a few brief external shots of the city, it cuts the Paris which lies at the heart of Zola's novel almost in its entirety. Cardinal conceptualizes this act of amputation via a series of window shots. Whilst Zola desired his fiction to be a window onto the world, Cardinal inverts this image using his camera to peer voyeuristically from the outside world into the claustrophobic interiors his characters inhabit.[2] However, whilst Cardinal may bar Zola's panoramas, his television voyeurism liberates another aspect of the novelist's fiction: Zola's intent to show, in extreme close-up, the disintegration of his hero and heroine beneath the forces acting upon them and the invasive gaze of their creator. Zola's pen dissects his characters and Cardinal's camera invades their consciousness, offering a prolonged series of point-of-view shots that offer access to their being. In just one of many shots monumentalizing and elevating Claude as painter, Cardinal offers a point-of-view shot from the lowly perspective of Christine as she poses fearfully for the painting and painter, the combined causes of her ultimate destruction.[3] Cardinal's adaptation thus curtails aspects of Zola's vision, whilst simultaneously liberating others.

It is clear that vision and its power are central themes in Zola's novel. The text's key moments are, by and large, visual ones. Claude's request for Christine to pose for him is made without words. His eyes speak in their place:

> Les yeux brûlants dont il la regardait, disaient clairement: 'Ah! il y a vous, ah! ce serait le miracle attendu, le triomphe certain, si vous me faisiez ce suprême sacrifice! Je vous implore, je vous le demande, comme à une amie adorée, la plus belle, la plus chaste.' Elle, toute droite, très blanche, entendait chaque mot: et ces yeux d'ardente prière exerçaient sur elle une puissance. (p. 525)

Her eyes signal her agreement and neither she nor Claude speaks of their pact because words would bring the shame that visual communication occludes. The closeness of the lovers manifests itself in their shared vision as they walk through Paris: 'ils regardèrent l'eau bouillonner à travers la fôret des charpentes de l'Estacade [. . .], les yeux au loin sur le Port-au-Vin et le jardin des Plantes' (p. 514). Vision is precisely what empowers Claude as an artist. Yet his vision ultimately fails, a failure predicted by the novel from the outset. Zola paradoxically situates blindness at the core of Claude's powerful sight: 'il travaillait avec l'obstination aveugle de l'artiste' (p. 602). Claude laments the fracture of his vision, the inability of his painting truly to see the object it depicts:

> pourquoi de brusques trous? Pourquoi des parties indignes, inaperçues pendant le travail [. . .]? Et il se sentait incapable de correction, un mur se dressait à un moment, un obstacle infranchissable, au-delà duquel il lui était défendu d'aller [. . .] Il s'énervait, ne voyait plus. (p. 604)

However, where the vision of individual characters fails, the more powerful external vision of Zola's narrative compensates. Whilst Claude does not paint or cannot complete the majority of the Parisian landscapes he sees, Zola's narrative does it for him, visualizing in words a series of landscapes for the reader. However, even Zola's narrative ultimately offers an intriguing, tempered portrait of its own visual power. Like its protagonist's offerings, the novel's verbal paintings of the landscape are frequently built around the vocabulary of fracture and blockage: 'une trouée s'ouvrait à gauche, jusqu'à l'île Saint-Louis, une fuite de miroir d'un raccourci aveuglant; [. . .] l'écluse de la Monnaie semblait boucher la vue de sa barre d'écume' (p. 609). The landscape is comparably barred and pierced at the novel's close:

> à gauche les maisons du quai du Louvre, à droite les deux ailes de l'Institut, masses confuses de monuments et de bâtisses qui se perdaient ensuite, en un redoublement d'ombre, piqué des étincelles lointaines. Puis, entre ces cordons, fuyant à perte de vue, les ponts jetaient des barres de lumières. (p. 716)

Vision, a sense at once potent and fractured, drives Zola's *L'Œuvre* as the nineteenth-century novelist explores the force and frailties of both his and his characters' ability to see.

Vision proves equally central, at the level of plot, to Cardinal's adaptation. Whilst the dialogue Cardinal includes in his work is extremely faithful to Zola's text, his adaptation in television, a medium usually heavy in dialogue, elides language in key scenes and privileges the visual. Christine and Claude escape to live in the country in Zola's novel. In Cardinal's adaptation the couple escape not only Paris but language itself. They find happiness in silence. Cardinal has Claude speak only to order food and Christine to echo her approval of the rent of their accommodation. Such words aside, the lovers' idyll is depicted entirely by visual means. In a series of shot reverse shots Christine mimics Claude's actions teasingly, replicating the manner of his consumption of meat, wine and an apple.[4] The symmetry of their desires is reinforced visually by the series of point-of-view shots that convey wordlessly their love in the remainder of their time in Bennecourt. Accompanied by an idyllic soundtrack of birdsong, Cardinal offers the viewer a point-of-view shot from the perspective of Christine as she gazes lovingly down at Claude as he lies at her feet. It is immediately followed by a reverse shot up from Claude's perspective which slides sensuously over her body, allowing the reader to access and share in Claude's desire before he kisses his mistress's feet. Speech, when it intrudes at the close of the Bennecourt sequence, heralds the end of the idyll. Claude embraces an unhappily pregnant Christine only to be asked to leave her alone in her discomfort. In Cardinal's adaptation, happiness is to be found in the visual while language symbolizes a fall from paradise.

Zola's novel not only explores the power of vision, but also the force of the painting that Claude's vision produces. It imbues painting simultaneously with a sense of potency and incapacity by problematically personifying the incomplete canvas. The figure in the painting that Claude cannot bring to life steps down from the canvas in spectral form to chase the artist who would render her: 'Cette fois, il s'était juré de ne rentrer jamais, il courait Paris depuis midi, comme s'il avait entendu galoper derrière ses talons le spectre blafard de la grande figure nue, ravagée de continuelles retouches, toujours laissée informe, le poursuivant' (p. 640). Painting's potency is far less problematic in Cardinal's adaptation and, indeed, although Claude never completes the masterpiece on which he works, Cardinal underlines its dominance via three key tropes: music, the predominance of the colour yellow and the personification of the canvas itself. Cardinal introduces a musical motif from the moment Christine undresses and sleeps in the initial pose in which Claude will subsequently draw her. Whilst this musical motif is initially associated with Christine's attractions, it soon supersedes her to represent the pull of the painting, with its mythical female figure, the sea-bound seductress whose siren song lures Claude to his death. The power of this painted figure is reinforced by the adaptation's use of colour. Christine is first associated with the colour yellow (she brings Claude yellow flowers in a yellow dress and the Bennecourt interlude in which she reigns supreme culminates in a yellow interior whose shades are intensified by those of the fire). The sketches and paintings created from Christine all resonate with the same shade. However, as the painted copy of Christine replaces her in Claude's affections and desires, Christine herself is gradually stripped of this colour. In the adaptation's closing images a pale Christine, dressed entirely in white, lies broken on the floor beneath a resplendently yellow portrait which, having absorbed her life force and colour, bathes the studio in which it stands in yellow. Moreover, Zola's personification of his painting finds an echo in the life force with which Cardinal imbues the canvas. Whilst point-of-view shots from Christine's perspective abound at the adaptation's outset, they gradually disappear and are replaced by highly unusual point-of-view shots from the perspective of the painting itself as Cardinal personifies its vision. One of Christine's final point-of-view shots takes place as Claude criticizes her for being inferior to the copy he has created of her. It is immediately followed by a point-of-view shot from the elevated perspective of the painting itself. The object so often looked at now actively looks as Cardinal underscores, in visual form, the power of painting at the heart of his adaptation.

Cardinal's adaptation not only explores vision at the level of plot, but, intriguingly, assesses the power of its own adaptive vision to see or convey Zola's novel in a different medium. Adaptations, whatever their form, promise some sense of revelation of the original source they adapt. And revelation itself lies at the heart of Zola's concept of artistry. The nineteenth-century novelist's alter ego Sandoz in L'Œuvre apparently reveals all in his works:

> la vie enfin, la vie totale, universelle [. . .] la conviction que tout doit se dire, qu'il y a des mots abominables nécessaires comme des fers rouges, qu'une langue sort enrichie de ces bains de force; et surtout l'acte sexuel, l'origine et l'achèvement continu du monde, tiré de la honte où on le cache, remis dans sa gloire, sous le soleil. (p. 590)

Sandoz's text may promise revelation in general, and bodily revelation in particular, but Cardinal's adaptation cannot, its director makes clear, deliver it. Cardinal both promises and frustrates the revelation of the naked body upon which both Claude's painting and consequently his own adaptation are predicated. David Baguley, writing on Zola's 1880 novel Nana, characterizes the novel as an extended striptease, 'one long frenzied, vertiginous peep show, a veritable orgy of voyeurism.'[5] Cardinal's adaptation might be characterized in similar terms. The director repeatedly has Christine begin to undress or shows the consequences of such a process (the character's clothes on the floor), but, somewhat coyly, never fully reveals the body behind this teasing peepshow. Peter Brooks suggests that Zola's Nana is never fully divested of the literal and metaphorical veils that shield the body which remains so visible throughout the novel. Cardinal's Christine is similarly never truly unveiled.[6] Cardinal bars her body in a variety of respects. Sexual interludes occur in the ellipses between scenes. The camera cuts solely to Christine's face as Claude paints her naked torso. It again homes in on her face when she subsequently strips in order for Claude to paint her. While the camera then offers a vision of her naked image on canvas, it does so in such extreme close-up that nothing of her body or even its contingent parts is distinguishable. Finally, when Christine stands naked for Claude to paint, Cardinal's adaptation literally bars her from its gaze as Claude paints a vertical line of paint on the camera screen which has positioned itself as his canvas, blocking the model he copies from our view.

Cardinal's coyness in relation to Christine's naked body, a body that the audience seizes only in glimpses, could perhaps be attributed to the time and context of the programme's broadcasting. However, it acquires an increased significance since this coyness extends beyond questions of the bodily to encompass painting in the programme as a whole. The paintings Cardinal's work depicts are always in some sense fundamentally blocked. In his studio, Claude flicks through a portfolio that the viewer is not permitted to see. We witness Christine posing naked for Claude as he begins to take her likeness, but are initially prevented from seeing the work in question. Cardinal cuts directly from the model to a point-of-view shot from the perspective of the art work itself as the salon audience laugh at it, bathed in the colours of the canvas they mock. The viewer is subsequently allowed to see mere fragments of this canvas as the camera moves across brief sections of it, refusing to depict its entirety. When Claude paints in the country, his own body partially obscures the painted landscape he creates, blocking it from the audience's view. Cardinal's adaptation makes clear its inability to reveal its model – Zola's source novel symbolized in the form of Christine's body – in its entirety. So too does it repeatedly block the paintings, or adapted copies, which fill its images. Through them it bars metaphorically its own creative existence. Cardinal places his art under the aegis of partial obfuscation.

Yet, it could be argued that, far from blocking Zola's source text, Cardinal's art of obfuscation in many senses brings the viewer closer to it, for occlusion is a key theme in *L'Œuvre*. Not only do Zola's descriptions fracture, puncture and block themselves metaphorically, preventing the reader from accessing fully the reality behind them, but the novelist undertakes a complex exploration of the fraught, impossible relationship between model and adapted art work via the figure of Christine and the reproductions made of her. The artistic copy made of Christine does not reproduce her; rather, it precedes her. Claude looks at Christine in their first encounter and rather than creating painting from her, recognizes her as his pre-existing painting: 'C'était ça, tout à fait ça, la figure qu'il avait inutilement cherchée pour son tableau, et presque dans la pose' (p. 442). Christine exists artistically before she does ontologically in the novel as Zola reverses the precedence of original and reproduction from the outset. Consequently, Zola presents Christine's skin, even before its pictorial representation on canvas, as always already man-made: 'Brusque-ment, un frisson courut, pareil à une moire sur le satin de sa peau' (p. 443). Christine's reproduction subsequently attains more life force than its model: 'Et elle renaissait, cette image, elle ressuscitait, plus vivante qu'elle [Christine], pour achever de la tuer' (p. 644). As her copy attains a measure of life, Christine becomes a mere object, a 'mannequin vivant, qu'il [Claude] plantait là et qu'il copiait, comme il aurait copié la cruche ou le chaudron d'une nature morte' (p. 631). The reproduction does not translate the original; rather, it replaces the original as Zola underlines the complexity of the relationship between source model and reproduction. Christine's original body is thus as hidden and as inaccessible in Zola's original novel as it is in Cardinal's adaptation.[7]

Whilst adaptations are frequently reproached precisely for what they hide, for the inaccuracy of their visions of their source text, both Zola and Cardinal are interested in artistry, not as an originary moment, but instead as a revisionary process. Zola's novel borrows from and adapts the techniques of the visual arts and Cardinal's adaptation subsequently borrows from and adapts both the literary techniques of Zola and those of the painters to whom the nineteenth-century novelist is so indebted. Cardinal's act of adap-tation is thus, in some senses, double. Zola's interest in the world of art is well documented; Cézanne was one of his childhood friends.[8] Zola wrote in defence of Manet in 1867 and came to know the circle of artists around the painter.[9] He devoted a considerable amount of his art criticism to the Impressionist painters.[10] Probing the boundary between word and image, Zola's writing claims to paint pictures. Of his brochure on Manet, the novelist writes: 'J'espère qu'on cessera de traiter de rapin débraillé l'homme dont je viens d'esquisser la physionomie en quelques traits.'[11] Conversely, he attributes to painting the ability to speak. Surveying 'Le Moment artistique' on 4 May 1866, he writes: 'Sur ces deux mille toiles, douze ou quinze vous parlent un langage humain.'[12] The permeable boundary between writing and the visual arts is as visible in the novelist's fiction. Henri Mitterand suggests: 'on y dénote aisément les procédés et les instruments de la picturalisation, qui inscrivent à tout moment dans le texte du roman des simulacres des tableaux, et étendent ainsi à l'infini le musée textuel'.[13] Zola's *L'Œuvre* is indeed filled with metaphorical still lifes and portraits, but the *paysage* dominates and Zola's written narrative repeatedly invokes the language, structure and materials of the visual arts. The narration presents 'la silhouette des tours pointues du palais de Justice, charbonnées durement sur le vide' (p. 515). In other places ink is the preferred method for visual reproduction. In *L'Œuvre*'s closing scene, a train is described thus: 'on distingua nettement, comme sur un transparent d'ombres chinoises, les découpures des wagons [. . .] Et la ligne redevint nette, un simple trait à l'encre coupant l'horizon' (p. 734). Zola throws into relief for the reader the 'touches' and 'taches' of his brushstrokes in his descriptions:

> Paris allumé s'était endormi, il n'y avait plus là que la vie des becs de gaz, des taches rondes qui scintillaient, qui se rapetissaient, pour n'être, au loin, qu'une poussière d'étoiles fixes [. . .] Les plus reculés, sous les ponts, n'étaient que des petites touches de feu immobiles. (pp. 715–16)

Zola might even be seen to apply varnish to his word paintings: 'Sous le soleil, couleur de blé mûr, les rangées de marronniers avaient des feuilles neuves, d'un vert tendre, fraîchement verni' (p. 527). Ultimately, frames can be discerned around certain of his descriptions: 'Le long du Pont-Neuf, de grands omnibus jaunes, des tapissières bariolées, défilaient [. . .] Tout le fond s'encadrait là, dans les perspectives des deux rives' (p. 609). Zola's narratives sketch, paint and exhibit their word pictures.

As Zola's novel explores the interaction of print and paint, Cardinal's adaptation probes the interstices between camera and canvas. The camera provides the viewer with still lifes, framing, for example, a hat, candle and apple in Claude's studio. Likewise, not only do the desiring point-of-view shots from the perspective of Claude and Christine offer a series of intimate and reciprocal portraits in the Bennecourt sequence, but in a set of three static shots whose stillness isolates them from the flow of this television production, Cardinal offers us frozen pictures of Christine sprawled on Claude's chest and of Claude asleep across her breasts, and an intertwined shot of their hands. Landscapes also feature in Cardinal's artistic exhibition. When

Claude cannot sketch or even describe the landscapes he intends to put on canvas, Cardinal's adaptation inserts isolated static shots of the location in question, supplying the viewer with the landscape that its artist will never paint. That camera and canvas are complementary in Cardinal's adaptation is clear. The viewer is offered a shot of the painted figure of the back of Sandoz in a canvas before the camera cuts to its exact reflection, the front of the same figure in the same posture in the television adaptation. Camera and canvas appear as two halves of the same whole. The point-of-view shots from the perspective of the painting further the director's link between camera and canvas for they allow Cardinal to exchange and interchange both. He has his protagonist paint directly on the surface of the camera that has metaphorically become the canvas of this adaptation. Claude's actions simultaneously draw attention to television as the medium of this adaptation and highlight its links with the pictorial arts more generally.

However, Zola's interest in *L'Œuvre* lies not just with art in general, but with Impressionist art in particular. He famously stated: 'Je n'ai pas seulement soutenu les Impressionnistes, je les ai traduits en littérature, par les touches, notes, colorations, par la palette de beaucoup de mes descriptions.'[14] Zola in his novel finds literary equivalents for key Impressionist techniques and Cardinal adapts these painterly techniques into the medium of television. Zola, for example, characterizes focalization as one of the defining techniques of Impressionist painters:

> On les appelle aussi impressionnistes, parce que certains d'entre eux paraissent vouloir rendre surtout l'impression vraie des êtres et des choses, sans descendre dans une exécution minutieuse qui enlève toute sa verdeur et l'interprétation vive et personnelle.[15]

Zola's novel obsessively focalizes sections of the landscape in different seasons through the gaze of Claude, as the following quotation with its compulsive repetition of 'il la vit' underlines:

> il la vit fourrée d'hermine, au-dessus de l'eau couleur de boue, se détachant sur un ciel d'ardoise claire. Il la vit, aux premiers soleils, s'essuyer de l'hiver, retrouver une enfance, avec les pousses vertes des grands arbres du terre-plein. Il la vit, un jour de fin brouillard, se reculer, s'évaporer, légère et tremblante comme un palais des songes. (p. 624)

Whilst Cardinal's adaptation does not fixate on sections of the landscape, its repeated use of point-of-view shots echoes the Impressionist emphasis on focalization.

John Rewald situates the exploration of light and its effects on perception as key to Impressionism.[16] Zola's descriptions depict light in liquid terms, as a force eating into and altering the structures and lines of reality. In the sun's haze, a row of houses becomes 'une falaise rocheuse, s'enfonçant au milieu d'une mer phosphorescente' (p. 517). In a boating scene strongly reminiscent of numerous Impressionist paintings in its subject matter, Cardinal's camera not only traces the play of light over faces and water, but it turns to consider the source of that light, offering a direct shot of the sun. The sequence depicting the lovers' return to Paris also opens with a direct shot of the sun, a sun that is initially blue, subsequently yellow and ultimately orange. The colours with which this sun washes objects are colours to which Zola's Christine objects in Claude's paintings:

> Un jour qu'elle osait se permettre une critique, précisément à cause d'un peuplier lavé d'azur, il lui avait fait constater, sur la nature même, ce bleuissement délicat des feuilles. C'était vrai pourtant, l'arbre était bleu; mais, au fond, elle ne se rendait pas, condamnait la réalité: il ne pourrait y avoir des arbres bleus dans la nature. (p. 561)

Cardinal reproduces such colour washes and their effect in the medium of television. His adaptation opens in a studio flooded red and lilac by the storm raging outside. The audience that surveys Claude's painting, an audience depicted in a point of view shot from the painting itself, is washed by the colours of the work they contemplate. The faces of this audience are flooded lilac, yellow, pink, green, red and orange by the art work they dismiss. Impressionist experimentation in relation to notions of *décentrage* is echoed in Zola's fiction. Christine does not recognize Notre-Dame when it is seen from behind (p. 514). Cardinal's adaptation not only delights in filming from disconcerting vantage points, it also explores the Impressionist technique of cropping, of slicing images with the edge of the canvas to gesture towards the reality lying beyond the confines of the painting. The adaptation crops Paris from its vision as a whole, focusing instead on claustrophobic interiors. It situates events such as the wedding of Claude and Christine in the ellipsis of the fade to black between scenes. It shows the impact that Jacques's death has on his father and mother (his father paints and his mother weeps), but it refuses to show the viewer the source of that impact, the body itself. The camera moves to the edge of the cot, but this edge severs the shot, simultaneously gesturing towards and refusing the object that lies beyond it. Indeed, Jacques's body is revealed to the viewer only in adapted form, in the shape of Claude's painting of it. Cardinal's act of adaptation is thus intriguingly double. He reworks not only Zola's source novel, but also the Impressionist artistic techniques that informed it.

Cardinal thus adapts Zola who himself adapts the Impressionists. Yet, Zola's interest in adaptation extends even beyond this in *L'Œuvre* for he situates it as a key narrative theme. The painting by Fagerolles that is revered in the salon is a much adulterated adaptation of Claude's derided earlier work: 'Et il [Claude] retrouvait son *Plein Air* dans ce *Déjeuner*, la même note blonde, la même formule d'art, mais combien adoucie, truquée, gâtée, d'une élégance d'épiderme, arrangée avec une adresse infinie pour les satisfactions basses du public' (p. 671). Bongrand suggests that adaptation of Claude's work extends far beyond Fagerolles:

> Et, regarde! tu devrais être fier, car c'est toi le véritable triomphateur du Salon, cette année. Il n'y a pas que Fagerolles qui te pille, tous maintenant t'imitent, tu les as révolutionnés, depuis ton *Plein Air*, [. . .] Regarde, regarde! en voilà encore un de *Plein Air*, en voilà un autre, et ici, et là-bas, tous, tous! (pp. 679–80)

Adaptation, moreover, is not solely the preserve of painting in Zola's novel. Jory adapts his own work: 'Jory parut, enchanté de l'existence, racontant qu'il venait de retaper une vieille chronique, pour avoir sa soirée libre' (p. 591). Happiness, Zola's novel makes clear, may be found in the act of replication. Replication, as indicated by the use of the imperfect tense, is the foundation of the lovers' Bennecourt idyll:

> des mois coulèrent dans une félicité monotone. Jamais ils ne savaient la date, et ils confondaient tous les jours de la semaine [. . .] Et, le soir, ils mangeaient des soupes aux choux dans la cuisine, ils riaient de la bêtise de Mélie dont ils avaient ri la veille. (pp. 553–4)

The lovers find joy in the walk they take through Paris, 'cette promenade sans cesse répétée' (p. 515). However, Zola's novel makes clear that the act of replication is ultimately an impossible one in its fullest sense. Claude tries and fails to replicate his experience in Bennecourt:

> Alors, il eut un geste de malédiction, il jeta son chagrin à toute cette campagne si changée, où il ne retrouvait pas un vestige de leur existence. A quoi bon cette agitation vaine, si le vent, derrière l'homme qui marche, balaie et emporte la trace de ses pas? Il l'avait bien senti qu'il n'aurait point dû revenir, car le passé n'était que le cimetière de nos illusions, on s'y brisait contre des tombes. (p. 699)

Neither can Claude return to or recreate his time in the Café Baudequin: 'Le propriétaire avait changé trois fois; la salle n'était plus la même, repeinte, disposée autrement [...] les couches de consommateurs s'y étaient succédé, les unes recouvrant les autres, si bien que les anciennes avaient disparu comme des peuples ensevelis' (p. 701). Claude is unable ultimately to return to or adapt in paint the section of landscape that he so desires to render. This inability brings artistic death. Cardinal is equally aware of the fraught, perhaps impossible, nature of the endeavour to return to Zola's novel as earlier source. However, by conceptualizing and incorporating in the fabric of his production this inability by means of the blocked relationship between Christine's body and the portraits made of her, between source and repro-duction, he creates artistic, adaptive life out of what brought Zola's protagonist only death.

Cardinal's 1967 adaptation of Zola's 1886 *L'Œuvre* delivers, at first glance, a very different vision of the novelist's work, replacing its panoramas with an intimate, invasive close-up of the lives of the characters under its lens. However, Cardinal shares both the nineteenth-century novelist's fascination with the power of vision in general and, more particularly, the power of his own adaptive vision. Zola's text both assesses and conceptualizes the power of its words to capture a vision of reality as well as the methods of the Impressionist painters. Cardinal's adaptation integrates into the fabric of its fictions an analysis of the power of its own adaptive vision, of the programme's ability to render, in a different medium, the techniques and origin of Zola's source novel. Both novelist and film-maker offer nuanced portraits of their own creative vision, ultimately testifying to the inability of their art to return the reader-viewer fully to an earlier source, be it an experience, a model, a reality or a novel. However, whilst the recognition of such incapacity kills Zola's protagonist, it is precisely the dramatization of this same recognition that brings the revisionary narratives of Claude's creator and adaptor artistic life. Both Zola and Cardinal testify to the fraught, obstructed relationship between Christine and her reproductions, between original and adaptation, paradoxically creating art out of the recognition of artistic blockage.

Notes

[1] Emile Zola, *Œuvres complètes*, ed. Henri Mitterand, 15 vols (Paris: Cercle du Livre Précieux, 1962–9), V: *Les Rougon-Macquart* (1967), p. 600. Unless otherwise stated, all subsequent references are to this edition and are given in the body of the text.

[2] This inversion of direction through a window is not confined to Cardinal's adaptation. Roger Vadim's 1965 cinema adaptation of Zola's 1872 novel *La Curée*, an adaptation which, like Cardinal's *L'Œuvre*, amputates the source novel's broader social and historical context in order to focus on the central love triangle, does something comparable to underline what it omits. Vadim leaves his heroine, towards the film's close, peering in through a closed window at a world she cannot access. For further details, see Kate Griffiths, 'Hunt the Author: Zola, Vadim and *La Curée*', *Studies in European Cinema*, 2/1 (2005), 7–17.

[3] This monumentalizing shot offers something of a televisual transcription of Zola's descriptions of Christine's relationship with the painting: 'Cette peinture, qu'elle avait déjà acceptée sans restrictions, elle la haussa encore, au fond d'un tabernacle farouche, devant lequel elle demeurait écrasée' (p. 636).

[4] Christine's reflective function in relation to Claude is made clear in the novel. She has 'le front limpide, uni comme un clair miroir' (p. 442). Not only do her reactions mirror those of Claude ('Elle s'attristait, si elle le trouvait triste; elle s'égayait, quand il l'accueillait gaiement'), but so too do her words (p. 521). Whilst she cannot like Claude's painting, she nevertheless repeats Claude's 'mots d'artiste' in relation to it (p. 521).

[5] David Baguley, 'Zola, the novelist(s)', in Robert Lethbridge and Terry Keefe (eds), *Zola and The Craft of Fiction* (Leicester: Leicester University Press, 1990), pp. 15–27 (p. 23).

[6] See Peter Brooks, *Body Work: Objects of Desire in Modern Narrative* (Cambridge: Harvard University Press, 1993).

7   For further details on the relationship between artistic model and literary or painted reproduction, see Kate Griffiths, *Zola and the Artistry of Adaptation* (Oxford: Legenda, 2009).

8   For further details of the Cézanne–Zola relationship, see Robert J. Niess, *Zola, Cézanne and Manet: A Study of L'Œuvre* (Ann Arbor: University of Michigan Press, 1968).

9   For contrasting approaches to the Manet–Zola relationship, a relationship about which much has been written, see Robert Lethbridge, 'Manet's Textual Frames' in Peter Collier and Robert Lethbridge (eds), *Artistic Relations. Literature and the Visual Arts in Nineteenth-Century France* (New Haven: Yale University Press, 1994), pp. 144–58, and Elizabeth Briggs-Lynch, 'Manet's *Nana*: the connection with Zola's *L'Assommoir* and *Nana*', in Jean-Max Guieu and Alison Hilton (eds), *Emile Zola and the Arts* (Washington, DC: Georgetown University Press, 1988), pp. 9–14.

10 See Emile Zola, *Ecrits sur l'art*, ed. Jean-Pierre Leduc-Adine, (Paris: Gallimard, 1991).

11 Ibid., p. 145.

12 Ibid., pp. 109–10.

13 Henri Mitterand, 'Le Musée dans le texte', *Cahiers naturalistes*, 66 (1992), 13–22 (21).

14 Cited by Henri Hertz, 'Emile Zola, témoin de la vérité', *Europe 30* (1952), 83–4.

15 Emile Zola, *Ecrits sur l'art*, p. 313.

16 John Rewald, *The History of Impressionism* (New York: MOMA, 1961), p. 338.

Donner à voir: Poetic Language and Visual Representation according to Paul Éluard

Peter Hawkins

Paul Éluard is probably the best known and most widely read of the poets associated with the surrealist movement. He was an early supporter of Dada and one of the founder members of the surrealist movement in the early 1920s. Although less well known in the English-speaking world than the painters of the movement, his influence was considerable, not least on the British supporters of the movement such as Roland Penrose, with whom he collaborated on the 1936 London International Surrealist Exhibition. In general he left the theorizing of the movement to André Breton, but his version of surrealism is subtly different from that of the self-appointed 'Pope' of surrealism and guardian of its ideological purity. Éluard's surrealism grew out of very close collaboration with some of the pre-eminent visual artists associated with the movement, most notably Max Ernst in the early 1920s and Pablo Picasso in the 1930s, these two only the most famous of a long line of friends and fellow artists that includes Man Ray, René Magritte and Salvador Dali.

Donner à voir is a composite volume published by Éluard in 1939 that contains the essential elements of his theoretical writings on surrealism.[1] The date of 1939 is crucial: it coincides with Éluard's break with Breton and the surrealist movement proper. Éluard is henceforth free to formulate his own approach to the aesthetics of surrealism without submitting to the collective discipline of the group imposed by Breton. Ostensibly the break with Breton arose because of Éluard's increasing closeness to the French Communist Party, which he finally joined in the middle of the German Occupation, in 1942, after the breakdown of the Germano-Soviet pact and the invasion of Russia by Nazi forces.[2] From then on Éluard remained a loyal and questionably uncritical supporter of the Stalinist French Communist Party until his death in 1952, which is probably one reason for his relative neglect in the post-Cold War English-speaking world. Breton, on the other hand, remained a fervent supporter of Leon Trotsky and the notion of continuous revolution, and was from the first an acerbic critic of Stalinism.

Donner à voir thus appears at a crucial intermediary period in Éluard's development, between the years of commitment to the surrealist movement and to the Communist Party. Typically it is a volume that formulates its ideas poetically, rather than ideologically. *Donner à voir* is made up of a variety of texts, many of which had been published earlier, such as *L'Evidence poétique*, the lecture Éluard gave at the surrealist exhibition in London in 1936, and *Physique de la poésie*, a talk given at an international congress on aesthetics and art in Paris in 1937, covering Éluard's interpretations of Picasso, Ernst and Dali. These more discursive pieces are interspersed with surrealist prose texts and lyrical poems, but also poems directly inspired by the work of the many painters he had worked with over the previous two decades. Finally, the volume includes a long text called *Premières Vues anciennes*, also published earlier, which is made up of a collage of quotations from a range of literary figures from Shakespeare and Blake, through Lautréamont and German Romantics such as Goethe and Novalis, to Éluard's contemporaries, including Breton and Ernst. The principle governing these texts is that of 'signe ce que tu approuves', 'signing what you agree with'.[3] This represents Éluard's subversive use of systematic plagiarism as a way of formulating his own ideas in relation to those of a whole artistic heritage: in this he follows the principle formulated by Lautréamont, 'le plagiat est nécessaire'.[4] The principles of Éluard's aesthetics thus remain elusive, scattered across a collection of disparate texts, and many commentators have resisted attempting to synthesize them, whilst foregrounding their subtlety and their openness to myriad readings.[5] It will be necessary to extract and to interpret to some extent these lapidary statements in order to understand their broader aesthetic and cultural significance. My strategy is to juxtapose them thematically, in order to bring out their underlying coherence.

Eluard proposes here a general statement about the nature of the creative imagination:

> L'imagination n'a pas l'instinct d'imitation. Elle est la source et le torrent qu'on ne remonte pas. C'est de ce sommeil vivant que le jour naît et meurt à tout instant. Elle est l'univers sans association, l'univers qui ne fait pas partie d'un plus grand univers, l'univers sans dieu, puisqu'elle ne ment jamais, puisqu'elle ne confond jamais ce qui sera avec ce qui a été.[6]

It is interesting that Éluard gives precedence here to the importance of the poetic imagination, a relatively traditional post-Romantic idea, rather than to the notions of automatic writing or the Freudian unconscious that are more usually associated with surrealism. Even so, his view is resolutely subjective and obviously influenced by surrealist ideas of the imagination as a mysterious faculty that governs our consciousness, as something analogous to the unconscious: he calls it a 'sommeil vivant'. This suggests that it is a semi-conscious but continuous stream of psychic activity and thus very similar to the surrealist conception of the unconscious. For Éluard it is not part of the external world: it is an autonomous faculty where the rules governing 'reality' do not apply. It is not a mystical state, and he makes clear that for him it has no religious dimension, it is 'without God'; he seems to regard such notions as a lie. Yet it appears to be linked to an idea of human progress, a future fulfilment hinted at in the phrase 'ce qui sera'. It is a universe with no fixed patterns of association, 'sans association': in it all combinations are possible. This idea is explained in a second extract, a general statement of the principle of free association and surrealist imagery, opening up the creative possibilities of poetic consciousness: 'Tout est comparable à tout, tout trouve son écho, sa raison, sa ressemblance, son opposition, son devenir partout. Et ce devenir est infini.'[7] This often repeated maxim applies not simply to poetic free association, but also, by implication, to visual representation. Not only words, but concepts and images can be freely juxtaposed and associated: it is easy to see this principle at work in the paintings of Éluard's friends and associates, such as Ernst, Dali or Magritte. For Éluard, poems and paintings are both representations of this imaginative process, which for him reveals the hidden workings of the consciousness. It is this imaginative faculty that structures our awareness of the world, and surrealist poets as well as painters are involved in the exploration of its processes. What Éluard's statement of principle does not explain, however, is the nature of the relationships established in this way, the nature of the subterranean links created by poetry and painting. Éluard is content to gesture towards an infinity of possibilities, without wishing in any way to restrict the process of interpretation, or to determine what the results of such experimentation might be.

In the following two extracts, Éluard makes a polemical, almost Dadaist attack on the tradition of figurative painting, probably in order to explain more clearly the difference and the importance of surrealist practice and that of modern painting in general:

Les peintres ont été victimes de leurs moyens. La plupart d'entre eux s'est misérablement bornée à reproduire le monde. Quand ils faisaient leur portrait, c'était en se regardant dans un miroir, sans songer qu'ils étaient eux-mêmes un miroir. Mais ils en enlevaient le tain, comme ils enlevaient le tain de ce miroir qu'est le monde extérieur, en le considérant comme extérieur. En copiant une pomme, ils en affaiblissaient terriblement la réalité sensible. On dit d'une bonne copie d'une pomme: «On en mangerait.» Mais il ne viendrait à personne l'idée d'essayer. Pauvres natures mortes, pauvres paysages, figurations vaines d'un monde où pourtant tout s'agrippe aux sens de l'homme, à son esprit, à son cœur. Tout ce qui importe vraiment, c'est de participer, de bouger, de comprendre.[8]

Longtemps ravalés au rang de scribes, les peintres copiaient des pommes et devenaient des virtuoses. Leur vanité, qui est immense, les a presque toujours poussés à s'installer devant une image, devant un texte, comme devant un mur, pour le répéter. Ils n'avaient pas faim d'eux-mêmes. Les peintres surréalistes, qui sont des poètes, pensent toujours à autre chose. L'insolite leur est familier, la préméditation inconnue. Ils savent que les rapports entre les choses, à peine établis, s'effacent pour en laisser intervenir d'autres, aussi fugitifs. Ils savent que rien ne se décrit suffisamment, que rien ne se reproduit littéralement. Ils poursuivent tous le même effort pour libérer la vision, pour joindre l'imagination à la nature, pour considérer tout ce qui est possible comme réel, pour montrer qu'il n'y a pas

de dualisme entre l'imagination et la réalité, que tout ce que l'homme peut concevoir et créer provient de la même veine, est de la même *matière* que sa chair,
que son sang et que le monde qui l'entoure. Ils savent qu'il n'y a rien d'autre que
communication entre ce qui voit et ce qui est vu, effort de compréhension, de
relation – parfois de détermination, de création. Voir c'est comprendre, juger,
déformer, oublier ou s'oublier, être ou disparaître.[9]

The emphasis here is once again on the creative possibilities of the visual
imagination as the faculty of interpreting the real world in a new and adventurous way. Human consciousness and the material world are both conceived
as mirrors, each reflecting the interpretive process of the imagination. This
activity is presented as the inspiration for surrealist painting, but also as an
activity in which all human beings are engaged, and in which the spectator
is also implicated. The last sentence of the above quotation, 'Voir c'est comprendre [. . .]' becomes another of Éluard's talisman principles, which he
reasserts in many different contexts. It emphasizes the importance of the
creative processes involved in seeing, which are the opposite of a simple
process of recording and representing reality, as practised by figurative
painters, according to Éluard. What this leaves out of account is the process
of painting itself, which can make a still life or a self-portrait just as revealing
as a more avant-garde composition. It also ignores the extent to which
surrealist painters were still involved in the process of imitation and representation. The reference to apples in Éluard's polemical commentary recalls the
very lifelike apples meticulously painted by Magritte in many of his most
famous paintings. In order to juxtapose elements of reality in a subversive
way, a surrealist painter has first to represent them, and often in a more
conventional way, as in the paintings of Magritte or Dali. What is striking
even so, in the second extract, is the equivalence established by Éluard
between poets and painters: both are involved in the same activity of creative
reinvention of the world, in the light of their imaginative activity.

Éluard cites the example of Picasso, a close friend and collaborator in the
second half of the 1930s, when Picasso realized many portraits of Éluard's
wife Nusch and illustrated the texts of many of his poems.[10] The following
passage emphasizes the mutual inspiration of poet and painter, and the
exemplary creativity of Picasso's vision:

À partir de Picasso, les murs s'écroulent. Le peintre ne renonce pas plus à sa réalité qu'à la réalité du monde. Il est devant un poème comme le poète devant un tableau. Il rêve, il imagine, il crée. Et soudain, voici que l'objet virtuel naît de l'objet réel, qu'il devient réel à son tour, voici qu'ils font image, du réel au réel, comme un mot avec tous les autres. On ne se trompe plus d'objet, puisque tout s'accorde, se lie, se fait valoir, se remplace.[11]

One might summarize Éluard's polemical argument in terms of the opposition between denotation and connotation: figurative painting attempts to define the appearance of an object or a scene; surrealist painting invites the spectator to look beyond literal representation to the secondary associations of the images presented, and to the process of interpretation itself. Here again the process of free association is common to painters and to poets, and concerns both visual imagery and words. Picasso's creative vision is the same as that of the reader of a poem, and the same as that of a poet interpreting a painting: a process of imaginative interpretation expressed in words or in images. Éluard underscores the relevance of these ideas to poetry:

Le poète est celui qui inspire, bien plus que celui qui est inspiré. Les poèmes ont de grandes marges blanches, de grandes marges de silence où la mémoire ardente se consume pour créer un délire sans passé. Leur principale qualité est non pas, je le répète, d'évoquer, mais d'inspirer.[12]

The opening sentence of the above passage is another of Éluard's reiterated poetic principles, explaining and developing the idea of Lautréamont, often quoted by Éluard: 'La poésie doit être faite par tous. Non par un.'[13] The text of the poem is an invitation to the reader's creative imagination, to explore the resonances and connotations of the words in the space of the 'grandes marges blanches', in much the same way as the spectator of a surrealist painting might interpret the paradoxical images presented in it, using the space of a gallery to meditate on them. Éluard is concerned to go beyond the Romantic notion of the poet as privileged visionary, as the inspired communicator of higher truths: his aim is to democratize poetic inspiration, to make it accessible to all readers of his poems, as part of the process of reading. For him the role of the poem is not to evoke reality but, rather, to stimulate the reader's imagination. This is the function of poetic language, to which he ascribes this particular creative function, which is separate from that of accounts of dreams or automatic writing; in this respect he diverges from the surrealist orthodoxy, as we shall see. The following two extracts reiterate a point of contention between Éluard and Breton which dates back to as early as 1926, when these observations were first formulated:

> On ne prend pas le récit d'un rêve pour un poème. Tous deux sont des réalités vivantes, mais le premier est souvenir, tout de suite usé, transformé, une aventure, et du deuxième rien ne se perd ni ne change. Le poème désensibilise l'univers au seul profit des facultés humaines, permet à l'homme de voir autrement, d'autres choses. Son ancienne vision est morte, ou fausse. Il découvre un nouveau monde, il devient un nouvel homme.[14]

> On a pu penser que l'écriture automatique rendait les poèmes inutiles. Non: elle augmente, développe seulement le champ de l'examen de conscience poétique, en l'enrichissant. Si la conscience est parfaite, les éléments de l'écriture automatique extrait du monde intérieur et les éléments du monde extérieur s'équilibrent. Réduits alors à égalité, ils s'entremêlent, se confondent pour former l'unité poétique.[15]

For Breton the inspiration of dreams and the process of automatic writing were the primordial activities of surrealism, intended to supplant the formal notion of the poem, regarded by him as a superseded relic of bourgeois aesthetics.[16] Éluard had always disagreed, regarding the poem as the primary expression of the creative vision in textual form, as he explains here, open to the active participation of the reader and the possibility of a renewed human consciousness available to all. For Éluard the poem is aesthetically autonomous, even if automatic writing has played a part in its composition. This is a somewhat 'heretical' view in relation to the hard-line surrealist position represented by Breton, and it illustrates the way Éluard's ideas at this point are moving in the direction of a broad humanism and away from the total revolt against 'bourgeois' aesthetics championed by Breton.

Éluard's reflection on the nature of poetic language is captured in this statement: 'Il nous faut peu de mots pour exprimer l'essentiel; il nous faut tous les mots pour le rendre réel.'[17] Here he contrasts the reductive, analytical use of language with its creative poetic purpose and refuses any restriction in vocabulary that might limit his poetic vision and his ability to 'make it real', to share it with his readers. This fragment of his reflection coincides with an interesting poetic essay published by Éluard in 1937 entitled *Quelques-uns des mots qui jusqu'ici m'étaient mystérieusement interdits*, which might be described as a playful attempt to broaden his poetic vocabulary and its imaginative hinterland by a process of free association.[18] This illustrates how Éluard needs to feel unrestricted in his use of language, so as to render his vision accessible to as wide an audience as possible, to open up his poetic inspiration to the participation of his readers.

Éluard aspires to a synthesis between poetry and visual representation:

> Le langage est un fait social, mais ne peut-on espérer qu'un jour le dessin, comme le langage, comme l'écriture, le deviendra et qu'avec eux, il passera du social à l'universel. Tous les hommes communiqueront par la vision des choses et cette vision des choses leur servira à exprimer le point qui leur est commun, à eux, aux choses, à eux comme choses, aux choses comme eux. Ce jour-là, la véritable voyance aura intégré l'univers à l'homme – c'est à dire l'homme à l'univers.[19]

In spite of Éluard's pious hope, drawing is unlikely to become quite as fundamental to human society as language, but it is interesting to observe that in the years since Éluard's death the visual imagery of surrealism has been inducted into the cultural heritage of humanity: the canvases of Dali, Picasso or Magritte have become familiar icons at a global level, regularly referenced in advertising, graphic design and illustration. This has happened largely at the expense of their potential as imaginative stimulus, in the spirit of surrealism and of Éluard's utopian idealism. Éluard's poetry, on the other hand, has remained largely a prisoner of its linguistic context within French culture, even if it has maintained its poetic charge. For Éluard, poetic expression was spontaneously visual in its use of imagery in language, just as surrealist painting was spontaneously poetic in its juxtaposition of visual images. The two functions grew out of the same imaginative activity, which for him was an essential part of the interpretation of the world, for all human beings as well as for poets and artists. In this respect, surrealist poetry and painting for Éluard would contribute to an imaginative revolution accessible to all human beings, bringing about a transformation of their relations with the real world. The nineteenth-century poetic ideal of 'Voyance' would no longer be reserved for a few poetic visionaries like Hugo or Rimbaud, but would be available to all. This belief is one of the central elements of Éluard's later revolutionary commitment, and flies in the face of the values of 'socialist realism' propagated by the Communist Party in the post-war years.

In the late 1930s Éluard collaborated extensively with many visual artists on luxury limited editions of his poems illustrated with prints by famous artists, such as Picasso, Man Ray, Hans Bellmer, Stanley Hayter, Valentine Hugo and others.[20] Interestingly, he decided to reverse the usual process of composition of these collections when he 'illustrated' some drawings of Man Ray with poems inspired by them, rather than the other way round.

To gain an idea of Éluard's poetic practice in relation to visual material, we can turn to a typical example of this collaboration, 'L'Attente', from the collection *Les Mains libres* of 1938, where both image and text are reproduced in the Pléiade edition of Éluard's collected works.[21] Characteristically, Éluard interprets Man Ray's drawing of a 'cat's cradle' in the form of a cobweb between two hands in terms of an amorous relationship: he was most celebrated as a love poet, and eroticism is one of the main inspirations for his poetic vision. Thus it is tempting to read this juxtaposition of the line, an alexandrine in form, 'Je n'ai jamais tenu sa tête dans mes mains', with the image of the cat's cradle as suggesting the negative effect of the absence of the loved one on the poet's vision. The hands and their sensory responses are redundant and decaying in the absence of the loved one. The hypothetical space between the two hands is filled not by the head of the loved one, but with the threads of a cobweb linking the hands and fingers in its place. This, in the light of Éluard's interest in the process of free association, suggests the opposite of the decay evoked by the idea of the cobweb: rather, the links that can be established in the head of the loved one by her presence. As he was to declare later, 'Le mal doit être mis au bien', especially in matters of sentiment.[22] This 'free association' produces a reversal of the connotations of the image. The cobweb may then be seen to suggest the links, perhaps the neurones and synapses in the brain of both the loved one, the poet and his reader, which can be seen to exemplify the principle that 'Tout est comparable à tout', everything may be linked to everything else, as long as one has the inspiration to see it. For Éluard this inspiration is very much bound up with the presence of the loved one, with the stimulation of a sexual relationship. So the drawing and its text, in spite of its apparent negativity, can be taken to illustrate some of the latent themes of Éluard's aesthetic principles, as I outlined above. This is only one possible reading of the image and its accompanying text, of course, but it is one that can be justified in terms of the themes and pre-occupations that Éluard has formulated elsewhere, and in particular in the broadly contemporaneous volume *Donner à voir*.

Another key example of Éluard's 'illustrating' the work of a visual artist is provided by the famous poem 'La Victoire de Guernica,' broadly con-temporary with the composition of *Donner à voir* and with the period of close collaboration with Picasso.[23] The poem was clearly inspired by the notorious unprovoked bombing of the town of Guernica by the German aviation during the Spanish Civil War. It is often associated with the giant canvas *Guernica* painted by Picasso as a protest against the bombing, one of the first examples of a civilian population being attacked in such a way. The relation between the poem and the painting is an elusive one, however. It is clear that it also represents one of the first examples of Éluard's writing a poem in response to a political event, something which was to become much more prevalent in his later work, particularly during the German Occu-pation of France and the subsequent Cold War period. Jean-Claude Gateau has investigated the conditions of Éluard's composition of the poem, and contends that it was inspired not by Picasso's finished canvas, but by a series of etchings completed earlier by Picasso in preparation for the larger work, entitled 'Songe et mensonge de Franco'.[24] The fourteen sections of the poem were intended to correspond to the fourteen prints of the series, and it was Éluard's original purpose for them to be published together. Picasso had other plans, however, and published the prints accompanied by a text of his own. Éluard then published the poem separately, but it is clear that its origin lies in the inspiration of Picasso's series of prints. The relation is not a direct one, even so: Éluard's text is often an oblique commentary on the images rather than a direct illustration of them, as can be seen from the reproduction provided by Jean-Charles Gateau.[25] The imaginative hinterland of the poem is significantly different from the series of prints, not least in the bitter irony of the 'victory' of the title, achieved at the expense of an unarmed population, and the moral 'victory' of the final resolve to vanquish its perpetrators: 'Nous en aurons raison.' It is clear, however, that the poem does even so represent an example of shared inspiration between the painter and the poet, and all the more significant for being based on their response to a landmark political event. The powerful inspiration of the two works, the poem and the final, monumental canvas for readers and spectators is well illustrated by their iconic status, since they are often reproduced together, in spite of the indirect relation between them, and they have often been a point of reference for later artists, such as Alain Resnais in his short documentary film of 1952, *Guernica*. Together they illustrate the effectiveness of Éluard's aesthetic practice and the richness of his constant collaboration with the artists associated with the surrealist movement.

It is possible to extract from *Donner à voir* the elements of an aesthetic theory that, although broadly inspired by surrealism, remains particular to Éluard. *Donner à voir* shares with the movement the importance attached to the poetic imagination and the role of free association; it recognizes the contribution of the techniques of automatic writing and the accounts of dreams, but subordinates them to a conception of the role of the poem and poetic language which is central to the poem's function as popular inspiration. This is conceived as being analogous to the role of the surrealist painter, and it is clearly the influence of figures such as Max Ernst or Picasso that inspires Éluard's conception of poetry. For Éluard the poem is analogous to the surrealist canvas, and the painters with whom he works are conceived as poets as much as visual artists: he constantly blurs the distinction between the painter and the poet. The conscious work of the elaboration of the canvas is perhaps comparable to that of the composition of the poem, and certainly both invite an imaginative response on the part of the reader or the spectator. Éluard is attentive to the role of poetic form and language in much the same way as his painter collaborators to the effects of their medium, whether paint or ink.

Éluard's vision of poetry and visual imagery is resolutely utopian, as were most of the principles of the surrealist movement, which were not supposed to be restricted to the aesthetic elite who formulated them but in theory available to all human beings. Yet, even so, Éluard carried these beliefs into his later political commitment to the French Communist Party, in spite of the dictates of Stalinist socialist realism emanating from Moscow.[26] His poetry has remained remarkably popular and accessible in spite of the waning influence of the Communist Party. Now that the Cold War politics of the post-war era has receded, a reassessment of his importance as one of the major figures of surrealism and one of the major poets of the French twentieth century is urgent. As an interlocutor of some of the major painters of the modern era and a collector and commentator of their canvases, Éluard's contribution to the relation between literature and the visual arts has been astonishingly far reaching and critically undervalued.[27]

Notes

[1] References to the works of Éluard are to the *Œuvres complètes*, vols I and II, ed. Marcelle Dumas and Lucien Scheler (Paris: NRF/Gallimard, 1968 (Bibliothèque de la Pléiade)).

[2] See Jean-Charles Gateau, *Paul Éluard et la peinture surréaliste (1910–1939)* (Geneva: Droz, 1982, Histoire des idées et critique littéraire, vol. 204), pp. 257–8.

[3] Éluard, *Avenir de la poésie*, in *Œuvres complètes*, I, p. 527.

[4] Quoted in *Premières vues anciennes*, in Éluard, *Œuvres complètes*, I, 996.

[5] Even the authoritative commentator Jean-Charles Gateau remains daunted by the enterprise: 'Il n'entre pas dans notre propos d'étudier la dialectique de cet ouvrage, qu'une thèse n'épuiserait pas. Les effets de connexion y sont infinis, et le rassemblement des textes leur donne une «masse critique» propre à amorcer toutes les réactions', *Paul Éluard et la poésie surréaliste*, p. 333.

[6] Éluard, *L'Evidence poétique*, in *Œuvres complètes*, I, p. 514.

[7] Éluard, *Avenir de la poésie*, in *Œuvres complètes*, I, p. 527. It reappears in *Premières vues anciennes*, I, p. 971.

[8] Éluard, *Je parle de ce qui est bien*, in *Œuvres complètes*, I, p. 941.

[9] Éluard, *L'Evidence poétique*, in *Œuvres complètes*, I, p. 515.

[10] A typical example would be 'Grand air', reproduced in Louis Parrot and Jean Marcenac, *Paul Éluard* (Paris: Seghers, 1969) (Poètes d'aujourd'hui series, no. 1), p. 48.

[11] Éluard, *Physique de la poésie*, in *Œuvres complètes*, I, p. 938.

[12] Éluard, *L'Evidence poétique*, in *Œuvres complètes*, I, p. 515.

[13] As in the conclusion of *Premières vues anciennes*, in Éluard, *Œuvres complètes*, I, p. 553.

[14] This extract comes from *Premières vues anciennes*, in Éluard, *Œuvres completes*, I, p. 550, which was originally written as a preface to Éluard's 1926 collection *Les Dessous d'une vie ou La pyramide humaine*.

[15] Éluard, *Premières vues anciennes*, in *Œuvres complètes*, I, p. 979.

[16] As, for instance, in the definition of surrealism given by Breton in the first *Manifeste du Surréalisme*: 'Dictée de la pensée, en l'absence de tout contrôle exercé par la raison, en dehors de toute préoccupation esthétique ou morale', in André Breton, *Manifestes du Surréalisme* (Paris: Gallimard, 1972), p. 35.

[17] Éluard, *Avenir de la poésie*, in *Œuvres complètes*, I, p. 526.

[18] Éluard, *Œuvres complètes*, I, pp. 691–718.

[19] Éluard, *Je parle de ce qui est bien*, in *Œuvres complètes*, I, p. 944.

[20] The full range is given in the exhibition catalogue, Annick Lionel-Marie (ed.), *Eluard et ses amis peintres, 1895–1952* (Paris: Centre Georges Pompidou et Musée National d'Art Moderne, 1992).

[21] Éluard, 'L'Attente', in *Œuvres complètes*, I, pp. 636–7.

[22] See Éluard, *Œuvres complètes,* II, p. 304.

[23] See Éluard, *Œuvres complètes*, I, pp. 812–14 and notes, 1525–6.

[24] See Jean-Charles Gateau, *Éluard, Picasso et la peinture (1936–1952)* (Geneva: Droz, 1983, Histoire des idées et critique littéraire, vol. 212), pp. 52–6.

[25] See ibid. p. 54.

[26] See Gateau, *Paul Éluard*, pp. 325–6 and subsequent chapter.

[27] See the exhibition catalogue, Lionel-Marie (ed.), *Eluard et ses amis peintres, 1895–1952*.

'La lettre au cinéma n'est pas une excellente solution': A Heteromedial Analysis of Chantal Akerman's Proust Adaptation

Jørgen Bruhn

When probing the intricate relation between the visual and the verbal, often translated into the registers of the image and the text, it is salient to discuss the work of Marcel Proust. In this chapter I pursue what I call a 'heteromedial' point of view in order to focus on one of the fascinating relationships connecting Marcel Proust and the arts, namely the relation between his writings and later cinematic adaptations of his work. I begin by making a brief sketch of the reception of Proust in an interart/intermedial perspective, which will lead me to consider the relation of Proust's work to cinema. I shall concern myself almost exclusively with Chantal Akerman's film adaptation of Proust's *La Prisonnière*, entitled *La Captive*, focusing on the opening scene. The discussion of Akerman's work will first necessitate a short description of my theoretical framework, where I propose a wider understanding of intermediality.

Marcel Proust created a handful of fictive but extremely lifelike artists in *À la recherche du temps perdu*, each of whom had not only a physiognomy and a psychological profile, but represented a well-defined aesthetic theory, and each of whom created entire artistic (though fictional) oeuvres. Partly as a result of this, and also because Proust's narrator discusses the fine arts incessantly, Proust's work has been investigated from a comparative art perspective.[1] In one typical reception, the poetics of the narrator and the different theories and (fictive) aesthetic practices of the artists in the novel were read as masked descriptions of real artists: the author Bergotte 'was' Anatole France, Elstir the painter 'was' Monet and the composer Vinteuil 'was' Fauré or perhaps Saint-Saëns. Furthermore, models for the art pieces described in the novel were sought in 'real' works outside the fiction. After the first waves of biographical research a new trend emerged, where the fictive autonomy of the artists was respected to the extent that the fictive painter Elstir was taken seriously as an autonomous artist whose work could, paradoxically, be as interesting as Claude Monet's. Here, the poetics of the narrator in À la recherche, and of 'Bergotte', entered aesthetic discussions as if they occupied real, intellectually valid positions to be argued against.[2] Thus, where I approach Proust from a modified comparative arts point of view I am not adopting an entirely new perspective, even if the specific perspective I am interested in is among the least investigated.

The only interart relation in À la recherche du temps perdu that remained unresearched for many years was Proust's relation to cinema. That vacuum in Proust studies has been filled to a certain degree by a short overview by Peter Kravanja in Proust au cinéma, by Melissa Anderson's essay 'In search of adaptation. Proust on film', and by Yves Baudelle's more substantial article on 'Proust et le cinéma'; finally, in 2004, Martine Beugnet and Marion Schmid published the very significant Proust at the Movies (2004) which will be important for my discussion below.[3]

Beugnet and Schmid examine the question of 'Proust on film' on five different levels. Proust's personal views on and knowledge about cinema are established: 'He never set foot in a cinema in his lifetime', which did not prevent him from detesting this emerging, popular technological invention, which he could not imagine having any artistic merit worth the name.[4] Secondly, Beugnet and Schmid establish and discuss the way that Proust argues for his own poetological position (in Le Temps retrouvé) by criticizing cinema and a cinematographic approach to reality. A third aspect concerns so-called cinematographic aspects that have marked À la recherche, and reveals hitherto hidden sources of (probably unconscious) inspiration behind À la recherche.[5] A fourth aspect concerns the historical explanations behind the different adaptations of *À la recherche*: it is a colourful story of shipwrecked manuscripts, daring investors and persistent directors. Finally, Beugnet and Schmid discuss in depth the different versions of *À la recherche* that are turned into film script and/or film. Beugnet's and Schmid's book is highly informed when it comes to contemporary theories of adaptation, and offers important readings of the five full-length movies based on Proust's novel: Schlöndorff's *Un amour de Swann*, Ruiz's *Le Temps retrouvé*, Akerman's *La Captive*, and Carpio's *Quartetto Basileus* and *Le Intermittenze del cuore*.

The adaptation on which I shall focus in this chapter is Chantal Akerman's *La Captive*.[6] *La Captive* is a 'free' adaptation; indeed, the entire film questions the possibility of literary adaptation.[7] This may explain why Akerman has chosen to film the neurotically obsessed volume *La Prisonnière*, a volume almost exclusively focused on the extreme jealousy of the narrator towards Albertine whom he loves, desires and hates all at the same time. It is a novel that poses the question of the possibility of transforming literature into film in a particularly acute way, because, as Beugnet and Schmid ask: 'How can a film give visual form to a mental obsession?' (p. 171).

In contradistinction to Schlöndorff's faithful recreation of the belle époque elements in *À la recherche* and Ruiz's neo-baroque and dreamlike rereading of *Le Temps retrouvé*, Chantal Akerman's version is the least extravagant version of the three when it comes to *mise en scène*. Instead of choosing a luxurious setting, Akerman has reduced everything to a few locations in Paris and to a journey to (probably) Normandy at the end of the film: this may be interpreted as an implicit critique of the spectacular heritage film. But, if the geographic setting is recognizable, the historical period is much more difficult to define. A car typical of the 1950s is driven around a Parisian milieu of today, while mobile phones are juxtaposed with clothes reminiscent of the early decades of the twentieth century.

This perplexing historical setting is commented on by Beugnet and Schmid (p. 178), who explain it by referring to Proust's attempt to create a sense of timelessness for the reader of *À la recherche*. This may be one of the clues to the curious chronotopic setting of the film.[8] However, this aspect of the work can be better understood by referring to Jean Cocteau's important concept of 'poésie cinématographique', a technique which mixes high and low elements, stylized and everyday dimensions, dream and reality, and which has been defined as 'the intersection of legend with quotidian reality' and 'the incursion of the modern world of the quotidian into the normally timeless *fable*'.[9] With this technique Cocteau aimed to create a viewer-position split between reading the film mimetically and interpreting the film as emblematic of other dimensions of life. This split position may relate to Akerman's work where the realism of the everyday scenes combined with the ahistorical setting seems to suggest philosophical, existential and psychological dimensions integral to the film.

Akerman has been frank about her strategy for dealing with one of the canonical texts of French literature. She has stressed, for instance, that when she wrote the manuscript (with Erik de Kuyper) she relied on her rather blurred but nevertheless vivid memories of reading isolated parts of *À la recherche* in her adolescence. She has described the writing of the manuscript as a mixture of the recreation of an earlier reading and the creation of a wholly new cinematic universe.[10] This is, of course, further explanation of the strategy of the director when it comes to the chronotopic mixture – or *poésie cinématographique* – involving both the *elision* of a number of central elements from *La Prisonnière* and the *creation* of new scenes.

Interestingly, Akerman has stated that she had considered adapting Proust for the screen as early as 1975 after filming her breakthrough *Jeanne Dielman, 23 Quai du Commerce, 1080 Bruxelles*, but that she chose not to because of her reservations concerning the relation between literature and film. She has claimed, according to Beugnet and Schmid, that she was at the time 'too puritan and dogmatic' about the use of literary works in film:

> I thought that literary works should not be adapted to film, that music should not be used, that cuts and shots/countershots should not be used – these kind of prohibitions. I was very radical, undoubtedly too much so, but I needed to be in order to define myself, form myself as a filmmaker.[11]

This statement of Akerman's earlier assumptions is relevant here for two reasons. First, because her comments support one aspect of my concept of heteromedial studies, namely that the relations between the arts – here cinema versus literary narrative – are very often antagonistic, or at least rest on rather precarious foundations. Secondly, even if Akerman claims that her radical anti-literary approach belongs to an earlier chapter in her aesthetic development, it appears that traces of this sceptical relationship to literature prevail in her later aesthetic considerations (which we discover in her interviews) and in her aesthetic practice, namely her adaptation of *À la recherche*.

Related to the specific way she has handled the novel (altering the names, the forgetting and remembering of scenes and passages, the mixing of times and places), she states: 'La lettre au cinéma n'est pas une excellente solution surtout lorsqu'il y a une adaptation littéraire en jeu. On ne peut pas s'inspirer du livre sinon cela devient une sorte de bataille – perdue d'avance – contre la littérature.'[12] The remains of this more or less fierce *bataille* in her film are fascinating: Akerman cannot escape the antagonistic core inherent in almost all adaptations. Thus Akerman's adaptation exemplifies what might be termed the Hegelian master-and-slave relationship of cinematic adaptations. It is to this dialectic interdependence of intertwined powers that I turn now in order to analyse the opening scene of the film.

The three-minute opening scene of the film is preceded by a one-minute credit line, which in the background, behind the text, makes sound and image represent the sea at night, thus gesturing towards the end of the film where Ariane drowns. The credits directly anticipate the opening scene where Simon has filmed Ariane and her friends at the sea, in daylight. *La Captive* brims with intertextual references; the final scene, for instance, combines a visual reference to Böcklin's *The Isle of the Dead*, and to Rachmaninov's symphony of the same name.[13] Earlier on *Cosi fan Tutte* (a work exploring love and betrayal) dominates the soundtrack.[14] The choice of Ariane as the name of the protagonist may refer to the Cretan labyrinth as a metaphor for the labyrinths of love and jealousy in the novel that are recreated in the film. Undoubtedly the most persistent cinematic intertextual reference is to Alfred Hitchcock's *Vertigo*. *Vertigo* seems to have inspired the entire setting of the film, and possibly Akerman also wishes to remind us that Hitchcock himself, in his work on the obsessive love affair with the woman named Madeleine, may have made a kind of Proustian adaptation. Melissa Anderson notes that 'Akerman shrewdly makes the connection between Proust and *Vertigo*, visually quoting moments from Hitchcock's film' and, therefore, '*La Captive* makes *Vertigo* seem Proustian and *À la recherche du temps perdu* seem Hitchcockian.'[15]

In the chronological construction of the movie the introductory scene is supposed to be the very last of the scenes, that is, after Simon and Ariane ('Marcel'/'I' and 'Albertine' in the novel) have lived together, and after Ariane, probably as a result of a suicide, drowns at the end of the movie. The scene is highly complicated and deliciously simple at the same time. A young man is projecting what looks like a super-8mm film, probably at home: the short film strip, presumably made by him, in faded colours without sound, shows a number of young girls at the beach, playing volleyball, swimming, joking and posing for the camera. In particular, one of the girls seems to have caught the attention of the cameraman: the girl will later be isolated and distinguished as Ariane. Slowly the viewer detects the real purpose of Simon's rather neurotic and repetitive replaying of a single sequence, namely that he tries to lip-read Ariane's words, which, by repeating them aloud for himself, he reads, hears or sees as 'Je vous aime bien'. After having decoded and repeated these words, he sits in front of the projector, and, from the point of view of the spectator, he seems to share, symbolically, the same space as Ariane. A denotative, relatively objective reading of the sequence cannot take us much further, but a number of important aspects lurk under the surface of this cinematic text.

At first sight this opening scene might appear to recycle the mainstream cliché of the traditional sentimental longing for the lost loved woman, and this is, albeit in a sophisticated and mediated sense, an important part of the scene as well as the entire film. However, the scene clearly has a much wider significance. One way of approaching the richer meaning is by acknowledging the strong dichotomy between Ariane and Simon. Whereas the deceased Ariane is a silenced, passive, absent, seen, dead *woman*, Simon is a speaking, acting, seeing living *man*, who films and thus actively objectifies Ariane. Structured in this way, the content of the scene seems to be something of a textbook illustration of the well-known scheme in (traditional) psychoanalytic/ feminist film criticism. In 1975 Laura Mulvey defined an objectifying male gaze that was identified, *inter alia*, with the work of Hitchcock, which was seen as typical of the representation of the pleasures of the male gaze.[16] If we take a closer look at the scene, the apparently objectifying Hitchcockian gaze is not the most appropriate tool of analysis. Instead of trying to establish a kind of visual monologue, which would justify the male-gaze thesis, Simon is instead establishing a dialogue. The dialogue is not only part of the attempt to make Ariane speak; it is also, and perhaps more importantly, part of the economy of gazes suggested in the scene. Ariane seems to object to being objectified, mainly by looking back at the recording Simon, but her very direct gaze *into the camera* is also aimed at the spectator who is confronted by a very lively and subversive subjective subject. Ariane's 'to-be-looked-at-ness' (Mulvey) is redirected *against* both Simon and the spectator.[17]

The neat dichotomy also breaks down in the succeeding narrative where the content and ideological substance of most elements of the dichotomy is deconstructed. Ariane is, for instance, in many ways stronger and more self-confident than is Simon (partly because she contains the secret of lesbianism so mysterious and attractive both to Marcel in the novel and to Simon in the film), and even if she dies at the end of the film it might easily be argued that Simon is merely surviving her death. He is living a deathly existence, desperately trying to substitute the emptiness in his life by taking over and controlling Ariane's life. So when the dichotomy and the deconstruction of the steady contradictions are worked through, we may glimpse a complicated and disturbing configuration of death and absence penetrating not only the female part (the dead Ariane), but also the male protagonist of the film.

However, my concern is not the crippling absence of love (and the substitution of love with the intense emotions of jealousy), or the relation between depression and desire. Instead, I shall propose a heteromedial reading of this particular scene that may illuminate important parts of Akerman's entire cinematic adaptation of Proust.

Interart studies, with subcategories such as 'word and image studies' and 'music and image studies', has developed as an important subfield of comparative literature and art history in the twentieth and twenty-first centuries. The three arts commonly referenced are literature, the visual arts and music with their presumed basic components of words, images and sound. Interart studies deals with the relations *between* the arts, and the object of research of such studies has been conceptualized along different lines, but often focus has been on, for instance, studies of ekphrasis, of so-called artistic *Doppelbegabungen,* or adaptations from music to poetry. One of the most important parts of interart studies has been the investigation of adaptations of novels into film. However, with the impact of cultural studies from the 1960s (the critique of the traditional hierarchy of the arts in relation to other cultural forms of expression) and the influence of more recent trends in artistic and technological products (hybrids in the arts such as performance and happenings, and new digital media), the term 'interart studies' has since the 1990s been displaced by 'intermediality studies'.[18] Several definitions of intermedial studies have been suggested, but Mikko Lehtonen's formula is concise and clear: intermediality is 'intertextuality transgressing media boundaries'.[19] Interart studies and intermedial studies have inspired important critical work, and productive attempts to cross anachronistic disciplinary boundaries must be welcomed. I believe, however, that intermediality studies has a problematic tendency to focus on comparisons *across* media borders, instead of perceiving any cultural text as, internally, a mixed-media phenomenon.

I am, therefore, proposing a theoretical and analytical framework that develops out of intermediality studies. I have coined this new approach 'heteromedial studies'.[20] I consider heteromediality to be a condition for any conceivable cultural text (understood as a semiotic artefact), and, consequently, heteromediality is as foundational and as all-encompassing a cultural term as intertextuality. So, instead of comparing texts from different media, I wish to analyse a single text as necessarily a composite of different media, and to reveal the intermedial relations *within* the cultural text.[21] Consequently, any text is heteromedial, which has two implications: first, that all texts share a number of common 'modality features'.[22] This means that 'all media are mixed media', to quote W. J. T. Mitchell.[23] And, secondly, that the presence of the different media or art forms often expresses a tension-filled relationship: often a rivalry, sometimes a battle, and in fewer cases a happy marriage.[24] Furthermore, the relationship can often be related to larger contextual discourses and debates contemporary with the production of the work of art.[25] In short: all texts are mixed, openly or in less obvious ways, and the idea is that the specific constellation of the mixture expresses comprehensive historically charged questions related to struggles concerning, for instance, gender, class or aesthetics.

A reading of the opening scene following a heteromedial analysis 'programme' would de-emphasize the traditional discussion in intermedial adaptation of the quantitative comparison between novel and film (likenesses, differences). Instead, a heteromedial reading might start out with apparent banalities concerning the inherent multimedial and multimodal nature of the text in question. Such a categorization of media aspects of the text must be interpreted and analysed as a power struggle. Finally, this analysis should lead to provisional conclusions concerning the contextualization – in a more comprehensive frame – of the internal power struggle that characterizes the media *relations* in the text.

In order to pursue a heteromedial analysis one must begin by making an inventory of media and modalities. Here a sketch will suffice. We have the basic elements of any film sequence (after the era of silent movies). This includes sound (the well-known iconic sound of the sea gradually overtaken by the almost exaggerated noise of the film projector), and also the spoken words (symbolic signs) of Simon. Moving visual images disclose the time and space dimensions of Simon's room and the space of the film in the film, namely a beach filmed at an unknown time before the projection. We also note an unusually high number of elements referring explicitly to media and representational acts: we have the speaking protagonist as opposed to the silent (and silenced) object of his look; we have sound referring to both the sea and to the projector, we have 8mm footage of past events, and we have the filming event and the filming activity (in the past) as opposed to the projecting event that we witness (as a result of yet another film-projection, on screen, on a TV set or on a PC-interface)

From this introductory inventory we move on to the second step in a heteromedial analysis and suggest an interpretation of the scene based on the media relations within the cinematic text. These we can interpret as signs of more comprehensive historically charged questions related to struggles over gender, class and aesthetics. The scene is first and foremost a metafictive scene discussing itself as fiction and representation. It is, in Mitchell's terminology, a (moving) 'metapicture'.[26] This is old news for readers familiar with the postmodernist obsession with transforming all texts into more or less self-enclosed reflections of their own self-representational reflexivity. The scene is of course an elegant *mise en abyme* of the entire film, and even of Proust's novel (not only *La Prisonnière*, but the complete *À la recherche du temps perdu*). However, Derrida has taught us not to rely too heavily on the self-representational force of *mise en abyme*. Derrida's concept of *contre-abyme* reminds us that to *place in abyss* works more than one way; the smaller part represents the whole, the whole represents the part and the entire work always represents something outside itself as well. The *mise en abyme* does not, in short, work in a closed, logically ordered system. *Mise en abyme* complicates for instance levels of enunciation and symbolic dimensions, instead of clarifying matters. Rather than being a sign of the self-enclosed work of art, the *mise en abyme* here spills the signification of the scene into other themes and problematics.[27]

The scene is, therefore, not only a self-representation for it offers a number of partly internally contradictory allegories, mostly dealing with the relation between represented and representer, between different media, and between male and female. Besides the metafictive dimension, the scene appears initially to express a thesis common to many feminist approaches to film theory: the existence of a destructive and ultimately misogynistic and violent male gaze. As early as 1975, in her feminist classic *Jeanne Dielman, 23 Quai du Commerce, 1080 Bruxelles*, Akerman investigated the possibilities of depicting an objectified woman on terms other than from a patriarchal position, so the thematic is familiar to her. Akerman in her Proust adaptation appears to ask, from a feminist point of view, *what does cinema do?* The answer is that filming equals *distinguishing* and thus objectifying one of the young girls – but the question is whether this act of distinguishing also means isolating and, eventually, killing the object of the gaze. It appears not to, I would argue, given that an overly pedagogical feminist critique of cinema as an extension of the male, murderous gaze is not exemplified in *La Captive*. One of the strongest achievements of this scene (and *La Captive* in general) is, on the contrary, that it demonstrates how the male gaze is fatal for the male viewer-position as well. Moreover, even if Simon is alive in contrast to Ariane in the opening scene (and also lives in the fictive time 'after' the film), he is existentially and psychologically petrified and dumb. The scene is perhaps best understood as one that establishes a dialogic *contact* between subjects, instead of representing a monologized object. Akerman appears to copy the formal frame of a beautiful, if pessimistic, allegory of the destructive male gaze and its possible connection to an essential feature of narrative cinema – but only in order to turn this upside down by installing a strong and dialogically able subject in the role assumed to be occupied by a numb, objectified feminine object. We might even ask ourselves if Simon is really trying, like Scottie in *Vertigo*, to make Ariane come to life again, or if he is really trying to relive the moment of filming her, thus being able to stay on 'the right side' of the camera.

The scene also expresses a specific media tension between the cinematic representation and the literary, novelistic representation. If Simon's filming Ariane cannot be read as a rather obvious representation of the male gaze and thus for the specular regime of cinema, then the question is: what can cinema do to other represented objects?

The speculative answer, at a more abstract level, is that cinema in this particular example 'objectifies' the literary precedent. Notwithstanding the expressions of respect for the literary precedent, including those made by Akerman herself, we often detect another desire lying behind film adaptations. In the words of Linda Hutcheon:

> Adaptation is repetition, but repetition without replication. And there are manifestly many different possible intentions behind the act of adaptation: the urge to consume and erase the memory of the adapted text or to call it into question is as likely as the desire to pay tribute or copying.[28]

My point here is that, even if Akerman in her statements on her adaptation seems to remain on friendly terms with her literary precedent, something else may be at stake. One telling sign of this suppression of the literary antecedent is that (almost) all references to books, reading or literature seem to be eradicated in the film despite the centrality of literature and reading in Proust's novel.

Therefore, the film, possibly despite the conscious intentions of its director and scriptwriter, expresses a negative relationship to Proust's *La Prisonnière*. But the novel, at least in this particular case, seems to return in repressed form – to paraphrase Freud's idea of the unconscious – as telltale signs of the literary precedent in the film. So, even if Akerman has created an extremely 'free' or even 'repressing' adaptation that celebrates its cinematic freedom from the literary precedent, Proust's novel strikes back. Because whose gaze is it that the spectators 'follow' in the scene? For whom, if for anyone or anything, is Simon a stand-in? Clearly, Simon is identical to the narrator 'Marcel' in Proust's novel. And to a certain extent the 'I' of *À la recherche* shares a number of traits with its author, Marcel Proust. Therefore, we might read the scene as a transposed, metafictive illustration of the destructive forces that might be ascribed to Marcel Proust's work (including his narrator): *À la recherche* constructs the relationship between Marcel and Albertine as a dangerously destructive one, so dangerous that Marcel might be said to destroy Albertine. Consequently Akerman, perhaps without having realized it, probes the deepest layers (in terms of aggression and destruction) of the Proustian novel. In other words: the freest adaptation, an adaptation bordering on an anti-adaptation (compared to Ruiz's and in particular Schlöndorff's earlier versions) turns out to be the most 'faithful' one, to use an ambiguous, not to say infected, term in adaptation studies.[29] Or, to phrase it in a less dramatic way: the film has not been able to free itself from the literary precedent.

I propose to take the interpretation a step further and test one final possible subject–object relation in the scene. Let us remove Simon from behind the projector (in the present time of the film) and the camera (and the film of the film), and replace him with the director Chantal Akerman. Now Akerman is a representative not only of her own project, but of the entire concept of adapting novels to film, and my final suggestion is to view the scene as a heteromedial allegory: Akerman, representing film adaptation at large, demonstrates the inherently paradoxical fight for acknowledgment in the master-and-slave relation between film and literature that lies hidden in any adaptation. Akerman is helplessly in love with a literary work, of which she has admitted that she has mostly fragmentary but strong and cherished memories, exactly as is the case with Simon longing for Ariane. But these scattered, partly lost memories she must continuously try to *re-present*, in her case represent in the *film* medium, in order to make the work come alive again; and to have the work reassure her that 'je vous aime bien'.

The literary work does not and cannot reply, nor can the dead Ariane answer Simon, except on 8mm film. But in this scene Akerman has created a powerful metaphor reaching far beyond her own adaptation, perhaps unwittingly representing what screen adaptations are all about: trying to force the absent, silent text to become a living, speaking film.

Notes

1 Among the numerous works on Proust and the arts, see, for instance, Luc Fraisse, *L'Œuvre cathédrale. Proust et l'architecture médiévale* (Paris: José Corti, 1990); Stephanie A. Moore, '"Bâtir un livre": the architectural poetics of *À la recherche du temps perdu*', in Manfred Schmeling and Monika Schmitz-Emans (eds), *Das visuelle Gedächtnis der Literatur* (Würzburg: Königshausen und Neumann, 1999), pp. 188–202; J.-J. Nattiez *Proust musicien* (Paris: Christian Bourgois, 1984); M. E Chernowitz, *Proust and Painting* (New York: np, 1945); and Mieke Bal, *The Mottled Screen: Reading Proust Visually* (Stanford: Stanford University Press, 1997).

2 Proust scholarship has given rise to several key interpretations of the function of the artists of the work. Anne Henry argued powerfully for the idea that the entire work, and in particular Proust's fictive artists, was part of a huge philosophical framework and that the artists were thus pedagogical steps in the narrator's process of *Bildung*. See Anne Henry's influential *Proust romancier: Le tombeau égyptien* (Paris: Flammarion, 1983) and her *Marcel Proust: Théories pour une esthétique* (Paris: Klincksieck, 1983). For philosophical readings, see also Vincent Descombes, *Proust: Philosophie du roman* (Paris: Éditions de minuit, 1987), and Gilles Deleuze, *Proust et les signes* (Paris: PUF, 1964/1970).

3 Peter Kravanja, *Proust à l'écran* (Brussels: Lettre volée, 2003); Melissa Anderson, 'In search of adaptation. Proust on film', in Robert Stam and Alessandra Raengo (eds), *Literature and Film: A Guide to the Theory and Practice of Film Adaptation* (Malden, MA: Blackwell, 2004), pp. 100–9; Yves Baudelle, 'Proust et le cinéma', in *Roman 20–50* (Lille: Lille University 1996), pp. 45–70; and Martine Beugnet and Marion Schmid, *Proust at the Movies* (Burlington: Ashgate, 2004).

4 Beugnet and Schmid, *Proust at the Movies*, p. 11.

5 This phenomenon has been labelled, in another context, 'filmische Schreibweise'. See Irina O. Rajewsky, *Intermedialität* (Tübingen and Basel: A. Francke Verlag, 2002), p. 197.

6 For a discussion of the Italian director Fabio Carpi's two films related to Proust's work *Quartetto Basileus* (1982) and *Le Intermittenze del cuoure* (2003), see Beugnet and Schmid, *Proust at the Movies*, pp. 206–28.

7 See Beugnet and Schmid, *Proust at the Movies*, p. 206.

8 See M. M. Bakhtin, 'Forms of time and the chronotope in the novel', in *The Dialogic Imagination* (Austin: Texas University Press, 1981), pp. 84–258.

9 See Joan Tasker Grimbert and Robert Smarz, '*Fable* and *Poésie* in Cocteau's *L'Éternel Retour* (1943)', in Kevin J. Harty (ed.), *Cinema Arthuriana: Twenty Essays* (Jefferson, NC: McFarland and Co., 2002), pp. 220–41 (p. 221). I have discussed Cocteau's idea

of *poésie cinématographique* in 'Tristan transformed: bodies and media in the historical transformation of the Tristan and Isolde-Myth', in J. Arvidson, M. Askander, J. Bruhn and J. Führer (eds), *Changing Borders: Contemporary Positions in Intermediality* (Lund: Lund Intermedia Press, 2007), pp. 339–60.

10 Beugnet and Schmid, *Proust at the Movies*, p. 172.

11 Ibid., p. 171.

12 Ibid., p. 172.

13 Ibid., p. 175.

14 Mentioned by Bérénice Reynaud in 'Alluring absence', which is available at *http://sensesofcinema.com/2004/cteq/la_captive/*, accessed 30 January 2013.

15 See Melissa Anderson, 'In search of adaptation: Proust on film', p. 108.

16 See Laura Mulvey's 'Visual pleasure and the narrative cinema' (1975), reprinted in Leo Braudy and Marshall Cohen (eds), *Film Theory and Criticism* (6th edn, New York and Oxford: Oxford University Press, 2004), pp. 839–48.

17 For this particular reading of the scene I am indebted to comments made by my colleague Anna Sofia Rossholm.

18 See Claus Clüver's historical overview, 'Intermediality and interart studies', in Arvidson, Askander, Bruhn and Führer (eds), *Changing Borders*, pp. 19–37.

19 Mikko Lehtonen, 'On no man's land: theses on intermediality', *Nordicom Review*, 4/2000, 71–83 (71).

20 See Jørgen Bruhn, 'Heteromediality', in Lars Elleström (ed.), *Media, Modalities, and Modes* (New York and London: Palgrave/Macmillan, 2010), pp. 225–36.

21 For a comparable point of view which has been an important inspiration for me, see W. J. T. Mitchell, 'Beyond comparison: picture, text, method', in *Picture Theory* (Chicago and London: Chicago University Press, 1994, pp. 83–107.

22 Lars Elleström discusses the possibilities of constructing a theory of media on the basis of multimodality in his essay 'The modalities of media: a model for understanding intermedial relations', in Lars Elleström (ed.), *Media, Modalities, and Modes*, pp. 11–.50.

23 'If all media are mixed media, they are not all mixed in the same way, with the same proportions of elements.' See W. J. T. Mitchell, 'There are no visual media', *Journal of Visual Culture*, 4/2 (2005), 257–66.

24 Concerning different metaphors for the relations between the arts, see Walter Bernhart, 'Words and music as partners in song: "Perfect Marriage" – "Uneasy Flirtation" – "Coercive Tension" – "Shared Indifference" – "Total Destruction"', in Arvidson, Askander, Bruhn and Führer (eds), *Changing Borders*, pp. 85–94.

25 For a stimulating, contemporary discussion of the meaning of context, see chapter 5 in Linda Hutcheon, *A Theory of Adaptation* (London: Routledge, 2006).

[26] See W. J. T. Mitchell's essay 'Metapicture', in *Picture Theory*, pp. 35–82.

[27] For a substantial discussion of the term *mise en abyme*, see Moshe Ron, 'The restricted abyss: nine problems in the theory of mise en abyme', *Poetics Today*, 8/2 (1987), 417–38, who develops the terminology proposed in Lucien Dällenbach, *The Mirror in the Text*. Derrida uses the term 'contre-abyme' in his essay on Kafka, 'Before the Law', translated in Derek Attridge (ed.), *Acts of Literature* (New York and London: Routledge, 1992), pp. 183–220 (pp. 217 and 220). I became aware of the concept in Nicholas Royle's idiosyncratic introduction to Derrida, *Jacques Derrida* (London: Routledge, 2003), p. 89.

[28] See Linda Hutcheon, *A Theory of Adaptation*, p. 7.

[29] For a useful critique of the concept of 'faithfulness' and 'loyalty' in adaptation studies, see Thomas M. Leitch, 'Twelve fallacies in contemporary adaptation theory', *Criticism*, 45/2 (spring 2003), 149–71.

Translation sources

The following is a list of suggested sources of translations, where these exist, of a number of the key primary or secondary works explored in *The Art of the Text*.

Adorno, Theodor

Detlev Claussen, *Theodor W. Adorno. Ein letztes Genie* (Frankfurt am Main: S. Fischer, 2003) is available in English as *Theodor W. Adorno: One Last Genius* (Harvard University Press, 2008).

Stefan Müller-Doohm, *Adorno. Eine Biographie* (Berlin: Suhrkamp, 2003) is available in English as *Adorno: A Biography* (Cambridge: Polity Press, 2005).

Benjamin, Walter

Walter Benjamin's classic essay is available as 'The work of art in the age of mechanical reproduction', in *Illuminations*, trans. Harry Zohn (London: Pimlico, 1999).

Breton, André

Nadja is available as *Nadja*, trans. Richard Howard, with an introduction by Mark Polizzotti (London: Penguin, 1999).

Manifestes du surréalisme is available as *Manifestoes of Surrealism*, trans. Richard Seaver and Helen R. Lane (Ann Arbor: University of Michigan Press, 1972).

Colette

Le Voyage égoïste is available as *Journey for Myself: Selfish Memories*, trans. David Le Vay (London: Peter Owen Publishers, 1971).

Lamartine, Alphonse de
Lamartine's *Méditations* is available as *Poetical Meditations*, trans. G. Hittle
(Lewiston, NY: Edwin Mellen Press, 1993).

Michaux, Henri
Some of the works discussed in chapter 4 are available in *Darkness Moves:*
An Henri Michaux Anthology, 1927–1984, ed. and trans. David Ball (Berkeley
and Los Angeles, CA: University of California Press, 1994).

Modiano, Patrick
Voyages de noces is available as *Honeymoon*, trans. Barbara Wright (London:
Harper Collins, 1992).

Proust, Marcel
À la recherche du temps perdu is available as *In Search of Lost Time*, trans. C. K.
Scott Moncrieff and Terence Kilmartin, and revised by D. J. Enright, in 6
volumes (London: Vintage, 2000) as follows: *Swann's Way; Within a Budding*
Grove; The Guermantes Way; Sodom and Gomorrah; The Captive & The
Fugitive; Time Regained & A Guide to Proust.

Penguin Classics published a new translation in 2003:
The Way by Swann's, trans. Lydia Davis, ed. Christopher Prendergast (London:
Penguin Classics, 2003).
In the Shadow of Young Girls in Flower, trans. James Grieve, ed. Christopher
Prendergast (London: Penguin Classics, 2003).
The Guermantes Way, trans. Mark Treharne, ed. Christopher Prendergast
(London: Penguin Classics, 2003).
Sodom and Gomorrah, trans. John Sturrock, ed. Christopher Prendergast
(London: Penguin Classics, 2003).
The Prisoner and The Fugitive, trans. Carol Clark and Peter Collier, ed. Christopher
Prendergast (London: Penguin Classics, 2003).
Finding Time Again, trans. Ian Patterson, ed. Christopher Prendergast (London:
Penguin Classics, 2003).

Verne, Jules

Many of Jules Verne's novels are freely available in English translations of variable quality at *http://jv.gilead.org.il/works.html#novels* (accessed 18 October 2012).

A comprehensive critical bibliography of modern translations of Verne is provided by Arthur B. Evans, 'Jules Verne in English: A bibliography of modern editions and scholarly studies', *Verniana*, 1 (2008–9), 9–22, available at *http://www.verniana.org/volumes/01/index.en.html* (accessed 18 October 2012).

The reader may also wish to consult the following recent translations of texts referred to in chapter 1:

De la terre à la lune and *Autour de la lune* are available as *From the Earth to the Moon* and *Around the Moon*, introduction and notes by Alex Dolby (Ware: Wordsworth Editions, Wordsworth Classics, 2011).

Le Pays des fourrures is available as *The Fur Country*, trans. Edward Baxter (Toronto: NC Press Ltd, 1987).

Le Rayon vert is available as *The Green Ray*, trans. Karen Loukes (Edinburgh: Luath Press, 2009).

Vingt mille lieues sous les mers is available as *Twenty Thousand Leagues under the Seas*, ed. William Butcher (Oxford: Oxford University Press, Oxford World's Classics, 2009).

Le Tour du monde en quatre-vingts jours and *Cinq semaines en ballon* are available as *Around the World in Eighty Days* and *Five Weeks in a Balloon*, introduction and notes by Roger Cardinal (Ware: Wordsworth Editions, Wordsworth Classics, 1994).

Voyages et aventures du capitaine Hatteras is available as *The Adventures of Captain Hatteras*, ed. William Butcher (Oxford: Oxford University Press, Oxford World's Classics, 2009).

Zola, Emile

L'Œuvre is available as *The Masterpiece*, trans. Roger Pearson (Oxford: Oxford Paperbacks, 2008).

Bibliography

Adorno, Theodor, 'Picture book without pictures', in *Minima Moralia: Reflections from Damaged Life*, trans. E. F. N. Jephcott (London: NLB, 1974), pp. 140–1.

——, *The Culture Industry: Selected Essays on Mass Culture*, ed. J. M. Bernstein (London: Routledge, 1991).

Anderson, Melissa, 'In search of adaptation: Proust on film', in Robert Stam and Alessandra Raengo (eds), *Literature and Film: A Guide to the Theory and Practice of Film Adaptation* (Malden, MA: Blackwell, 2004), pp. 100–9.

Annink, Ed and Max Bruinsma (eds), *Gerd Arntz: Graphic Designer* (Rotterdam: 010 publishers, 2010).

Aragon, Louis, 'Du décor', *Le Film*, 16 September 1918, repr. in *Écrits sur l'art moderne*, ed. Jean Ristat (Paris: Flammarion, 1981).

——, *Anicet ou le panorama, roman* (Paris: Gallimard/Folio, 2001).

—— and Elsa Triolet, *Œuvres romanesques croisées* (Paris: Robert Laffont, 1964)

Arrouye, Jean (ed.), *Écrire et voir: Aragon, Elsa Triolet et les arts visuels* (Aix-en-Provence: Publications de l'Université de Provence, 1991).

Aydelotte, Winifred, 'Hollywood, the World's sculptor', *Photoplay*, March 1934.

Bakhtin, M. M., 'Forms of time and the chronotope in the novel', in *The Dialogic Imagination* (Austin: Texas University Press, 1981).

Bal, Mieke, *The Mottled Screen: Reading Proust Visually*, trans. Anna-Louise Milne (Stanford: Stanford University Press, 1997).

——, *Reading 'Rembrandt': Beyond the Word-Image Opposition* (New York and Cambridge: Cambridge University Press, [1991] 1994) (Amsterdam: Amsterdam University Press, 2006).

Balakian, Anna, *The Snowflake on the Belfry: Dogma and Disquietude in the Critical Arena* (Bloomington: Indiana University Press, 1994).

Bann, Stephen, *The True Vine: On Visual Representation and the Western Tradition* (Cambridge: Cambridge University Press, 1989).

Barante, Prosper Brugière de, *Histoire des ducs de Bourgogne de la maison de Valois*, 13 vols (4th edn, Paris: Ladvocat, 1826).

Barrère, Jean-Bertrand, 'Victor Hugo et les arts plastiques', *Revue de littérature comparée*, 30 (1956).

Barthes, Roland, *S/Z* (Paris: Seuil, 1970).

——, *Leçon* (Paris: Seuil, Collection Points Essais, 1978).

——, *La Chambre claire: note sur la photographie* (Paris: Seuil, 1980).

——, *L'Empire des signes* (Paris: Seuil, Collection Points Essais, 2005).

Baudelle, Yves, 'Proust et le cinéma', in *Roman 20–50* (Lille: Lille University 1996), pp. 45–7.

Becker, Andrew Sprague, *Rhetoric and Poetics of Early Greek Ekphrasis: Theory, Philology and the Shield of Achilles* (London: Rowman & Littlefield, 1995).

Benjamin, Walter, 'The image of Proust', in *Illuminations* (London: Pimlico, 1999).

Benjamin, Walter, 'The work of art in the age of mechanical reproduction', in *Illuminations* (London: Pimlico, 1999).

Berger, John, 'Why look at animals', in *About Looking* (London: Writers and Readers, 1980), pp. 1–26.

Beugnet, Martine and Marion Schmid, *Proust at the Movies* (Burlington: Ashgate, 2004).

Blanchot, Michel, 'L'ange du bizarre', in *Henri Michaux ou le refus de l'enfermement* (Tours: farrago, 1999).

Blondel, M. and P. Georgel (eds), *Victor Hugo et les images* (Dijon: Aux amateurs du livre, 1989).

Blount, Margaret, *Animal Land: The Creatures of Children's Fiction* (London: Hutchinson, 1974).

Bodmer, Frederick, *The Loom of Language: A Guide to Foreign Languages for the Home Student*, ed. Lancelot Hogben (London: George Allen and Unwin, 1943).

Bowie, Malcolm, *Henri Michaux: A Study of his Literary Works* (Oxford: Clarendon Press, 1973).

——, *Proust Among the Stars* (London: Harper Collins, 1998).

Breton, André, *Nadja* (Paris: Gallimard, 1964).

——, 'Manifeste du surréalisme' (1924), in *Manifestes du surréalisme* (Paris: Gallimard, 1972).

Brooks, Peter, *Body Work: Objects of Desire in Modern Narrative* (Cambridge: Harvard University Press, 1993).

Bruhn, Jørgen, 'Heteromediality', in Lars Elleström (ed.), (London and New York: Palgrave/Macmillan, 2010), pp. 225–36.

Bruno, Giuliana, *Atlas of Emotion: Journeys in Art, Architecture, and Film* (London: Verso, 2002).

Brunot, Ferdinand, *Histoire de la langue française des origines à nos jours* (Paris: Armand Colin, 1968).

Bull, Malcolm, *The Mirror of the Gods: Classical Mythology in Renaissance Art* (London: Allen Lane, 2005).

Burke, Christopher, *Active Literature: Jan Tschichold and New Typography* (London: Hyphen Press, 2007).

Burke, Edmund, *A Philosophical Enquiry into the Origin of our Ideas of the Sublime and the Beautiful*, ed. Adam Phillips (Oxford: Oxford University Press, 1998 [1757]).

Butor, Michel, *Improvisations sur Henri Michaux* (Fontfroide-le-Haut: fata morgana, 1985).

Byron, Lord, *The Major Works*, ed. J. J. McGann (Oxford: Oxford University Press, 2000).

Cartwright, Nancy, Jordi Cat, Lola Fleck and Thomas E. Uebel, *Otto Neurath: Philosophy between Science and Politics* (Cambridge: Cambridge University Press, 1996).

Chateaubriand, François-René de, *Génie du christianisme*, 2 vols (Paris: Flammarion, 1966 [1802 by Migneret]).

Chelebourg, Christian, *Jules Verne. L'Œil et le ventre, une poétique du sujet* (Paris: Minard, 1999).

Chernowitz, M. E., *Proust and Painting* (New York: np, 1945).

Chiassaï, Marc, *Aragon/Peinture/Écriture. La Peinture dans l'écriture des 'Cloches de Bâle' à 'La Semaine Sainte'* (Paris: Kimé, 1999).

Claussen, Detlev, *Theodor W. Adorno. Ein letztes Genie* (Frankfurt am Main: S. Fischer, 2003).

Clüver, Claus, 'Intermediality and interart studies', in J. Arvidson, M. Askander, J. Bruhn, and J. Führer (eds), *Changing Borders: Contemporary Positions in Intermediality* (Lund: Intermedia Studies Press, 2008), pp. 19–37.

Colette, *Le Voyage égoïste*, in *Œuvres*, vol. 2 (Paris: Gallimard, Bibliothèque de la Pléiade, 1986), pp. 1091–1181.

Collier, Peter and Robert Lethbridge (eds), *Artistic Relations: Literature and the Visual Arts in Nineteenth-Century France*, (New Haven: Yale University Press, 1994).

Compagnon, Antoine, *Les cinq paradoxes de la modernité* (Paris: Seuil, 1990).

Cordova, Richard de, *Picture Personalities: The Emergence of the Star System in America* (Urbana: University of Illinois Press, 1990).

Dachy, Marc (ed.), *Projet d'histoire littéraire contemporaine* (Paris: Gallimard, 1994).

Daguerre de Hureaux, Alain, *Delacroix* (Paris: Hazan, 1993).

Danius, Sara, *The Senses of Modernism: Technology, Perception and Aesthetics* (Ithaca and London: Cornell University Press, 2002).

Daspre, André, *Hommage à Claude Digeon* (Paris: Les Belles Lettres, 1987).

Deleuze, Gilles, *Proust et les signes* (Paris: PUF, 1964/1970).

——, *Cinéma 1: L'Image-mouvement* (Paris: Minuit, Collection Critique, 1983).

—— and Claire Parnet, *Dialogues* (Paris: Flammarion, Collection Dialogues, 1977).

Derrida, Jacques, 'Before the Law', in Derek Attridge (ed.), *Acts of Literature* (New York and London: Routledge, 1992), pp. 183–220.

Deschamps, Émile, *Études françaises et étrangères* (2nd edn, Paris: Urbain Canel, 1828).

Descombes, Vincent, *Proust: Philosophie du roman* (Paris: Éditions de Minuit, 1987).

Diderot, Denis, *Œuvres esthétiques*, ed. Paul Vernière (Paris: Garnier, 1959).

Didi-Huberman, Georges, *La Ressemblance informe ou le Gai Savoir visuel selon Georges Bataille* (Paris: Macula, Collection Vues, 1995).

Diesbach, Ghislain de, *Le Tour de Jules Verne en quatre-vingts livres* (Paris: Perrin, 2000 [1969]).

Dubois, Philippe, *L'Acte photographique et autres essais* (Paris: Nathan, 1990).

Dyer, Richard, 'Charisma', in Christine Gledhill (ed.), *Stardom: Industry of Desire* (London: Routledge, 1991), pp. 57–9.

——, Richard, *White* (London: Routledge, 1997).

Elkins, James (ed.), *Photography Theory* (London and New York: Routledge, 2007).

Ellis, John, 'Stars as a cinematic phenomenon', in *Visible Fictions* (London: Routledge, 1992), chapter 6.

Éluard, Paul, *Œuvres complètes*, vols I and II, ed. Marcelle Dumas and Lucien Scheler (Paris: NRF/Gallimard, 1968, Bibliothèque de la Pléiade).

Evans, Arthur B., 'Optograms and fiction: photo in a dead man's eye', *Science-Fiction Studies*, 20/3 (1993), 341–61.

Farwell, Beatrice, 'Sources for Delacroix's *Death of Sardanapalus*', *Art Bulletin* 40/1 (1958), 66–71.

Fer, Briony, *On Abstract Art* (New Haven and London: Yale University Press, 1997).

Fischer, Barbara K., *Museum Meditations: Reframing Ekphrasis in Contemporary American Poetry* (New York and London: Routledge, 2006).

Fischer, Lucy, *Designing Women: Cinema, Art Deco and the Female Form* (New York: Columbia University Press, 2003).

Flusser, Vilem, *Towards a Philosophy of Photography* (London: Reaktion, 2000).

Foster, Robert, 'In the spring of a young man's fancy', *Picture-Play*, April 1916, 63.

Fraisse, Luc, *L'Œuvre cathédrale. Proust et l'architecture médiévale* (Paris: José Corti, 1990).

Freadman, Anne, 'Breasts are back!: Colette's critique of flapper fashion', *French Studies*, 60/3 (July 2006), 335–46.

Fussell, Paul, *The Great War and Modern Memory* (London: Oxford University Press, 1975).

Gaines, Jane, *Contested Culture: The Image, the Voice and the Law* (Durham, NC: University of North Carolina Press, 1991).

Gateau, Jean-Charles, *Paul Éluard et la peinture surréaliste (1910–1939)* (Geneva: Droz, 1982, Histoire des idées et critique littéraire, vol. 204).

——, *Éluard, Picasso et la peinture (1936–1952)* (Geneva: Droz, 1983, Histoire des idées et critique littéraire, vol. 212).

Genette, Gérard, *Figures III* (Paris: Seuil, 1972).

Georgel, Chantal, *La Forêt de Fontainebleau: Un atelier grandeur nature* (Paris: Réunion des Musées Nationaux, 2007).

Getsy, David J., *Body Doubles: Sculpture in Britain, 1877–1905* (London: Yale University Press, 2004).

Geuss, Raymond and Ronald Spiers (eds), *The Birth of Tragedy* (Cambridge: Cambridge University Press, 1999).

Gide André, 'Découvrons Henri Michaux', in *Essais critiques*, ed. Pierre Masson (Paris: Gallimard, Bibliothèque de la Pléiade, 1999).

Gindine, Yvette, *Aragon: prosateur surréaliste* (Geneva: Droz, 1966).

Griffiths, Kate, 'Hunt the author: Zola, Vadim and *La Curée*', *Studies in European Cinema* 2/1 (2005), 7–17.

Griffiths, Kate, *Zola and the Artistry of Adaptation* (Oxford: Legenda, 2009).

Grimbert, Joan Tasker and Robert Smarz, '*Fable* and *Poésie* in Cocteau's *L'Éternel Retour* (1943)', in Kevin J. Harty (ed.), *Cinema Arthuriana. Twenty Essays* (Jefferson, NC: McFarland and Co., 2002), pp. 220–41.

Grojnowski, Daniel, *Photographie et langage: fictions, illustrations, informations, visions, théories* (Paris: Corti, 2002).

Grossiord, Sophie and M. Asakura (eds), *Les Années folles* (Paris: Paris Musées, 2007).

Guieu, Jean-Max and Alison Hilton (eds), *Emile Zola and the Arts* (Washington, DC: Georgetown University Press, 1988).

Hamon, Philippe, 'Images à lire et images à voir: "images américaines" et crise de l'image au XIXe siècle', in Stéphane Michaud, Jean-Yves Mollier and Nicole Savy (eds), *Usages de l'image au XIXe siècle* (Paris: Editions Créaphis, 1992).

Hamon, Philippe, *Imageries: littérature et image au XIXe siècle* (Paris: José Corti, 2002).

Hanney, Roxanne, *The Invisible Middle Term in Proust's* A la recherche du temps perdu (New York: Edwin Mellen Press, 1990).

Hanoosh, Michèle, *Painting and the Journal of Eugène Delacroix* (Princeton: Princeton University Press, 1995).

Hansen, Miriam, 'Mass culture as hieroglyphic writing: Adorno, Derrida, Kracauer', *New German Critique*, 56, special issue on Theodor W. Adorno, (spring–summer, 1992), 43–73.

Hardy, Alain-René, *Art-Deco Textiles: The French Designers* (London: Thames & Hudson, 2003).

Heffernan, James A. W., *Museum of Words: The Poetics of Ekphrasis from Homer to Ashbery* (Chicago and London: University of Chicago Press, 1993).

——, *Cultivating Picturacy: Visual Art and Verbal Interventions* (Waco, TX: Baylor University Press, 2006).

Henry, Anne, *Proust romancier: Le tombeau égyptien* (Paris: Flammarion, 1983).

——, *Marcel Proust: Théories pour une esthétique* (Paris: Klincksieck, 1983).

Hertz, Henri, 'Emile Zola, témoin de la vérité', *Europe 30* (1952), 83–4.

Hugo, Victor *Œuvres poétiques*, vol. 1 (Paris: Gallimard, 1964).

——, *Œuvres complètes* (Paris: Laffont, 1985).

Hunt, Susan and Paul Carter (eds), *Terre Napoléon: Australia through French Eyes 1800–1804* (Sydney: Historic Houses Trust of New South Wales, 1999).

Hutcheon, Linda, *A Theory of Adaptation* (London: Routledge, 2006).

Imbert, Maurice (ed.), *Correspondance Adrienne Monnier & Henri Michaux 1939–1955* (Paris: la hune, 1995).

Ingold, Tim, *Lines: A Brief History* (London and New York: Routledge, 2007).

Jones, Michael Allan, *Foundations of French Syntax* (Cambridge: Cambridge University Press, 1996).

Kaufmann, Walter (ed. and trans.), *The Portable Nietzsche* (London and New York: Viking Penguin, 1982).

Kinross, Robin, 'On the influence of Isotype', *Information Design Journal*, 2/11 (1981), 122–30

——, 'Emigré Graphic Designers in Britain: Around the Second World War and Afterwards', *Journal of Design History*, 1, 3 (1990), 35–57 (p. 44)

Krauss, Rosalind, 'The Photographic Conditions of Surrealism', *October*, 19 (1981), 3–34

Kravanja, Peter, *Proust à l'écran* (Brussels: Lettre volée, 2003)

Lacambre, Jean and Isabelle Julia, *Les Années romantiques: La Peinture française de 1815 à 1850* (Paris: Réunion des Musées Nationaux, 1995).

Lamartine, Alphonse de, *Méditations poétiques et Nouvelles méditations poétiques*, ed. Aurélie Loiseleur (Paris: Livre de poche, 2006).

Larkin, Áine, *Proust Writing Photography: Fixing the Fugitive in 'À la recherche du temps perdu'* (Oxford: Legenda, 2011).

Lecaudé, Jean-Marc, 'Le Narrateur et sa disparition', in John Flower (ed.), *Patrick Modiano* (Amsterdam and New York: Rodopi, 2007), pp. 239–56.

Lehtonen, Mikko, 'On no man's land: theses on intermediality', *Nordicom Review*, 4/2000, 71–83.

Leitch, Thomas M., 'Twelve fallacies in contemporary adaptation theory', *Criticism*, 45/2 (spring 2003), 149–71.

Lethbridge, Robert and Terry Keefe (eds), *Zola and The Craft of Fiction* (Leicester: Leicester University Press, 1990).

Levy, Oscar (ed.), *The Complete Works of Friedrich Nietzsche*, 18 vols (Edinburgh: T. N. Foulis, 1909), vol. XIV.

Lionel-Marie, Annick, *Paul Éluard et ses amis peintres, 1895–1952* (Paris: Centre Georges Pompidou et Musée national d'art moderne, 1982).

Long, Christopher, *Josef Frank: Life and Work* (Chicago: University of Chicago Press, 2002).

Löwith, Karl, *Nietzsche: philosophie de l'éternel retour du même* (Hamburg: Calmann-Lévy, 1991).

Maynard, Patrick, *The Engine of Visualization: Thinking Through Photography* (Ithaca and London: Cornell University Press, 1997).

Michaux, Henri, *Documents année 1929*, vol. I (Paris: Éditions Jean-Michel Place, 1991).

——, *Œuvres complètes*, vol. II, ed. Raymond Bellour with Ysé Tran (Paris: Gallimard, Bibliothèque de la Pléiade, 2001).

——, *Œuvres complètes*, Vol. III, ed. Raymond Bellour with Ysé Tran and the collaboration of Mireille Cardot (Paris: Gallimard, Bibliothèque de la Pléiade, 2004).

Mitchell, W. J. T., 'Ekphrasis and the Other', *South Atlantic Quarterly*, 91 (1992), 695–719.

——, 'Beyond comparison: picture, text, method', in *Picture Theory* (Chicago and London: Chicago University Press, 1994), pp. 83–107.

——, 'There are no visual media', *Journal of Visual Culture*, 4/2 (2005), 257–66.

Mitterand, Henri, 'Le Musée dans le texte', *Cahiers naturalistes*, 66 (1992), 13–22.

Modiano, Patrick, *Vestiaire de l'enfance* (Paris: Gallimard/Folio, 1989).

——, *Voyage de noces* (Paris: Gallimard/Folio, 1992).

——, *Chien de printemps* (Paris: Seuil, 1993).

Moore, Stephanie A., '"Bâtir un livre": the architectural poetics of *À la recherche du temps perdu*', in Manfred Schmeling and Monika Schmitz-Emans (eds), *Das visuelle Gedächtnis der Literatur* (Würzburg: Königshausen und Neumann, 1999), pp. 188–202.

Morin, Edgar, *The Stars* (Minneapolis: University of Minnesota, 2005 [1957]).

Müller-Doohm, Stefan, *Adorno. Eine Biographie* (Berlin: Suhrkamp, 2003).

Mulvey, Laura, 'Visual pleasure and narrative cinema' (1975), reprinted in Leo Braudy and Marshall Cohen (eds), *Film Theory and Criticism* (6th edn, New York and Oxford: Oxford University Press, 2004), pp. 839–48.

Munster, Wil, *La Poétique du pittoresque en France de 1700 à 1830* (Paris: Droz, 1991).

Nattiez, J.-J., *Proust musicien* (Paris: Christian Bourgois, 1984).

Neurath, Marie and Robert S. Cohen (eds), *Otto Neurath: Empiricism and Sociology*, (Dordrecht: D. Reidel, 1973).

Neurath, Marie and Robin Kinross, *The Transformer: Principles of Making Isotype Charts* (London: Hyphen Press, 2009).

Neurath, Otto, *International Picture Language: The First Rules of Isotype* (London: Kegan Paul, Psyche Miniatures,1936).

——, *From Hieroglyphics to Isotypes: A Visual Autobiography*, ed. Matthew Eve and Christopher Burke (London: Hyphen Press, 2010).

Niess, Robert J., *Zola, Cézanne and Manet: A Study of L'Œuvre* (Ann Arbor: University of Michigan Press, 1968).

Nietzsche, Frederich, *The Gay Science: with a prelude in German Rhymes and an Appendix of Songs*, trans. Walter Kaufmann (New York: Random House, 1974).

——, *Beyond Good and Evil; Prelude to a Philosophy of the Future*, trans. Walter Kaufmann (New York: Vintage Books, 1989).

——, *Human, All Too Human: A Book for Free Spirits* (Cambridge: Cambridge University Press, 1996).

——, *Thus Spoke Zarathustra* (Cambridge: Cambridge University Press, 2006).

O'Reilly, Chiara, 'Paul Huet: natural history and Romantic landscape painting' (unpublished doctoral thesis, University of Sydney, Australia, 2006).

Ortel, Philippe, *La Littérature à l'ère de la photographie: enquête sur une révolution invisible* (Nîmes: Jacqueline Chambon, 2002).

Parish, Nina, *Henri Michaux: Experimentation with Signs* (Amsterdam: Rodopi, 2007).

Parrot, Louis and Jean Marcenac, *Paul Éluard* (Paris: Seghers, 1969, Poètes d'aujourd'hui series, no. 1).

Paulson, William (ed.), *Les Genres de l'hénaurme siècle* (Ann Arbor: University of Michigan Press, 1989).

Perec, Georges, 'J'ai fait imploser le roman', *Galerie des arts*, 184 (1978), 73.

Plato, 'The Simile of the Cave', in *The Republic* (London: Penguin Books, 2003), pp. 242–3.

Poli, Doretta Davanzo, *Tissus du XXe siècle. Designers et manufactures d'Europe et d'Amerique* (Paris: Editions Skira, 2007).

Postle, Martin (ed.), *Joshua Reynolds: The Creation of Celebrity* (London: Tate Publishing, 2005).

Potts, Alex, *The Sculptural Imagination: Figurative, Modernist, Minimalist* (London: Yale University Press, 2000).

Proust, Marcel, *À la recherche du temps perdu*, ed. Jean-Yves Tadié (Paris: Gallimard, 1987–9).

Rabb, Jane M., *Literature and Photography: Interactions 1840–1990* (Albuquerque: University of New Mexico Press, 1995).

Rajewsky, Irina O., *Intermedialität* (Tübingen and Basel: A. Francke Verlag, 2002).

Reginster, Bernard, *The Affirmation of Life: Nietzsche on Overcoming Nihilism* (Cambridge, MA and London: Harvard University Press, 2008).

Rewald, John, *The History of Impressionism* (New York: MOMA, 1961).

Richardson, Michael, *Surrealism and Cinema* (Oxford and New York: Berg, 2006).

Roche, Roger-Yves (ed.), *Lectures de Modiano* (Nantes: Éditions Cécile Defaut, 2009).

Roelens, Nathalie, 'Écrire le visage: Michaux, Blanchot, Klossowski, Genet', *Word & Image*, 15/4 (October–December 1999), 309–22.

Roger, Jérôme, '"Le phrasé même de la vie" ou la vie plastique d'Henri Michaux', in Pierre Vilar, Françoise Nicol and Guénaël Boutouillet (eds), *Conversations avec Henri Michaux* (Nantes: Cécile Défaut, 2008), pp. 75–98.

Ron, Moshe, 'The restricted abyss: nine problems in the theory of mise en abyme', *Poetics Today*, 8/2 (1987), 417–38.

Royle, Nicholas, *Jacques Derrida* (London: Routledge, 2003).

Rykiel, Sonia, *Colette et la mode* (Paris: Éditions Plume, 1991).

Sainte-Beuve, Charles Augustin, 'Prospectus sur les œuvres de Victor Hugo', in *Premiers lundis*, vol. 1, ed. Maxime Leroy (Paris: Gallimard, 1949), pp. 297–303.

Savage, Robert, 'Adorno's family and other animals', *Thesis Eleven*, 78 (August 2004), 102–12.

Schaeffer, Jean-Marie, *L'Image précaire: du dispositif photographique* (Paris: Seuil, 1987).

Schlöndorff, Volker, 'A propos de l'adaptation de *Un amour de Swann*. Notes de travail', in *Bulletin de Société de Marcel Proust et des Amis de Combray*, 1984, pp. 178–91.

Scott, David, *Pictorialist Poetics* (Cambridge: Cambridge University Press, 1988).

Séché, Léon, *Le Cénacle de Joseph Delorme (1827–1830)* (Paris: Mercure de France, 1912).

Smith, Paul (ed.), 'The nineteenth century art novel', special issue, *French Studies*, 59/1 (2007).

Sontag, Susan, *On Photography* (London: Penguin, 1977).

Spinoza, Baruch, *Ethics* (London: Dent, 1970).

Staël, Madame de (Anne-Louise-Germaine). *De l'Allemagne*, 2 vols (Paris: Garnier-Flammarion, 1968).

Stendhal, *Le Rouge et le noir* (Paris: Flammarion, 1964).

Tadié, Jean-Yves, *Regarde de tous tes yeux, regarde!* (Paris: Gallimard, 2005).

Thélot, Jérôme, *Les Inventions littéraires de la photographie* (Paris: Presses Universitaires de France, 2003).

Tisseron, Serge, *Le Mystère de la chambre claire: photographie et inconscient* (Paris: Flammarion, 1996).

Townsend, Gabrielle, *Proust's Imaginary Museum: Reproductions and Repro-duction in* À la recherche du temps perdu (Oxford: Peter Lang, 2007).

Trotter, David, *Cinema and Modernism* (Oxford: Blackwell, 2007).

Twyman, Michael, *Graphic Communication through ISOTYPE* (Reading: Reading University 1975).

Unwin, Timothy, 'Eat my words: Verne and Flaubert, or the anxiety of the culinary', in John West-Sooby (ed.), *Consuming Culture: The Arts of the French Table* (Newark: University of Delaware Press, 2004), pp. 118–29.

Verne, Jules, *Les Œuvres de Jules Verne*, 50 vols (Lausanne: Rencontre, 1966–71).

Vierne, Simone, *Jules Verne: mythe et modernité* (Paris: PUF, 1989).

Vološinov, V. N., *Marxism and the Philosophy of Language* (Cambridge, MA: Harvard University Press, 1973).

Wagner, Peter, *Icons–Texts–Iconotexts: Essays on Ekphrasis and Intermediality* (Berlin and New York: Walter de Gruyter, 1996).

Wegner, Frank, 'Photography in Proust's *À la recherche du temps perdu*' (un-published doctoral thesis, University of Cambridge, 2004).

Williams, Michael, *Ivor Novello: Screen Idol* (London: BFI, 2003).

Wohrne, Maria Wennerström, 'Att översätta världen: Kommunikation och subversivt ärende i Henri Michaux "Voyage en Grande Garabagne"' (un-published doctoral thesis, University of Uppsala, Sweden, 2003).

Wollen, Peter, 'Modern times: cinema, Americanism, the robot', in *Raiding the Icebox: Reflections on Twentieth-Century Culture* (London: Verso, 1993).

Wood, Michael, 'Other eyes: Proust and the myths of photography', in *The Strange M. Proust* (London: Legenda, 2009).

Zhang, Dora, 'A lens for an eye: Proust and photography', *Representations*, 118/1 (spring 2012), 103–25.

Zola, Emile, *Œuvres complètes*, ed. Henri Mitterand, 15 vols (Paris: Cercle du Livre Précieux, 1962–9).

INDEX

Index

Index